MODERN MAN

BOOKS BY ANTHONY FLINT

*Wrestling with Moses: How Jane Jacobs Took On New York's
Master Builder and Transformed the American City*

This Land: The Battle over Sprawl and the Future of America

*Smart Growth Policies: An Evaluation of Programs and
Outcomes*

MODERN MAN

The Life of Le Corbusier, Architect of Tomorrow

Anthony Flint

New Harvest
Houghton Mifflin Harcourt
Boston   New York   2014

Copyright © 2014 by Anthony Flint

This edition published by special arrangement with Amazon
Publishing

For information about permission to reproduce selections
from this book, go to www.apub.com.

www.hmhco.com

Library of Congress Cataloging-in-Publication Data
Flint, Anthony, date.
Modern man : the life of Le Corbusier, architect of tomorrow /
Anthony Flint.
pages cm
ISBN 978-0-544-26222-5 (hardback)
1. Le Corbusier, 1887–1965. 2. Architects – France – Biography.
3. Architects – Switzerland – Biography. I. Title.
NA1053.J4F59 2014
720.92 – dc23
[B]
2014016740

Book design by Greta D. Sibley

Printed in the United States of America
DOC 10 9 8 7 6 5 4 3 2 1

To Melissa, who went her own way also

CONTENTS

INTRODUCTION

...

The Ascent

He watched her for what seemed like hours, her chest rising and falling, as the big boat did the same on the waves of the Atlantic. They had left Rio de Janeiro for the long trip back to France, nestled in crisp white sheets in a first-class cabin aboard the *Lutetia,* the black ocean outside the portal window. Time was a relative matter as the ship made a vector for the equator. The year was 1929. The Roaring Twenties were about to end with the stock market crash, but no such realities would intervene in that stateroom. Propped up on one elbow, he could hardly believe his good fortune, meeting Josephine Baker in Buenos Aires several days before. In Rio they sipped caipirinhas and sauntered along Ipanema beach, and she was so lovely he created portraits of her using the colored pencils he had brought for work. On board, they attended an elaborate costume party. He dressed as an Indian soldier with a polka-dot bandanna, and she was a china doll. "What a pity you're an architect, Monsieur Le Corbusier!" she had said. "You'd have made a sensational partner!"[1]

He smiled, knowing their worlds were not so far apart. As his stateroom companion well knew, he was no ordinary draftsman.

He had been welcomed in South America as a celebrity just as much as she was: the man from Paris, stepping out in tailored suit with a pocket square and bow tie, filling lecture halls across the continent with those eager to hear his radical new theories in architecture and urban planning. He was breaking the mold in building homes and entire cities — just as Pablo Picasso had in painting and Ernest Hemingway with the novel — sculpting smooth, white, streamlined buildings that had never been seen before, forgoing wood and brick and stone for concrete, replacing staircases with spirals and ramps, wrapping exteriors with long ribbons of black-framed windows, and planting gardens on rooftop terraces. Everything about his architecture was different. He perched his buildings on sturdy yet elegant concrete columns he called *pilotis,* freeing the ground for cars and open space, and making the structures appear to float in air. And his formula was repeatable — efficient housing built with low-cost construction methods, whether three-story town houses or towers set in parks, linked by spacious high-speed roadways and ultimately served by planes and helicopters. The turn of the twentieth century had brought the machine age — cars, locomotives, planes, and the factories of mass-production manufacturing — and that most fundamental of life's functions, the habitation of homes and cities, required the same modernization. The dapper visitor with the slicked-back hair and round black eyeglasses was delivering a new way to live.

Becoming Le Corbusier — not just a man, but a force — had required no little marketing. He adopted the pseudonym in 1920, leaving behind his given name, Charles-Édouard Jeanneret-Gris. Taking a single moniker was popular among the bohemians and artists in Paris at the time, and for him the act had a symbolism all its own. While inspired in part by his great-grandfather

Monsieur Lecorbesier of Brussels and the eighteenth-century French actress Adrienne Lecouvreur, a former resident of the town house where he lived in Paris, the renaming signaled his break with the past, with Victorian and bourgeois traditions, and the embrace of the modern. But it was also an exercise in branding. The original star architect would be forever distinguished from all other innovators in design, including his American rival, Frank Lloyd Wright. The name was reminiscent of a mystic bird of Celtic lore, the highly intelligent hunter and scavenger *le corbeau*, "the raven." He had taken to drawing himself as the sleek black bird, peering down from a tightly gripped perch, assessing the landscape, ready to launch in acrobatic flight.

All of Paris, wealthy clients and bohemians alike, knew where to go to find new ideas in design: 35 rue de Sèvres, the bustling atelier next door to the department store Le Bon Marché. The equivalent of a start-up in a garage, the top floor of an unremarkable building in the sixth arrondissement served as his headquarters, little more than a long corridor with drafting tables and adjustable black lamps, one after the other, and papers and plans hanging on the walls and sprouting from the floor in rolled-up bunches, like some kind of crazy shrubbery. The apprentices reported each morning, eager to work for the visionary master, alongside the team partners and like-minded innovators: his cousin Pierre Jeanneret and the furniture designer Charlotte Perriand. Each month, it seemed, brought a new building design, a new way to organize life: the places for living, for business, for government, for recreation and culture.

The atelier was the fountainhead for all manner of innovations — a car that was the precursor to the Volkswagen Beetle; furniture made of aluminum tubing, black leather, and spotted horsehair; even, in time, a women's clothing line, an ensemble of V-neck blouses, pleated skirts, and go-anywhere sandals, submitted to America's first fashion magazine, *Harper's Bazaar*. At night the team would celebrate with wine and champagne in the bistros of the Latin Quarter, and in the morning, after the master had done calisthenics or played basketball and painted, his life-long side pursuit, they would all reassemble and get back to the blueprints and do it all over again.

It was gratifying, and utterly intentional, that the people of Latin America, a hemisphere away, would hear about all the excitement. The trip there was one of many international forays for the ambassador of the new order. The fast-growing cities of Argentina and Brazil needed his help to be better-organized, cleaner, more orderly places. Le Corbusier was the man with the plan. In standing-room-only lecture halls, he sketched the next city with charcoal on tan newsprint, never reading from prepared remarks but instead creating a storyboard on the spot. He drew chains of apartment buildings set in open space, awash in sunlight and fresh air, with recreation areas and circulation all around, proposing it all as the most natural of evolutions. To demonstrate how cities cannot be frozen in time, he drew the cathedral of Notre Dame and the Eiffel Tower, and then his towers in the park; the progression honored the past but didn't stay stuck in it, not least because cities of the future needed to be prepared for ever-increasing populations. But as he wrote, the critics and the mandarins in academia were saying no to all of it. They thought it outrageous, to move on from convention and propose new forms. And that just made Le Corbusier more exciting, a true rebel. The Argentineans and Brazilians felt like they were part of something – that they were being given the keys to the future. They could even leapfrog places like Paris and New York City in embracing the modern.

In one rendering from the perspective of being out at sea and looking onshore, he painted a set of three proposed apartment buildings in Rio, rendered in a soft yellow in a purplish haze, as if glowing with the promise of a happy future. It was a thrilling prospect, and Le Corbusier relished the role of messiah. THE PROPHET OF THE NEW ARCHITECTURE, blared the headline of an advertisement for a Spanish translation of the book he published in Europe years earlier, *Vers une architecture* (*Toward an Architecture*), touted in the copy as "the bible of the perfect dwelling."[2]

In the august interior of the Jockey Club in Buenos Aires, fellow diners whispered to each other about the famous architect visiting from Paris. On the streets he was stopped for autographs. In a bar one night, a group bought him so many beers he lost count, saluting and toasting him and all but letting him leave. By day he scheduled appearances at universities, meetings with government officials, and lunches with the wealthy elite, such as Victoria Ocampo, editor of the literary journal *Sur,* which featured such writers as Jorge Luis Borges. Le Corbusier viewed Ocampo as possessing singular good taste and strength; she reciprocated by helping him with the logistics of his lecture appearances.[3] While the urban planning schemes had broad appeal, the rich and powerful had something more selfish in mind. They wanted him to build a modern architectural masterpiece as a villa of their own.

It didn't take much time for Josephine Baker to have that idea as well. From the time the fellow Parisian introduced himself after her performance in Buenos Aires, it was clear this was not just another fan eager to meet her backstage. She was charmed and curious. Within a few days of their paths crossing, she was asking him to design a house for her on the Right Bank in Paris, close to Montmartre and the nightclub that helped make her famous, the Maud de Forest.

He appreciated a gifted artist at work – an artist traveling the world just as he was, creating excitement. In 1929, the twenty-three-year-old was not so much a singer and dancer, but a phenomenon. La Femme Sauvage, the Black Venus, she shimmied across the stage in sparse pink flamingo feathers at the Théâtre des Champs-Élysées, and in a skirt of uptilted bananas at the Casino de Paris.[4] A mixed-race daughter of St. Louis, she was an impossibly exotic sight, whether warbling tunes with a snake draped around her neck onstage or walking her pet leopard, Chiquita, down the Champs-Élysées. Everything about her – her hairstyle with a slicked-down curl on her forehead, her gold-painted nails, her designer-made gowns, her caramel-colored skin that inspired a sun-tanning craze at the Côte d'Azur, even her American accent – was soaked up in France and around the world. She was the new thing, lifting the people out of their seats and making audiences feel they were part of something.

As luck would have it, they were on the same boat, the *Giulio Cesare*, from Buenos Aires to São Paulo, he in white slacks and shoes, suit jacket and bow tie, she in white skirt and top and pillbox chapeau adorned with a flower. The architect and the jazz singer kept connecting. "I can't give you anything but love," she sang at a performance in what was then Brazil's second-largest city. Despite her fame, she seemed to him entirely natural, modest, and without vanity. She found him irresistible and funny. When they reconvened in Rio, the bond was confirmed.

And so he drew her, sleeping like a child under a comfortable blanket, and in front of Rio's Sugarloaf Mountain, too, wearing a knee-length skirt and accompanied by a man in a fedora smoking a pipe – Le Corbusier himself. Both of them had their chins up and gazed hopefully to the horizon.

That was what he did with the things that held his attention. He drew everything, rushing to put pencil or paintbrush to paper, before the thoughts could race out of his head. He was exceptionally good at what would become a forgotten art, made obsolete by the camera and then the smartphone. In an instant he would set down perfectly placed lines that framed a three-dimensional volume, parse light and shadow, and fill in perspective, proportion, and scale.

His steady hand was noted early on, as a young man growing up in French-speaking northwest Switzerland, in the town
of La Chaux-de-Fonds. Urged on by the master of his art school,
he produced lush watercolors of brown and green, replicating
the symmetrical fir trees of the region amid the wide, V-shaped
valleys and undulating hills. Charles L'Eplattenier, a lover of the
outdoors who took his classes out into the countryside to record
the power of nature, saw how adroitly Le Corbusier perceived
the patterns all around him, the woven tapestry of the alpine
meadows and forests, thatching and dovetailing into one another.

In the classrooms of the École d'Art, Le Corbusier dutifully re-
produced the ornamentation of interiors and buildings that was
the mainstay of design at the turn of the twentieth century, the
decorative arts of the Arts and Crafts movement. L'Eplattenier, a
big, intense man with dark eyes and long goatee, marveled at the
young man's obvious talent. It was a gift to be able to sort out the
world all around. "The greatest thing a human soul ever does in
this world is see something, and tell what it saw in a plain way,"
said John Ruskin, the guru of the Beaux-Arts schools of the era.
"Hundreds of people can talk for one who can think, but thousands can think for one who can see. To see clearly is poetry,
prophecy, religion, all in one."[5]

He was grateful for his training under L'Eplattenier, an inspiring and charming master, and his classmates were a fine
bunch of lads. But his birthplace remained a complicated memory and a contradictory influence. A place of Swiss precision and
order and Calvinist discipline, La Chaux-de-Fonds was his birthplace and the location of his first buildings – and the hometown
he was eager to flee.

The city of just over thirty-five thousand was an outpost, settled by medieval pioneers who traveled north from the provincial
capital of Neuchâtel, fleeing religious persecution and wanting

to be left alone. When the village, built with the timbers of the clear-cut forests of the Jura Mountains, burned to the ground in 1794, civic leaders decided to rebuild according to a strict plan: a grid based around one long and straight east-west boulevard, with buildings of uniform size, height, and color lining all the parallel avenues and cross streets. Order was all around. Each rooftop featured systems for shedding and draining the heavy snow in winter; each doorstep had an upside-down metal stirrup for scraping boots. And almost every structure was capped by strips of windows, letting in light to top-floor ateliers, perfect for the business that had formed the basis of the local economy: making watches. Ever since one of the early settlers repaired a timepiece for a visitor, La Chaux-de-Fonds found its calling in watchmaking, the signature industry of the nation.

At one point over half of all watches in use around the world came from there – many of the most sturdy and glamorous brands: Breitling, TAG Heuer, Omega, Movado, Cartier, and Girard-Perregaux. The fire and reconstruction provided the opportunity to dedicate the city to the business with single-minded zeal. Most workers lived in the buildings where they worked, at the benches in the top-floor ateliers; eradicating the medieval clutter gave them abundant light, and the wider streets made it easier to clear snow and allowed watch parts to be ferried from one building to another. It was a brilliant marriage of physical arrangements and an economic machine, based on the *établissage* system, where each piece of the product was assembled in a different place. Everybody had a role, from the material supplier to the maker of the second hand to the engraver of the pocket watch case. Workers got training in the specialized functions where there was the most need and settled into their niche. Karl Marx marveled at what he called the perfect example of full-participation, heterogeneous manufacturing: the city as one big factory. Jean-Jacques Rousseau and Vladimir Lenin paid visits as well.

It was indeed a glorious machine, and Le Corbusier was supposed to be a cog in it. His father was a watch engraver and fully expected the son to be his successor in the trade.

Georges-Édouard Jeanneret-Gris was stern and tender, a fastidious and practical man, Swiss in every sense. His diary contained not only the daily events of life but also a meticulous spreadsheet of the family finances, including fluctuations in the price of groceries.[6] He married Marie-Charlotte-Amélie Perret, the daughter of a local craftsman, in 1883, and their first son, Albert, was born three years later. In twenty months, the second son arrived, delivered at home at 38 rue de la Serre on October 6, 1887. He was christened Charles-Édouard Jeanneret-Gris, the name he would abandon thirty-three years later, though he would continue to sign letters to his family as Édouard, or simply Ed, or sometimes the affectionate nickname "Doudou."

Home was the second floor of one of the uniform apartment buildings in the center of town, and then, when he was six years old, the fifth floor of an equally drab town house on the central boulevard, rue Léopold-Robert. Behind the cold exterior – it was an unspoken tradition not to be flashy on the outside, even for increasingly wealthy residents – the interior of the Jeanneret home was warm and tasseled, arrayed with Victorian furniture and bric-a-brac, and the prize possession, a piano, which Marie played with considerable talent. Music was often the only respite from the intentional self-denial and sobriety, a home life where the script seemed to be never to have too much fun.

The core of the family was the four of them, the parents and the two boys, though Aunt Pauline lived with them for a time as well. His mother was, and would remain, the most important woman in his life, the recipient of hundreds of letters, penned from faraway places and throughout his career. Yet his parents always seemed more impressed with Albert. He was robust, while Édouard seemed frail, as Georges, an enthusiastic senior member of the local mountaineering club, observed after taking both boys out for long hikes. Music seemed to be Albert's calling, even as he developed a bit of a stutter.[7] In school, Édouard never appeared quite as conscientious. One thing his parents did notice was how much he liked to play with blocks.

The École d'Art, a short walk from home, was the place where he was to be trained in design and engraving and ornamental composition, to take his place at his father's side, supplying finely decorated cases for major makers such as Longines. The precocious young man sped through the curriculum, designing a table clock, jewelry boxes, pendants, and a silver cane handle for his father, shaped as an eagle-dog hybrid. And he dutifully crafted the watchcases of silver and inlaid steel and brass, cut with burin and chisel, sculpted with intricate patterns of geometry and the vestiges of the natural world, all to be held in the palm of a hand. Though his prizewinning designs were in line with the emerging art nouveau movement of the time, he found it all as tedious as the mindless copying of decorative patterns that was required in his schooling. It was also increasingly hurting his eyes. He was saved from the life of a journeyman engraver by an ocular condition that appears to have been a detached retina, requiring thick glasses and effectively making him blind in one eye. Squinting to etch hair-thin lines on metal watchcases was out of the question.

Fortunately, L'Eplattenier, the man who stood patiently beside him at the drafting tables of the art school, was ready with the suggestion of an alternative vocation. Le Corbusier drew so beautifully, and perceived space and shapes in such an extraordinary way. He should consider architecture.

The pride and precision of watchmaking, and the high-functioning order of La Chaux-de-Fonds, rebuilt on ashes, would always stay with him. But his hometown never offered enough to hold him there. Like the city's other famous son, Louis-Joseph Chevrolet – the maker of cars so hugely popular in America was also born there – his only chance at greatness was to leave.

If he was to be an architect, as L'Eplattenier had advised, he would need to do two things, both of which required a clean departure: talk his way into apprenticeships with the leading designers of the day and, at the same time, get out and see the world.

On board the *Lutetia,* he padded around with the confidence of a veteran traveler. Transportation was an increasingly glamorous business, and he made the most of it, from the grand ocean liners to the Graf Zeppelin, the hydrogen-filled airship that he would take when he returned to Brazil in 1936, to, later, the first passenger jets, whose shiny, ribbed silver fuselages were the backdrop for dozens of photographs, capturing him stepping off the rollaway stairs in a fresh suit wondrously free of wrinkles. He traveled like a head of state, demanding VIP treatment from governments and other clients, strictly first class and the finest hotels. As a nineteen-year-old leaving La Chaux-de-Fonds in September 1907, however, he carried a backpack and stayed in hostels and took the train, repeatedly excusing himself from the shared compartment to wash away the locomotive's black smoke that blew in through the windows. He would complain of indigestion, write home for fresh clothes, and miss the family so badly that he arrayed photos of them all in little bedside shrines. But the hardships, in what would be a total of four years of traveling through Europe, were footnotes in a remarkable journey of discovery.

He headed first to Italy, to Florence by way of Lugano, Milan, Genoa, and Pisa, carrying a copy of John Ruskin's *Mornings in Florence* as a travel guide. There he met his friend Leon Perrin,

a classmate from the art school, and the two young men set out
through the Renaissance city to tour the museums and cathedrals and great works of architecture. Amazed at the beauty he
was seeing – the most beautiful things the human spirit was capable of producing – he filled his sketchbook with encyclopedic
detail, page after page of Byzantine grandeur, lovingly rendered
in pen, pencil, and watercolor paintbrush: columns and capitals
and vaulting arches, tombs and basilicas, checkered with twirling lines and mystical beasts. A statue in an alcove amazed him
for its perfect proportions and the way the figure seemed to be
ready to step out from its inlaid-marble niche. He stood in cathedrals in a daze, observing, oblivious to mealtimes, a head-in-
the-clouds target for pickpockets, who relieved him of his wallet
early on.

Michelangelo and Rubens, Titian and Botticelli, all of them
bestowed gifts, slaking his thirst for the beautiful. He lingered
at the piazza, sharing his lunch with a cat, watching the pretty
women go by. A side trip to the Carthusian monastery at Val
d'Ema put him in the ultimate swoon. The hillside complex featured small rooms, each with high ceilings, a little private garden, and a view to the Tuscan countryside; the cells, the spaces
accommodating individual privacy, were juxtaposed with the
common areas, close at hand, for prayers and communal dinners.
It was a modern city built in the fifteenth century, "the noblest
silhouette in the landscape . . . I had never seen such a happy interpretation of a dwelling," he recalled.[8] The monastery and its
"radiant vision" would inspire his housing schemes for the rest
of his career.

The journey went on, from Venice to Vienna, where he
bought a felt hat and replaced his worn shoes, and started knock-
ing on doors in hopes of an apprenticeship somewhere among
the city's esteemed architectural offices. He was in for a rude
awakening. He found the people in the Austrian capital to be

"undiscoverable," and that it was impossible to get anywhere without a network of connections. He used his spare time to listen to music, getting a standing-room ticket for a five-hour performance of Wagner's *Siegfried* at the opera house, conducted by Gustav Mahler,[9] and, as the evenings drew on, consorting with the prostitutes at the Stephansplatz.

There was no work in Vienna. But there were infinite possibilities in Paris. And in Paris, there was concrete.

The material he would sculpt so effectively throughout his career was in the midst of being discovered at the turn of the century, and two brothers who had set up shop in Paris were doing most of the early experimenting. Auguste and Gustave Perret, immigrants from Belgium, were part of an avant-garde in architecture and the arts, and their specialty was using new building methods and materials to create an entirely new class of buildings — different in the way they looked and the way they functioned. The Perret brothers, working from a combination of a construction company and an architectural office, specialized in reinforced concrete made with ferro-cement — *béton armé*, threaded with steel — that allowed them to build taller and wider, reduce seams and joints, and open up interiors. The awesome strength of the material meant that fewer interior walls were needed. Yet the material could also be decorated and carved and even made to look like wood. The Perret brothers built their headquarters just across the Seine from the Eiffel Tower, adjacent to the Trocadéro; it was typical in its transparent logic and open plan. The recent arrival from Vienna made a cold call, showed Gustave Perret his drawings, and was hired on the spot as a part-time apprentice.

His parents told him not to go to Paris. So did L'Eplattenier for many of the same reasons: They believed the city was decadent, a Babylon where he would be hopelessly distracted. When he first arrived he worried they might have been right — it was

pouring down rain, he couldn't see any of the city's famous landmarks, and the hotel room was a hovel. But he would look back
on the fourteen months he spent there with great fondness, for
setting him on his way. In the mornings he worked on blueprints
for apartment buildings and hunting lodges for the Perret brothers, immersing himself in the mathematics and geometry of
the spaces made possible by concrete. In the afternoons he ex-
plored the city. He took a top-floor flat in the Latin Quarter overlooking the cathedral of Notre Dame, which he repeatedly and
thoroughly visited; he painted a watercolor of the view out his
window, across the ubiquitous mansard rooftops, to the Gothic
towers on the Île de la Cité, and had himself photographed, in his
student hat and cape, on the balcony.

In those days, he was mostly alone, and there was always a
book he was reading. His program of self-education included
Don Quixote by Miguel de Cervantes (the man of La Mancha
was a tortured protagonist with whom he identified his whole
life) and *The Life of Jesus* by Ernest Renan, and an immersion
in classic literature worthy of a university core curriculum:
Homer, Nietzsche, Rousseau, Flaubert, Baudelaire.[10] His parents
could not help but be impressed when they came to visit, bringing along the increasingly aimless Albert, who celebrated the re-
union with his brother by staying up late and consuming copious
amounts of wine.

Le Corbusier had come to Paris, he said, "to know." His expectations were equally high for the rest of his journey. After con-
cluding the apprenticeship with the Perret brothers, and a brief
sojourn home in La Chaux-de-Fonds, he headed to Germany, the
focus of his next investigations, thanks to an assignment to write
a report for the École d'Art on architectural innovations there.[11]
The destinations included Frankfurt, Dresden, Hamburg, and
Munich, where he met William Ritter, a journalist, painter, and

art and music critic who impressed him with his contrarian flair; the two exchanged intimate letters for years. In Berlin Le Corbusier talked his way into working as an apprentice for Peter Behrens, a pioneer of the modern movement best known for his AEG Turbine Factory, an imposing yet elegant structure of concrete and glass. Behrens's other apprentices included Ludwig Mies van der Rohe and Walter Gropius, later directors of the influential Bauhaus modern design school. Le Corbusier found Behrens to be an incorrigible tyrant who paid his minions next to nothing. He endured drudgery at the drafting tables, and it was all he could do to pay for his rented room. He eagerly ate dinners prepared by the rooming house frau for the cost of one mark.

He again found solace in music, moved by a concert of Tchaikovsky. But his chief respite was always in drawing and painting, filling a pocket notebook of graph paper, its leather cover creased and worn like a catcher's mitt: buildings, town squares, public gardens, and cathedrals. On page after page, front and back, he colored in browns and deep purples and scribbled notes in the margins. His analysis of how humans functioned in cities was evolving, building on the wisdom of Camillo Sitte, a founding theorist of urban planning and design. The city, he began to think, was like an organism, and it must accommodate its inhabitants with both well-functioning order and joyous discovery to maintain vitality and happiness. The first inklings of a new order were forming, some way to improve on the walled medieval maze.

Just as his apprenticeship in Paris, he was satisfied with his accomplishments in Germany. It was time to leave again for the final segment of his wanderings through Turkey and Greece – the *Journey to the East*, as his travel diary was titled, published many years later. Taking a train back to Vienna and a boat down the Danube to Belgrade and then on to Istanbul, he viewed the five-month excursion as a reward for his penitence at the Behrens studio. He had no way of knowing that what he saw would inspire him, and his architecture, for decades to come.

His companion was Auguste Klipstein, whom he had met in Germany, equally dedicated to having some fun. From Istanbul they traveled by mule to the remote male-only monastery at Mount Athos, drank retsina and dined on octopus, shopped in the bazaar, and swam nude in the Aegean Sea.[12] But the mood turned serious at the Athens Acropolis, which Le Corbusier saw first from the water. The collection of temple ruins set on a pedestal, white stone contrasting with the blue of the sea, seemed to him the most perfect placement of buildings on earth by man.

He put off the visit to the site itself for several days, knowing it would be a big event. On the day he decided to go, he sipped coffee at a café all afternoon, waiting until sunset – the perfect time to enter the ancient compound. He returned again and again, visiting the Parthenon every day for nearly two weeks, circling it as if it were prey, sketching the ribbed columns both standing and fallen, and mapping the organization of the temple. He was both astonished and disturbed by its powerful presence. "It harbors the essence of artistic thought," he concluded.[13] He sensed a mystical mathematical formula at work for creating great architecture. He would tour other places on the return to Switzerland – Naples, Pompeii, and Rome – but the time in Athens had him thinking even more intensely, if that was possible, about what he might be capable of.

Something else stirred deep within him on the *voyage d'Orient*. He was beginning, in earnest, his lifelong love of women, as much of an obsession as architecture. He had flirted in Paris and stolen a kiss in Vienna, but the fantasies of full-mouthed, big-breasted women intensified as he headed south. He wrote to Ritter, who was openly gay, about his throbbing erections in the hostel rooms at night. But while women fascinated him, they were un-approachable. He couldn't think of what to say to them. His passions were unleashed only with prostitutes, and then only, as he neared the age of thirty, when he returned to Paris in 1917. The sex was remarkably solitary, yet he felt a power that coursed through all of life. "Women so pretty, so well dressed and fresh and cheerful, Paris still so much a bouquet of pink flesh. The heart remains alone when the body does its thing. There's no time for love . . . ," he wrote to Ritter. "The naked man is for him who has overcome himself and satisfied his body. He is a complex of firm, rectilinear planes. For me the naked man is architecture. When I'm not doing architecture, I see everything as women."[14]

For someone who lived so much in his head, thinking so intensely, with all the dials turned up high, sex took him away – like a beer at the end of a factory shift or losing oneself in a basketball game. And he sought to extend the immersion. Because he drew everything else, he painted watercolors of the prostitutes, too – naked women in recline, pleasuring each other, curves everywhere, buttocks raised up, heads thrown back in ecstasy. "My women are bestially lascivious, prurient, in heat," he wrote in his journal.[15] He gave one of the watercolors to his escort early one morning in Paris, and she had accepted it with a laugh.

The prurience went on, until finally, in Paris in 1922, he met a woman he could talk to. They would become partners for life.

Yvonne Gallis was a salesgirl and fashion model in a couture house where Le Corbusier had shown some of his artwork. She was close to his height, buxom and alluring, all painted lips and dark mascara, a full-figured Gypsy from Monaco. They were drawn to each other immediately. She was no match for his intellect and shared few interests. After they were married, she forbade the discussion of architecture at home and at dinner parties. As they began dating, they talked about other things and drank wine and had picnics in the countryside. She was elegant and exotic, dressed in clingy skirts and accessorized with a bell-jar cloche and hoop earrings, and made a legendary spicy aioli. He liked her fondness for practical jokes. She once steered a visiting church dignitary to sit down on a whoopee cushion; other guests tried to plunge their spoons into soup bowls to find themselves blocked by a thin, invisible plastic cover, or got fake sugar cubes that failed to dissolve in their coffee, or found a little phallus poking up out of a mustard ramekin. She would regularly ask guests – whether a fellow architect or a messenger boy – "Have you seen it?" When asked what "it" was, she'd respond, *"Mon cul* [my ass]."[16]

While a wild child and sometimes "skittish as a gazelle," she "makes our undertakings easy," he wrote to his mother.[17] They would marry in a simple ceremony attended by friends in Dampierre-en-Yvelines outside Paris, and planned to honeymoon in Switzerland, but Yvonne's passport wasn't processed in time, so the newlyweds separated for their first Christmas. It was the first of many times they would be apart. He seemed to spend as much time writing to her as being with her, assuring her of his return, the letters shot through with baby-talk affections. She was his "dear Vonvon." He was her "Doudou." She would set aside the envelopes with the far-flung postmarks and return to domestic busywork, sewing a bedspread, making dresses for the outings when they were together again, canning cornichons and pickles, trying new makeup and hairstyles.[18] And she would smoke cigarettes and sip pastis – the cloudy, high-alcohol, licorice-flavored liqueur that was popular in the South of France following bans on absinthe – earlier and earlier in the day.

She was waiting for him to return on the *Lutetia.* At the time, they were not yet married. But his dalliance with Josephine Baker would set a familiar pattern; he would be unfaithful throughout their partnership. He was living for the moment and adept at compartmentalizing. The jazz singer had an even more expansive approach. Her partner, Pepito Abatino, a Sicilian stonemason who passed himself off as a count and served as her manager, was actually on board the very same ship. Le Corbusier had met him. There seemed to be an understanding that she would go her own way, sleeping with men and women, whenever it felt right.

As the ocean liner cleaved through the heaving Atlantic, the passengers gathered at precise hours for cocktails and Brazilian steak arrayed on starched white tablecloths, then dispersed again for the privacy of their staterooms. "I am a little blackbird looking for a bluebird," she trilled in a private concert for the architect, strumming a ukulele.

The moment was to be relished, because it, too, would pass. He was acutely aware of the passage of time, as if the second hands of the pocket watches of La Chaux-de-Fonds were ticking loudly in his head. There was so much to do: commissions to chase, new renderings to draw. He never stopped thinking of how he could better house humanity. The boat itself was an inspiration; with all its amenities organized so efficiently, it was like a big apartment building on the water. What if he could build an ocean liner on land?

Her chest was rising and falling, and the waves were swelling and receding. He could feel the power of the muscular propellers beneath him, bringing him back to France, where he would return to the business of changing the world. He had what had become a familiar feeling, of being on the brink of something. Crossing the time zones, ready to launch.

MODERN MAN

1 ▪ THE ROAR

The shopkeepers in Saint-Germain-des-Prés might have made a game out of guessing which outfit it would be at the front door of 20 rue Jacob in the late morning, long after the freshly baked croissants and baguettes had been set out. A three-piece suit of silk or tweed? A solid-color bow tie or a narrow necktie with neat horizontal stripes? Bowler, fedora, porkpie, or boater? Two things were givens: a pressed pocket square and the thick, round black eyeglasses perched on Le Corbusier's prominent nose.

The crisp dress belied the cluttered garret he was coming from. It was always a point of amusement, that he was designing villas of pure white, spartan and streamlined, for others, but that top-floor flat at 20 rue Jacob remained, for the most part, the messy quarters of a free man in Paris. Reached by a dark wood spiral staircase, it had been the servants' quarters in the sixteenth century – the time of Voltaire – when the town house was famously occupied by Adrienne Lecouvreur, the beloved actress poisoned by a rival. From the moment he arrived, the one-bedroom flat under the old building's mansard roof became both his private study and a place of convening, of dinner parties and late nights of tobacco and Calvados and ruby-red wine. It was here that he would collect his watercolors and sketches, and publish the early copies of the journal he founded, *L'Esprit Nouveau,* a guidebook of the modern. At first there was little more than a bed and his drafting table. A bare lightbulb dangled down from the ceiling. Soon the letters and postcards and books and manuscripts piled high, occupying every available surface. A shaggy gray house cat threaded its way among antique vases and pieces of sculpture, most of which propped up long rows of books. The untidy aerie embodied the kind of conditions he was requiring his clients to eliminate. But there was little time to practice what he preached.

Bounding out across the threshold, he would begin his daily walk to the atelier at 35 rue de Sèvres, about a half-mile journey through the heart of the Left Bank of the Seine. In late morning, rue Jacob, a narrow canyon lined on both sides with six-story apartment buildings with shops on the ground floor, was a patchwork of shadows from the angling sun. His neighbors stirred at their convenience. Gertrude Stein and the boyish writer Colette were known to come next door, where the American Natalie Barney gathered women in bountiful undress in her back garden, much to his delight.[1] Pablo Picasso and F. Scott Fitzgerald might have been at Café de Flore, where Coco Chanel could see her handiwork on the women around the bar. At Les Deux Magots, the question was not what but how much Ernest Hemingway had imbibed, though he always said he favored the bistro for serious talks.[2] Le Corbusier's favorite spot, where he would allow himself a glass of Chianti, was Le Petit Saint-Benoit, a bistro just about three blocks from the apartment. Down rue Bonaparte, past a stately church overlooking a cobblestone square, all the cafés and brasseries were a daily reminder of how the Latin

Quarter, alongside Montmartre to the north, was bohemia's ground zero, the throbbing center of intellectual and artistic life. It was Florence in the time of the Renaissance, Greenwich Village in the 1960s, Silicon Valley at the start of the twenty-first century. And it was right out his front door.

There was never a question that he had to be in Paris.

The city pulled at him like a magnet. He was smitten from the time he rented the flat with the view of Notre Dame, during his apprenticeship with the Perret brothers. "The laboratory that is Paris is at every hour a temptation, the attempt to test the mechanism of mysterious tools," he said.[3]

When he left for the apprenticeship in Berlin with Peter Behrens, he promised himself he would be back. That moment came in 1917, a terrible and risky time to try to start anew in Paris, as the German bombardment rained down. He claimed to want to serve as a soldier, but near blindness in one eye excluded him from Swiss military conscription. So he boarded a train as just another civilian, with suitcases packed full and with money in his pocket from the design work he did on a cinema in La Chaux-de-Fonds, and left his hometown for good. Returning to Paris at that time, while a generation was being lost all around him, required discipline and determination. His solution was to adopt an attitude of bravado, pitying his neighbors cowering in the bomb shelters, huddling under blankets, and nibbling on crackers; unflinching when a friend was killed as he went to enlist, or after a building just across the street was destroyed by an explosion. He even viewed one bombardment of a bridge over the Seine, a spectator of war, perilously close to the fiery destruction.[4]

Yet where there was devastation, there would be rebuilding. Inherent in the armistice was the hope that mankind would turn to better things, applying advances in technology to improve the human condition, rather than lay waste to it. Le Corbusier saw the moment as one of possibility and promise, ripe for new ideas and a fresh start.

His source of income at the beginning of his permanent relocation was unglamorous: designing and managing a brick factory and a slaughterhouse. He was once again going it alone, occupying his time reading, writing letters, and bringing prostitutes home. For the project of ushering in the modern era, however, he would need a collaborator. Common cause arrived in the form of Amédée Ozenfant, heir to a construction company, painter, and manager of a couture salon. Auguste Perret made the introduction. "He's an odd duck," Perret told Ozenfant, "but he'll interest you."[5]

The two men conferred on the idea of a clean break with the past. Ozenfant vowed to part with virtually all his material possessions as a symbol of parting with the culture of the bourgeois; Le Corbusier jettisoned the name Charles-Édouard Jeanneret-Gris. They came to call it "purism," a cleansing, the stripping away of extras, whether ornamentation on buildings or flowery detail in a painting. Together they wrote the manifesto of the movement, obliquely titled *Après le cubisme* (After cubism), and mapped out the next steps of their avant-garde: science and art, marching forward, hand in hand. A new journal, *L'Esprit Nouveau,* headlined with a simple, industrial font, would be the paper of record for the transition to the modern, featuring the best and most daring ideas of how to embrace the postwar industrial age. "There is a new spirit abroad: a spirit of reconstruction and unification, guided by a clear notion of things," they wrote, as coeditors, in the maiden issue. "A great new epoch has begun."[6] They ran off mimeograph flyers advertising the magazine, and filled the pages with their own essays and those of others, pictures, and poetry.

He was an intense man, Ozenfant was, and their friendship ratcheted up to a fever pitch. When he split with his Russian wife, he said it was to spend more time with his compatriot. Le Corbusier returned the favor, lavishing attention on the relationship. He had not so much as boiled a potato in La Chaux-de-Fonds, but one night, in his Paris apartment, he served Ozenfant an elaborate dinner of oysters and pork chops and Saint-Émilion wine.[7] They went to Rome together; they had themselves photographed in a studio portrait in the basket of a hot-air balloon. Yet in what would become a familiar script, the relationship seemed destined to burn up. The first signs of discord emerged over painting, which Le Corbusier eagerly pursued in those early days in Paris, moving from his detailed and realistic watercolors to the abstract forms that were de rigueur. Sitting at easels side by side, he and Ozenfant sought to express the value of purist focus by portraying simple objects like a book on a mantel, a vase, a carafe, or a guitar. But when the works were displayed, they were deemed mediocre, far outside the league of Picasso, Matisse, and Cézanne. They quarreled over the placement of artwork in a benefactor's gallery, then over who deserved the credit for founding purism and *L'Esprit Nouveau*. The tight bonds loosened. They went from adoring best friends to publishing caricatures of each other.

Le Corbusier would paint for the rest of his life. He would drape his buildings with art, with giant tapestries and intricate sculptures. But the falling-out with Ozenfant reminded him of the real reason he was in Paris; it wasn't painting, but architecture and urban planning. Just as Charles L'Eplattenier had said, that was his gift. That was his true calling. He would keep his canvases to himself, ceding the medium to Picasso and the rest. Hemingway and Fitzgerald and Steinbeck could reinvent the novel, T. S. Eliot the poem. Le Corbusier's contribution to those times of churning and disruption and innovation was to change the way people lived – beginning with the very city he was walk-ing through.

The home was a machine for living in, he said, and the villas he would build were masterworks. But he was never content to pro-duce individual homes alone. His utopia was affordable housing for the masses, in cities arranged for maximum order and effi-ciency. It required thinking fresh in every way.

One of his first breakthroughs was astonishingly simple, as he calculated the massive task of building on the ashes of World War I. To quickly house the homeless, he proposed three floors of rectangular concrete slabs supported by thin columns all around the perimeter. The design obviated the need for load-bearing walls and allowed inhabitants to configure their interior living space however they wished. It was the world's first truly open plan. He called it Maison Dom-ino – a pun on the Latin word *domus*, "house," and on the playing pieces from the game. It was a matter of going back to the building blocks he played with as a child.[8]

His next housing prototype was another tribute to simplic-ity. The Maison Citrohan was a staggered three-story shoe box of reinforced concrete painted white. Le Corbusier deliberately named it after the popular French car the Citroën, hoping to enter into a development partnership with the family-owned car company. His vision was to build houses just as Henry Ford was making the Model T on an assembly line. Homes and cars could both be mass-produced, saving on cost, and would function to-gether like a pas de deux in ballet. At the ground level was an-other first: a carport. The interior was arranged for maximum efficiency and functional flow, but also made to feel roomy and spacious.

The inspiration came from a bistro on the rue Godot de Mauroy – where he often had lunch – a space that was deep, long, and narrow, but felt expansive in part because of the doubling of the height of the ceiling. The kitchen was tucked away in a cube in the back, with room for tables on top.[9] The Maison Citrohan was at once compact and roomy, allowing the most modest homeowner to enjoy interior space on a par with a swanky art gallery and the outdoors on a wraparound balcony or the rooftop garden. The rooms would be best filled sparely with modern furniture; built-in features would take the place of dressers and wardrobes and bookshelves.[10]

With Immeubles Villas, he took the concept further still, sketching a giant apartment building that could hold 120 super-efficient versions of the Maison Citrohan, stacked in rows and on top of one another. He had jotted down the design on the back of a lunch menu, recalling the concise grandeur of the monastery at Val d'Ema, one of the highlights of his journey to Italy. One could either be horrified by the conditions of the city, he said, or try to do something about them. The modern city required a complete rethinking of the apartment, he believed.[11]

He would not stop there. What the world needed was housing and more housing. He built a company town for the industrialist Henri Fruges, who desperately needed workforce housing for his sugar cube factory in the town of Pessac, near Bordeaux. The fifty-one row houses were part of a system that allowed both uniformity and variety: the same basic framework, built with what was intended to be a low-cost concrete construction method and a unified heating and cooling system, but with components – modular building blocks – that could be arranged in different configurations. Residents could forsake the open-air terrace and add another room, for example. The three-story homes were packed gracefully close together on tree-lined streets.[12]

The need for housing, he recognized, was so great that something even more dramatic was necessary. Thousands of people were streaming into the French capital each year, doubling the population to six million in the first half of the twentieth century. The furious pace of urbanization required a completely new approach to city building. The housing needed to be bigger, taller, and denser. The city of the future needed towers in the park.

The plans for Ville Contemporaine, a "City for Three Million People," debuted at the Salon d'Automne in 1922. The scheme was a Rorschach test for a new kind of urbanism, towers spaced in regular intervals in vast open spaces, served by streets wider and longer than any in existence. As a stepping up of scale, it was a natural evolution, from Maison Dom-ino to the Immeubles Villas to Pessac and now to this, an explosion of building in concrete, steel, and glass, upward to the heavens and across the landscape – and, once established, a template of urban form, infinitely repeatable. For the first time, Le Corbusier separated the functions of life into distinct and orderly zones: one for offices and business, one for retail, one for residents, yet another for recreation. He separated motor vehicles and pedestrians as well, making the network of streets and sidewalks three-dimensional, with viaducts and raised platforms and terraces. The congested city needed to be supersized. In New York City, planners had established a grid of avenues and cross streets, from lower Manhattan to Harlem. Le Corbusier saw the need for a grid that was even bigger in all its components, the blocks and the streets and the parks, in a more realistic preparation for the burgeoning population.

Le Corbusier rendered the City for Three Million People with thin lines of ink on delicate tracing paper, a portrait of uncluttered order. The cruciform towers were drawn rising up amid spacious plazas and trees, under open skies with one puffy cloud; the horizon was clear and unfettered. But it was a conceptual blueprint and received by some as science fiction. Three years later, he unveiled a more specific plan that showed how the scheme could be implemented – in a proposal so brutal, so un-flinching, that he would be known for it for the rest of his life.

Like the Maison Citrohan, the Plan Voisin was another at-tempt at a partnership with a car manufacturer. He had con-sidered the Peugeot and Michelin empires as well, but Gabriel Voisin, a friend and patron who had written an essay for *L'Esprit Nouveau,* was a natural partner. Voisin's cars were the toast of the town, the symbol of a new era. The movie star Rudolph Val-entino had one, as did Maurice Chevalier and Josephine Baker; Le Corbusier himself owned the C7-10 Lumineuse, and he would park the car in front of several projects for photographs. The car and the city would go hand and hand – but only if the city could be retrofitted to better accommodate motorized travel.

The Plan Voisin called for eighteen cruciform office towers of glass and steel, sixty stories high, on a sweeping rectangular grid that was a huge open park, with raised terraces for pedestrians and broad roadways slicing through, east and west, north and south. An adjacent area of residential, government, and cultural buildings was also an orderly arrangement of big structures, each on its own pedestal of a city block. As a place of commerce and living, the Plan Voisin could accommodate current and future populations, providing ample office space and housing twelve hundred people per acre – triple the most crowded parts of Paris at the time. And the city of the future would be served by high-ways, train and subway lines, even an airport that would become the grand entryway to the city. Le Corbusier was poetic in his de-scription of his creation:

> [The] delicate horizontal lines span the intervals between the huge vertical piles of glass, binding them together with an attenuated web. Look over there! That stupendous col-onnade which disappears into the horizon as a vanishing thread is an elevated one-way autostrada on which cars

cross Paris at lightning speed. For twenty kilometers the undeviating diagonal of this viaduct is borne aloft on pairs of slender stanchions.

In the new business centre office work will be performed, not in the persistent dimness of joyless streets, but in the fullness of daylight and an abundance of fresh air.

Do not smile incredulously. Its 400,000 clerks will be able to scan a landscape such as that one looks down on from the lofty crests above the Seine near Rouen and behold a serried mass of trees swaying beneath them. The stillness is absolute. . . .

When night intervenes the passage of cars along the autostrada traces luminous tracks that are like the tails of meteors flashing across the summer heavens.

Two hundred meters above it lie the spacious roof-gardens of these office-skyscrapers, planted with spindle-berries, thuyas, laurels and ivy. They are gay with beds of tulips or geraniums and the herbacious borders of bright-eyed flowers that wind along their stone-flagged paths. Overhead electric lamps shed a peaceful radiance. The depth of the night makes the prevailing calmness but the deeper. Armchairs are scattered about. There are groups in conversation, bands playing, couples dancing. And all around are the suspended golden discs of other gardens floating at the same level.[13]

The winding lanes and cross streets lined with shops and cluttered with cafés would no longer be tolerated. "The street as we know it will cease to exist," he proclaimed.[14]

The futuristic vision was no flight of fancy. A new Paris was urgently necessary. Behind the romantic facade, the icons of the Eiffel Tower and the Arc de Triomphe, Paris in the 1920s was

burgeoning, unwieldy, and unhealthy, teeming with substandard housing and shantytowns. The metropolis was at capacity
and every day seemingly closer to collapse. The evidence of this
looming failure was all around him, on his walk to work and all
around town. So many people, crowded together, doubling and
tripling up in apartments built for another time. They jostled in
the streets, where the horse-drawn buses were outnumbered
by double-decker trams and, increasingly, private automobiles.
Every fall, when the vacationers of August returned, it seemed
like there were more cars in Paris than ever before. Their headlights lit up the Champs-Élysées. Everywhere the streets were a
cacophony, the building facades slathered with advertisements,
the sidewalks dotted by overflowing garbage pails, everything
covered in soot and grime.

The technological advances of the day had reached the factory and transportation – the car, the locomotive, the ocean
liner – but not the basic human function of how people lived
their daily lives. To Le Corbusier it was an insult to human dignity to be stuck in the nineteenth century in this way, an unac-
ceptable shortcoming. Cities were not worthy of the age and no
longer worthy of mankind.[15] Their centers needed to be decon-
gested, with better-planned green and open spaces, allowing the
traffic to circulate, while at the same time accommodating more
density.[16] The height restrictions on buildings, imposed by long-
dead kings, should be lifted, he thought. Cluttered city blocks
needed to be redesigned entirely, purged and simplified and consolidated. The street, so perilous to pedestrians, would cease to
exist in its current form. The urban future would be cleansing,
calm, and powerful, the metropolis set in the fullness of daylight
and abundance of fresh air.

The reimagined city required starting over – cutting away at
the old to make way for the new. The demonstration would be
vivid; the site Le Corbusier had chosen for the Plan Voisin was

two square miles in the heart of Paris, on the Right Bank north of the Île de la Cité and Notre Dame, the third and fourth arrondissements. In the bull's-eye was the neighborhood known as Le Marais.

A patchwork maze literally translated as "the swamp," Le Marais had once been an aristocratic stronghold, built from scratch by King Henri IV and centered on the big square park, the Place des Vosges. But when the royal court decamped for Versailles, the grand mansions, the *hôtels particuliers,* were chopped up into slipshod workers' tenements. Immigrants poured in, sanitation couldn't keep up, and the overcrowding bred disease. Virtually every home in one precinct was condemned as uninhabitable because of a stubborn outbreak of tuberculosis.[17]

He promised to save major churches and landmarks, including the Place des Vosges. Everything else would be cleared away—a comprehensive and necessary act to supersede "the medley of silly little reforms with which we are constantly deceiving ourselves."[18] "The city is crumbling," he proclaimed, "it cannot last much longer; its time is past. It is too old . . . the disequilibrium grows day by day." He continued: "Surgery must be applied at the city's centre. . . . We must use the knife. . . ."[19]

It couldn't have been clearer. To save Paris, he would have to destroy it.

The idea wasn't entirely outrageous. Rue de Rennes, the quickest route to the atelier, was a reminder of how Paris not so long ago had been similarly reinvented. The wide boulevard was one of two dozen blasted through the medieval city by Georges-Eugène Haussmann.

At the midpoint of the nineteenth century, conditions were even worse than in Le Corbusier's day. The city was a maze of squalor and chaos. Thousands lived in substandard housing no landlord would bother to fix, so great was the demand for shelter. Congestion stifled commerce and the basic functions of life, as the carriages stood off on the narrow lanes, unable to pass one another. Even longtime residents routinely got lost in the crazy quilt of streets sprouting off in every direction, turning corners, zigzagging, dead-ending, diverting into dark alleyways. Bands of thieves preyed on the citizenry, accosting victims in the labyrinths dimly lit by oil lamps.

From upper floors the cry of *"Attention! De l'eau!"* signaled waste tossed down to the streets, which funneled effluent, via open gutters in the center of the roadways, to latrine reservoirs where workers shoveled it into barrels to be carted off to a forest outside city limits.[20] The drinking water, straight from the Seine, was so poisonous that it killed many foreigners, including Mozart's mother.[21] Disease spread quickly in the close quarters, killing thousands in outbreaks of cholera.

Haussmann, summoned by Louis-Napoléon Bonaparte in 1853, set himself to the task of starting over. From his offices in the Hôtel de Ville, he commanded fourteen thousand laborers wielding pickaxes and trowels, working all day and into the night, the excavations illuminated by floodlights powered by the emerging new energy source, gas. Over twenty-two years, he transformed the city, beginning with the Île de la Cité, site of Notre Dame, and moving outward on both sides of the Seine, conjuring wide boulevards radiating in straight lines and punctuated by new grand monuments and public buildings; eighty-five miles of new streets with an average width of eighty feet, and wider sidewalks, rotaries, and public squares. He doubled the numbers of streetlamps and trees, rebuilt the aging bridges vaulting the Seine, installed a modern water and sewer system that became a model for the world, and bracketed the city center with expansive landscaped parks, the Bois de Vincennes and the Bois de Boulogne. New housing took the form of uniform seven-story apartment buildings occupying whole blocks, a hundred thousand new structures with consistent facades, entrances, cornices, and ironwork balconies. Notre Dame was refurbished, the Louvre expanded, and grand new public buildings rose up, chief among them, L'Opéra (now Palais Garnier), designed by the architect Charles Garnier, whose ego matched the task at hand. "One must be God," he said, "or else an architect."[22]

The *grand travaux,* funded through a private bank owned by the Péreire family, was lauded around the world as an act of extraordinary creation, the original urban renewal. Camille Pissarro painted the new streetscapes, images that endure as iconic Paris. Mark Twain wrote that the city had been tamed – making much of the legend that above all the other public benefits, the Haussmann plan deprived the periodically rebellious masses of alleyways to duck into, and they could be fired upon down the long straight boulevards as a matter of regime preservation. But it had required massive destruction. More than 27,000 existing buildings were demolished, and 350,000 people, 20 percent of the city's population, were evicted. The backlash was inevitable, led by Victor Hugo and Charles Baudelaire, who lamented the purging of the old city, and residents, such as those around the Jardin du Luxembourg, opposed to the plans for redevelopment. An enterprising journalist revealed the financial house of cards; the actual cost was fifteen times greater than initially advertised. Crédit Mobilier, the Péreire brothers' bank, collapsed. Haussmann was hounded out of town, and, not long after, Napoléon went into exile.

The lesson was not lost on Le Corbusier. To take the modernization of Paris to the next level, new forms of persuasion would be necessary.

A central task was to convince the city that such a sweeping redevelopment would work financially and deliver huge economic returns. For this he turned to the principles espoused by Henry George, the nineteenth-century American political economist who ran for mayor of New York City and whose ideas led to the game Monopoly. George believed that government set the stage for private real estate development with comprehensive planning and investments in infrastructure, and it could tax the resulting enormous increases in land and property values – a win-win creation of immense wealth. Le Corbusier courted real estate developers, carmakers, and business leaders to make the case; what he needed then was a big event to showcase the plan as part of a package of all his ideas for embracing the modern. Happily, a perfect venue was at hand: the International Exposition of Modern Industrial and Decorative Arts of 1925.

The massive gathering was billed as a clarion call to the future: "You have to be modern and let it be known" was its slogan. It was a world's fair marking the transition from art nouveau – the initial embrace of a new industrial aesthetic, expressed in the parabolic arches of the Eiffel Tower and the Paris Métro's ornate headhouses – to art deco, the new style of the machine age inspiring the sleek designs of luxury sedans and the Chrysler Building in New York City.

Le Corbusier had little use for art nouveau or art deco, which he viewed as superficial and commercialized. It wasn't his idea of the modern. The organizers, in turn, didn't care for Le Corbusier, and assigned him a remote site, occupied by a tree in the middle, at the fringe of the grounds. Relishing the challenge, he built his pavilion, called L'Esprit Nouveau, so the tree poked up through a neat circle in the ceiling. He was handed further ammunition when the exposition bureaucracy also ordered the construction of a high fence obscuring his handiwork. What was it they were trying to hide? Visitors flocked there, curious to see what the fuss was about. He had successfully crashed the party.

While the other pavilions strutted and preened, L'Esprit Nouveau was a minimalist reduction: a white box with a giant checkerboard of black-framed windows at its front. It was in

every sense a model home, demonstrating how residential construction could be streamlined and standardized using industrial materials, stripped down and simplified, inside and out. The
double-height living areas, overlooked by a bedroom loft, were
sparsely furnished with simple wooden chairs and a leather sofa,
with an elegant built-in cabinet and a metal set of stairs, reminiscent of an ocean liner. The industrial style – re-created decades later by the likes of IKEA and Crate and Barrel – extended
to a coffee carafe, fashioned from a chemist's flask. And on the
walls, next to paintings by Le Corbusier's friend Fernand Léger,
was the storyboard of the Plan Voisin, showing how the new approach to living could be multiplied over and over.

Two press releases that Le Corbusier had circulated completed the masterful exercise in public relations. Even in a town
brimming with new thinking, the ideas were shocking; the death
of the street, clearing away the heart of Paris, was beyond audacious. The architect was prepared to be attacked – the occupational hazard of a rebel. It might take time to be understood, but
meanwhile people were talking and that was important. It sometimes seemed that he alone appreciated how the stakes were so
high, as he aimed to improve the lot of all humanity before conditions got worse. There can be architecture, he had written, or
there can be revolution.

The walk to work concluded at the stately park and metro station at the intersection of rue de Babylone, boulevard Raspail,
and rue de Sèvres. To the left was the Hôtel Lutetia, grande
dame of Saint-Germain, its café seats spilling out onto the sidewalk and crowded day and night. Straight ahead and across the
park was Le Bon Marché, the oldest department store in Paris.
On the south side of the greensward stood the Jesuit complex
at 35 rue de Sèvres, where Le Corbusier had rented space for
his burgeoning architectural practice. It was a step up from his

cramped first studio at 29 rue d'Astorg, north of rue de Rivoli and the Jardin des Tuileries, but the space was nothing more than a hallway the monks were no longer using, forty yards long and only five yards wide. On the second floor overlooking an inner courtyard, it was painted plain white and was lined with windows, providing abundant light. Against the far wall were the drafting tables one after the other, each equipped with a black spring-loaded movable lamp at the top corner, splashing down more light. Plans were everywhere, on the tilted surfaces, rolled up on shelves, and sprouting from containers on the floor. The modern architecture of the twentieth century came from this place, deep within a building with an unremarkable neo-Renaissance facade and adjacent to Saint-Ignace Church. Sometimes the team worked at the drafting tables while the sounds of Gregorian chants wafted in.[23]

When he walked through the door, arriving after everybody else, the draftsmen looked up with anticipation, trying to gauge the master's mood. He spent little time in the small windowless office he had reserved for himself; instead he would pace up and down and check on the progress of projects. This was his company, and these were his troops. Three generations of architects would get their training there, but there were two people who were especially important members of the team.

Pierre Jeanneret, his cousin, had the chiseled good looks of a Swiss mountaineer and was seldom seen without his dirty-blond hair neatly parted and swept across his broad forehead. Nine years younger than Le Corbusier, and a few inches shorter with a stocky build, he had excelled in painting and drawing at L'École des Beaux-Arts in Geneva, where he was born. Le Corbusier met him in 1920 in Paris, where he had come to further study architecture, and saw great potential in his thoughtful, if not worldly wise, cousin. He recommended Pierre apprentice with the Perret brothers, just as he had done, and the two men began what would be a lifelong partnership; the name of the firm in Paris was initially Jeanneret, Architects. They complemented each other well. Pierre would often take the first run at renderings for a commission, understanding his cousin's creative direction but keeping in mind the practical limitations of site, materials, structural engineering, and all manner of construction details. He was also effectively the office manager, making sure the accounting was in order, becoming a liaison between Le Corbusier and the rest of the team, and smoothing relationships with clients when they frayed. In the early days, the two of them would often stay up until one a.m. or later, and Pierre would never flinch. If Le Corbusier thought of himself as Don Quixote, Pierre was without question Sancho Panza: his more sociable cousin was "always right," and indispensable for the operation of the business.[24]

A few years after the duo settled into a well-functioning routine, the atelier got its other critical addition. Le Corbusier well remembered the day Charlotte Perriand walked through the door.

Twenty-four years old, she was a doll-faced brunette fresh from art school with a boy's haircut and a necklace of shiny ball bearings. She was struck by Le Corbusier's description of architecture in *Vers une architecture* – the "masterly, correct and magnificent play of volumes brought together in light" – and had seen the L'Esprit Nouveau pavilion. Heading over from her photography studio in Saint-Sulpice, she knocked on the door at 35 rue de Sèvres. If Le Corbusier was thinking as males often do – seconds after meeting a woman, making the calculation of his chances of sleeping with her – he didn't let on.

"What do you want?" he asked, peering over his eyeglasses.

"To work with you," she said.

He glanced at the drawings she had brought. "We don't embroider cushions here," he sniffed, and showed her the door. She left him her card and an invitation to see her work – interior design – at an exposition in town, never thinking she'd see him again and feeling a little bit relieved, given the frosty encounter.[25]

In fact, the very next morning, Pierre and Le Corbusier headed straight for her booth at the Salon d'Automne, the annual exhibition of painting and decorative arts that had been a stage for Rodin, Cézanne, Matisse, and many others, as well as Le Corbusier, who debuted his City for Three Million People there. Perriand's booth featured a snazzy lounge, with a bar capped by a nickel-plated cornice and stools made of four aluminum tubes braced by a succession of three circles of the metal, ascending like cartoon radio waves. A coffee table topped with glass – an unusual choice of surface in those days – was supported by a cruciform stand. Part space age, part jazz age, the Bar sous le Toit, as she called it, was a smash hit at the salon. People were crowding around, as if they wanted to start mixing martinis right then and there. The two cousins looked at each other in silent agreement. She was hired.

Perriand brought flair and joie de vivre to the atelier, and most of all, she was the spark for the furniture line that would soon be recognized around the world and mimicked in interiors from suburban ranch homes to dentists' waiting rooms. Furniture had been an important part of the business – sleek and tailored tables and chairs went hand in hand with the minimalist interiors, as part of a package. Though it could be thought of as mere add-on accessory, Le Corbusier considered furniture to be a powerful statement, something that needed to shed its privileged past – the precious settees and painted dressers, descendants of the ancients in Egypt, Greece, and Rome – and become functional once again. From the temple to the castle to the Victorian sitting room, furnishings had become prized and dainty possessions, trophies of wealth and power, rather than practical tools to store books or eat dinner at or to sit in and recline. In that sense, Le Corbusier was said to have remarked, sofas were bourgeois – whereas chairs should be architecture. The gambit, pursued by fellow modernists Charles and Ray Eames, Marcel Breuer, and Ludwig Mies van der Rohe, among others, was to design furniture that was comfortable, functional, and visually striking, in the modern style.

For the task, Perriand shopped in hardware stores and gathered armfuls of steel tubing intended for bicycles, and visited a friend's shop for fine English leather. The results were stunning. The boxy armchair, with overstuffed leather cushions set in silver tubing at right angles, held the dinner party conversationalist upright; the LC4 chaise longue, a chrome crescent set in a black lacquer base, cradled the human body in recline. Perriand herself served as the model for photographs of the "relaxing machine," feet in high heels raised up, body serene on the taut ponyskin upholstering and leather headrest. The use of industrial materials, Le Corbusier hoped, would lead to mass production and an affordable option to furnish the similarly mass-produced modern home.

That same promise – efficiency, affordability, comfort, and function – was the inspiration for yet another new business line for the atelier: the development of a compact car. Like furniture, the car was a critical component of Le Corbusier's vision for a new way of living, part and parcel of the homes and apartment towers he was designing. The focus of the burgeoning automobile business in Europe in the 1920s was on luxury sedans and race cars, turned out by Porsche and Bugatti, all aerodynamics and muscle and speed. Le Corbusier was himself fascinated; he loved his Voisin and eagerly took the wheel at a Fiat factory that had an oval test track on the roof. But if the car was to fulfill its promise as a liberating force for personal mobility, it would have to be more compact and affordable. Henry Ford was leading the way in that sector with his Model T, and Citroën and Renault and Peugeot followed suit. There clearly was an opening, however, for him to jump in and build a vehicle himself to go with his homes. With the expansion into the new product line, he could provide every element of modern living.

He and Pierre called it the Voiture Minimum: a rolling half-crescent on four wheels. The rectangular windshield dropped down sharply, with headlights below; the rear sloped down more gently, accommodating the engine in the back. Two thin doors opened outward toward the front, welcoming driver and passenger into an interior that was as simple and spartan as the furniture the atelier was turning out.[26] No bulbous fenders, no garish grilles: It was a means of transportation.

Over several years, Le Corbusier and Pierre Jeanneret revised the designs for the prototype until it was ready for production. But they could never close a deal with a manufacturer. The compact car of destiny would belong to someone else: Ferdinand Porsche's Volkswagen Beetle, the people's car. Le Corbusier could reasonably argue that he had the idea first.

The homes, the urban schemes, the car, the furniture – even at one point a brief foray in designing women's clothes: The innovation going on at 35 rue de Sèvres was something that legions of young designers eventually sought to be part of. They came from all around the world: Georges Candilis from Greece, Nadir Afonso from Portugal, Junzo Sakakura from Japan, and Josep Lluís Sert, future dean of the Harvard Graduate School of Design, from Spain. The time working in the atelier was universally inspirational, informing each of their personal styles. They weren't in it for the money; actual paychecks were sporadic. And they were roughly treated.

The role of unforgiving boss was scripted in Berlin, when Le Corbusier labored for the autocratic Peter Behrens. Now it was his turn. The draftsmen, arriving long before the master, braced themselves for the late-morning dressing-down over plans they had worked on until late the night before. Compliments were rare. He scolded them like children, for not being better organized. A big blowup might result in an on-the-spot firing. Though Pierre would often intervene, welcoming the chastened back into the fold, on at least one occasion Le Corbusier changed the locks on the door to keep an ousted young architect from returning. On the days when the master left before 5:30, when Yvonne preferred to have him home, the team would repair to the Hôtel Lutetia to commiserate.[27]

There was always a moment of inspiration to keep them there, like when he put a Bach cantata on the record player while the team put the finishing touches on the interior of a villa.[28] They all sensed they were part of something big. Working in the atelier was a privilege to be earned daily.

The intensity would not ease, even with the triumphs that lay ahead.

2 ▪ THE MASTERPIECE

The icon of the International Style came by way of a reluctant insurance agent with a weakness for golf.

Pierre Savoye was a diligent entrepreneur. His fortune was made insuring textile, mining, and chemical companies at the turn of the century. Savoye was a founding partner, with Gustave Gras, of an insurance company called Gras Savoye, which would rival Lloyd's of London in the business. What he was particularly good at was judging risk, the calculus of the value of property and the odds of disastrous loss. If there were further conflicts on the scale of World War I, and he was convinced that was inevitable, all manner of individuals and organizations would need protection. He was matter-of-fact but insistent in explaining this dark side of owning property and land and buildings and businesses, and dozens of customers came to trust him. His polished art in laying out the options would be copied by later generations of agents. By 1929, he was atop an empire, albeit based on impending doom, that ultimately included insuring the Louvre and the *Mona Lisa*. There was money to spend.

The idea of a country house, a second home, was automatic for a man in his position. Yet Pierre Savoye, insurer to the wealthy, shied away from possessions himself, particularly land and property. It was an occupational hazard. The more he knew about the risks of mass destruction following World War I, the more he was convinced that such investments would end in peril. He was content to rent an apartment in the building his family owned, in the seventeenth arrondissement. The woman he married had no such hesitations. Eugénie Savoye was a cardinal's niece from an aristocratic family in Lille, where her husband had started his insurance business. She had smooth skin and stern features, with thin lips and a nose that poked at the cheeks of the people she kissed on both sides. Eugénie was a dedicated choreographer of the couple's social life, entertaining and attending dinner parties, introducing and being introduced, being connected – Charles de Gaulle was the best man at their wedding – and otherwise reveling in the role as an aristocratic lady who had become a very successful businessman's wife. She wanted a weekend house, but with one big difference. It didn't need to be a big estate; she had no castle or manor in mind, like what Pierre's sister was building then, outside the Paris periphery. She would be satisfied with simple accommodations a short distance from the city, a place to relax and entertain.[1]

Her argument was bolstered by something her husband found harder to resist: proximity to a country club, a relatively new phenomenon, to enjoy a sport that was just catching on at the time. A maddening game requiring a clear mind and precision of movement, golf was being made at least a little bit easier by advances in equipment technology. The Prince of Wales had recently played a round at Saint Andrews with steel-shafted clubs, which were beginning to replace wood. Pierre Savoye liked the feeling of smacking the white ball down lush green fairways and chipping onto carpeted greens at the freshly opened Saint-Germain golf club, or La Boulie in Versailles. It was a tempting vision – to drive a half hour or so from the center of Paris to a second home, shed the compulsory formal dark attire for comfortable, sporty leisure wear, play a round of golf, and end the day with cocktails with friends. The routine would be standard procedure in places like Fairfield County, Connecticut, in the years ahead, but at the time, the lifestyle of the newly wealthy was a work in progress. The Savoyes were in the avant-garde of leisure.

The location for the dream presented itself in a little town in the western suburbs of Paris, a short distance north of Versailles. Poissy was a mere fifteen miles west of L'Étoile, along the winding path of the Seine in Yvelines, a pastoral commune known for making a liqueur from apricot pits, and Ben Franklin's chosen home while in France as an envoy. Its rolling hills, a world apart from the city yet easily reached by car, were destined for suburban development and trophy homes. Nearby, Robert Mallet-Stevens had recently built a residence for Paul Poiret, the couturier who had freed women from corsets. The western suburbs were clearly becoming a fashionable neighborhood. So when a friend, the president of a mining company, bought the 128-acre estate of the Château de Villiers in Poissy and offered a 17-acre subdivision that included a hilltop meadow surrounded by forest and orchards, Pierre Savoye relented.

With the land purchased, his wife took over, turning to the all-important question of the architect. There were lots of things she wanted to be part of this house, but a great, modern kitchen was near the top of the list – and she coveted one in particular. Le Corbusier was working on a redevelopment of a collection of small buildings in Ville-d'Avray, adjacent to Versailles, for an American couple, Henry and Barbara Church. The interior was a spartan spread of chaise longue and easy chair on a tile floor, framed by a simple picture window. The light reflected off shiny sliding aluminum panels on long rows of triple-decked built-in bookcases.[2] She tracked down the man behind this design.[3]

The letter of introduction, delivered to 35 rue de Sèvres in the fall of 1928, was followed by a tidy list of specifications: a large pantry; electrical outlets for all the latest appliances including a washing machine; a living room where she could entertain, with a big fireplace; a spacious master bedroom, a room for their son, Roger, and a guest room; servants' quarters, a caretaker's lodge, and an apartment for the chauffeur; storage space for trunks and tools; a wine cellar; and a garage for three cars, including the Voisin they drove. She decreed that the project should stay on budget and suggested she might like to add on to the house down the road.[4]

Sharing the brief with Pierre Jeanneret at the atelier, Le Corbusier seemed only to see the words that sealed the deal: that in terms of the overall form of the weekend house, it should be anything the architect wanted. They would give him carte blanche.

He and Pierre exchanged knowing glances. There was not so much discussion between the two men but an increasingly unspoken understanding. The commission was added to the file, under the name that would grace the lower corner of the renderings, in capital letters: MME SAVOYE. A visit to the site was planned. The Savoyes wanted a house near a golf club. Le Corbusier went about the business of creating a work of art.

Of all the occupations of the atelier, from the furniture to the grand urban planning schemes, the housing and apartment buildings, and other projects including many that would ultimately be labeled "unexecuted," it was the villas that paid the bills. By the end of the 1920s, Le Corbusier had designed fifteen of them—distinctive white structures of smooth concrete and right angles, with thin metal black sash windows, handsome and austere and elegant. He had worked himself into the position that was the envy of any retailer: Everybody wanted one.

It was a gift, the ability to deliver a home that pleased the occupants but pushed the frontiers of design. Each one featured something new, in a steady evolution, beginning with more traditional structures and incremental touches of flair.

He built his very first house at the age of seventeen, from 1905 to 1907, in the town of his birth. With the project of the Villa Savoye before him, those days in La Chaux-de-Fonds seemed a lifetime away. But it was there that he first plunged into architecture and experimented with new building designs. Commissions for several homes, made possible by increasingly wealthy clients from the watchmaking industry, set him on his way. Once again, Charles L'Eplattenier opened the doors for him. The art school master telephoned René Chapallaz, the local architect who had designed his own house, and asked if he might team with one of his most promising students to build a house for the esteemed jeweler and watch enameler Louis Fallet. Le Corbusier eagerly went to work on the Villa Fallet, the first of several homes he would help design in an emerging neighborhood on a slope at the northwest fringe of the city. It was a typical chalet with a base of Jura stone and capped by a triangular crown. But the exterior was distinctive. The facade featured two balconies, one the full width of the house and the one above half as wide, framed all around with dozens of little conical fir trees etched onto the surface of the exterior and the roof brackets. With its subtle broadcast of geometry and nature, no home celebrated the natural setting of that northwest corner of Switzerland in quite the same way. The architect-in-training, foreshadowing his practice of public relations, arranged to have the place photographed, requesting that the images would be enhanced if the residence was speckled with new-fallen snow.[5]

With his first creation, Le Corbusier took great care and paid attention to details, but the greatest joy came in pushing the limits of convention. Of the Villa Fallet, he wrote, "There is nothing routine about its architecture. I understood then that a house is built with materials and by workmen, and that success or failure hinges on plan and section. This gave me a horror of official teachings, formulas, and divinely ordained preconceptions, and I became convinced . . . of the need to rely on my own judgment."[6]

Word spread about the charming home up on the hill, beginning with Fallet's extended family. Albert Stotzer, a professor of mechanics at the watchmaking school in La Chaux-de-Fonds, and Ulysse-Jules Jaquemet, a watch polisher, promptly commissioned similar homes of their own. Both those structures were capped by the vernacular pitched roof of the region, though the side walls were steadily stripped of ornament.[7]

The fees from those commissions formed the foundation of his career as a young architect; he used the money to finance his travels through Europe – the journeys where he filled his sketchbooks and returned with his head full of new ideas. For his next project, he turned to clients literally close to home. Although he only discounted his fee instead of working for free, he sought to build a grand home for his parents in the very same neighborhood as the Villas Fallet, Stotzer, and Jaquemet. A plot of land was available for what would be the outermost house of La Chaux-de-Fonds; beyond it was forest and the border with France. Marie and Georges Jeanneret-Gris, who had lived in the city center, beginning with the apartment building where Le Corbusier was born, would be installed in a pastoral setting, with a garden terrace and expansive views to the south. The Maison Blanche, so named for its unadorned white walls, marked the turning point for the personal style of the young architect, then twenty-five years old. Only the triangular pitched roof echoed the chalets of the Jura region; the house was his most modern in appearance to date, both outside and in, where the living area, kitchen, dining room, study, and bedrooms were arranged in stripped-down simplicity. The pergola at the entrance to the garden recalled one he had seen in Pompeii, while the overall form was a dreamy combination of Istanbul and Frank Lloyd Wright.[8] The Maison Blanche was designed to be experienced in a promenade, beginning with the steps from the road and, once inside, maintained by a constant relationship with the world outside. The study with its custom-built desk overlooked the garden, while the spot for Marie's piano was a place of refuge as well. In the master bedroom, Le Corbusier raised the bed up high, so his parents could gaze out over the rustic horizon. The front door handle was a salamander in the style of art nouveau – a parting gesture that signaled the beginning of a new era. Inside there were pegs where Georges could hang his boater and cane.

The Maison Blanche, the first house Le Corbusier designed completely on his own, required just six months to build and attracted even more attention in his hometown and beyond. The clients who came to call were increasingly wealthy, owners of watch-manufacturing companies employing hundreds. Georges Favre-Jacot, maker of Zenith watches, asked for a villa in the sister city of Le Locle, another mansion on a hill. So did Anatole Schwob, owner of Cyma and Tavannes watches, who chose a site that would become the first project in the city center of La Chaux-de-Fonds. The mustard-colored concrete surfaces of the Villa Schwob were smooth and alternatively boxy and bowed, sparely adorned with rectangular, square, and oval windows all around. It was a mansion in town, a celebration of what he had come to call "regulating lines" and an expression of his journey to the Orient; it was entirely fitting that the residence came to be known as the Villa Turque, or "Turkish House."[9] Though he had his first major quarrel with a client, over adjustments Schwob demanded, the final product was a standout on a prominent street corner, surrounded by traditional structures that appeared drab by comparison.

Nearby, yet another commission, this for a sleek cinema, also put the young architect's signature on the neighborhood. The architectural firm of Charles-Édouard Jeanneret-Gris was on a roll. His listed services included building villas, country houses, and apartment buildings; industrial design; *transformations et réparations;* and designing storefronts, interiors, and landscaping.[10] He could have continued and transformed even more of his hometown, but Paris beckoned.

It was Amédée Ozenfant who provided the first opportunity to build there. Ozenfant, who had not turned his back on quite all the family wealth in his break with the bourgeois, commissioned a residence and studio in the fourteenth arrondissement, on avenue Reille overlooking the giant Montsouris reservoir. On a corner with a lane gently rising from avenue Reille, surrounded by sober and traditional attached buildings of about four stories, the white town house with black metal sashes combined the look of a café and an industrial factory. At the base was a garage, a novelty at the time, and spacious quarters for a housekeeper. The light poured in from huge panels of windows that almost entirely occupied the exterior wall, wrapping around the corner of the building and up to the ceiling, all glazed right angles. The occupants ascended by way of a spiral staircase from the foyer to the main floor, then up steps through a trapdoor leading to the rooftop garden.

A dapper banker from Basel who had taken an interest in Le Corbusier was the next big break. Raoul Albert La Roche, the head of a major financial firm, deputized the architect to buy modern art for him; he got good deals on six Picassos, but Le Corbusier charged more for his own canvases. La Roche's burgeoning collection, including not only Picasso, Le Corbusier, and Ozenfant, but also Léger, Lipchitz, and Braque, needed an appropriate home. La Roche proposed a combination residence and art gallery in Le Corbusier's emerging sleek style, situated in Auteuil in the sixteenth arrondissement, then little more than a village. The Villa La Roche (1923–25) would be his most striking creation to date, white blocks supported by concrete columns, and inside, the first use of his signature ramp, the better to gaze at artwork. The configuration was a precursor to Frank Lloyd Wright's Guggenheim Museum many years later.

The interior was clean and spare and pure, with built-in bookcases and storage areas maximizing the use of space. Each wall got its own pastel hue, the first major deployment of his color palette, the *polychromie*. A loft library, up above like an aerie, overlooked the cubist volumes of living space, abundantly lit by skylights and dotted with tubular chairs, plump leather cushion sofas, and metal tables of Le Corbusier's emerging furniture line. Moving through the house was conscious and mesmerizing – an architectural promenade. On the top floors, the tips of trees appeared through the windows, adding to the serenity of the package.

All the while, as he was building momentum in the villa business in Paris, he had not left Switzerland entirely behind. There was unfinished business involving unhappy clients. For all its wonders, the Maison Blanche had become too much house for his parents, with an outsized mortgage that was an unsustainable burden for the watch engraver and part-time piano teacher. World War I had decimated the watchmaking industry, so his father was making much less from engraving. Furthermore, even the hardy Swiss, as they neared retirement, found the promenade a bit of a slog, especially in winter when the snow piled high; Georges had developed arthritis. By 1919 the Jeannerets decided to quit La Chaux-de-Fonds entirely, moving to the village of Les Chables initially and then Corseaux, near Montreux, on the shores of Lake Geneva. Their unrepentant son tried in vain to convince the real estate agent that the sale price should be much higher; it was sold at a loss. "This town. I hate it," he wrote to a friend. The new owner got an eleven-page letter from the designer, telling him how to furnish it and otherwise respect the architecture of the Maison Blanche.[11]

Whether driven by guilt or the determination he brought to all endeavors, Le Corbusier sought to make sure his parents enjoyed their retirement in proper fashion, leaving the watch-making capital far behind. While his parents stayed in rented quarters, he scouted out a site in Corseaux, part of Vevey, in 1923. The location was a more industrial, working-class town on the emerging Swiss Riviera – home to the invention of milk chocolate and Nestlé – but also a retreat for personages such as the philosopher Jean-Jacques Rousseau, the writer Graham Greene, and the actor Charlie Chaplin. Vineyards stretched up steep slopes from the shoreline, the mountainside served by narrow switchbacks and funicular trains. Shrewdly negotiating with farmers for a parcel of flat land right at the water's edge, he secured the perfect spot for the Villa Le Lac, also known as La Petite Maison: precursor to the suburban ranch, the most elegant trailer home ever created. For this exercise in rightsizing, he designed a thirty-six-foot-long rectangular box of corrugated aluminum, recalling the fuselage of a plane. Inside, every inch of space was used for maximum efficiency, from the parlor that doubled as a guest room, with a trundle bed hidden under a hatch, to the kitchen sink and stove set out for compact work flow. Building on his use of colors at Maison La Roche, he painted the walls aquamarine, cobalt, and rust. Up top he laid down sod and plantings, in what was arguably the first green roof. He inserted strategic skylights, illuminating unexpected spaces, like the tiny bathroom and the closet. The little house was like an ancient temple at the water's edge.[12] It was so fine, he later added a room for him and Yvonne to stay in when they came to visit.

The structure occupied most of the tiny site, but there was room for a little yard at the eastern edge, and for this Le Corbusier invoked a modest but powerful bit of landscaping: a simple cantilevered table stretched out beside a strange creation – a solitary wall fronting the lake with a rectangular opening at its center, like a picture frame. "In order for landscape to count it has to be limited," he said, "proportioned through drastic steps, blocking the horizons by raising walls and only revealing them at strategic locations through breaks."[13] The landscape was similarly framed on the inside of the house. At the kitchen window, Marie had a front-row seat in the theater of Lake Geneva: the peaks of the mountains across the vast body of water, the long steamboats moving steadily this way and that on the lake, the changing weather of mists and storm clouds and rays of sun shining down. She could peer outside and see all of it, and then turn back to her chores, whether putting away the dishes or washing the dog.

His father would live only one year at La Petite Maison, but his mother would live there until she was one hundred years old; his brother, Albert, would take up residence there after that. The projects for his parents had a special place in his pantheon, especially Vevey, although he might not have imagined that both La Petite Maison and the Maison Blanche would become painstakingly preserved museums, visited by thousands.

Back in Paris, after the successes of the Villa Ozenfant and especially the Villa La Roche, he was rapidly becoming the architect of choice for distinctive residences in and around town. By now it was a familiar feeling to be sought after, and he was determined to take advantage – just as he had done with his popularity in La Chaux-de-Fonds, but more so. The interest kindling among the intellectual avant-garde was especially gratifying, and the engagement with the Parisian elite played out nicely in the house he built for Michael Stein, whose sister Gertrude was the stout sage for Matisse and Picasso, Fitzgerald and Hemingway. Michael and his wife, Sarah, were art collectors who teamed up with Gabrielle de Monzie, ex-wife of the public works minister who had stepped in to rescue Le Corbusier's L'Esprit Nouveau pavilion at the 1925 exposition, for a double residence in the western suburb of Garches.[14] The complex was an ensemble of cubes and horizontal ribbon windows, sharp-lined loggias and cantilevered overhangs; Le Corbusier had his Voisin photographed by the sliding front metal gate and outbuilding garage. The building materials, so intrinsically heavy, seemed to float around a little landscaped park.

The client, who would come to be known as "Papa Stein," was intrigued by the construction process and would linger at the site, admiring the architecture as it came together. But the occupants were not entirely obedient – or satisfied. They insisted on bringing in all their old Italian Renaissance furniture, not the spare furnishing Le Corbusier had recommended. It was a harbinger of a bad fit. Like his parents and the Maison Blanche, they ultimately sold the property.[15]

There would be other tangles and not-so-happy endings. The sculptor Jacques Lipchitz, who had commissioned a residence in the sixteenth arrondissement at Boulogne-sur-Seine, recommended Le Corbusier to the American artist William Edwards Cook, who sought the ultimate cubist house in the same neighborhood. There wasn't much room to work with at the site, but Le Corbusier created another simple and hard-edged structure, with horizontal bands of windows, and an inversion placing the bedrooms on the ground floor and the living room and library up above. Cook, who had just collected a vast inheritance, second-guessed the designs at every turn, confronting Le Corbusier nose to nose like a baseball team manager facing an umpire. And then there was Raoul La Roche, the nicest, most generous man he could ever know, who was forced to point out that there were serious problems in Auteuil – plumbing that didn't work, insufficient heat and lighting, bedrooms that did not accommodate his wife or the staff, and a moldy wall, a perilous condition not only for day-to-day living but for the artwork. That which could be fixed was fixed, and La Roche quietly paid for it all.

These were insignificant details and glitches, patched up as part of the punch list. Some of the clients couldn't seem to keep the focus on the big picture. He was out to change architecture utterly; there was much more at stake than an occasional damp wall. The basic principles of modern architecture needed a clear listing, so he turned to the printed word yet again, publishing the five points of architecture, a blueprint for achieving greatness, the Le Corbusier way.

First, he wrote, the contemporary building worthy of the modern movement required pilotis, reinforced concrete columns, to lift up the structure by at least one story, freeing the ground underneath for gardens and traffic or air circulation. The next requirement, a flat roof, was similarly a way of maximizing the use of space, providing an additional level for a garden or lounge; jettisoning the pitched roof was also an artistic statement, so that buildings as sleek boxes and cubes retained clean lines, free of the ornament of a cornice or parapet.

The third component, the free plan, was the most essential, as a matter of engineering. In traditional buildings, the walls dividing interiors into rooms were load bearing; they were necessary or the building would fall down. Under the old rules, the living room, bedroom, dining room, and kitchen all needed to be arranged in fixed squares and rectangles, in what Le Corbusier called *le plan paralysé*, or "the frozen plan." The use of columns and reinforced concrete that he recommended provided structural support all around the perimeter, leaving the interior to be designed however the client and architect wished. The kitchen could be open to the dining room and then on to the living room. There need not be any interior walls at all.

The fourth ingredient, the free facade, was also possible because the supporting columns could be hidden within or behind the exterior walls. In traditional buildings, the outside of the house, including components like windows and doors, served a structural function. They had to be there. The structure was legible from the ground up. Pilotis and reinforced concrete liberated the facade, allowing it to be plain and smooth, and freeing the placement of doors, windows, and other elements to follow the dictates of function and design. The free facade, in turn, enabled the fifth and final touch, the horizontal strip window, a band of fenestration running uninterrupted from one end of the building to the other, letting the light pour in from the outside and bestowing panoramic views.

Le Corbusier published these essential ingredients of modernism in 1927, just before he received the first letter from Eugénie Savoye. The weekend house in Poissy would express the five points of architecture so fully that it would be the ultimate expression of perfection in contemporary design.

The sites for the villas around Paris and in La Chaux-de-Fonds varied from the urban – like the Villa Ozenfant and the Villa Schwob, squeezed into a streetscape – to more expansive settings, like the Maison Blanche and the Villa Le Lac. But there was nothing quite like the pedestal that would display the Villa Savoye.

The center of the land that Pierre Savoye had purchased was a convex dome, a meadow encircled by trees that swayed in the breeze, a hilltop oasis, and an obvious sun-trap. Down below, to the north, the Seine made a gentle bend on its convoluted journey to Paris. The site was reached by bushwhacking in from a lonely street that came up from the town center, and Le Corbusier immediately deemed it sacrosanct. "The view is very beautiful, the grass is beautiful and so is the forest. We will preserve this. The house will stand in the midst of the fields like an object, without disturbing anything around it," he wrote.[16]

The building would relate to the landscape, and vice versa — indoors and outdoors, in constant interplay. He pictured a white box floating in that green field, perched upon fifteen concrete stanchions, the pilotis from his five points of architecture, that would act as trestles to enable a free plan for the interior.[17] It would be an abstract object and a mystery, both declaring its outward form and tantalizing the visitor to learn of the secrets within: a white square, raised up, with a continuous band of black sashed windows wrapped all around. There would be no hesitations about the architectural play of space and mass.[18] Traditional country estates were imposed on the landscape, with a long driveway and a grand entrance. The Villa Savoye would have no obvious front door. It would have four fronts, all equal, facing north, south, east, and west.

Reached fundamentally and necessarily by car, the white gravel driveway nosed into the property and circled around, the exact turning radius of a 1927 Citroën. Subtle garage doors opened to the space Eugénie Savoye requested for three vehicles.

From the beginning, Le Corbusier envisioned the architecture as a theatrical experience. The visitor would approach down a rosebush-lined parallel driveway, not entirely sure what this creation was all about. It would unfold step by step — first the discovery of the front door, a simple entrance of black metal frame set in translucent glass, in a central shaft thrust down to the ground containing storage and the servants' quarters. Then the ascent into this flying saucer of a building by a gently rising ramp or, alternatively, a spiral staircase. A hostess in a prim and proper manor might greet visitors on a sweeping staircase in a flowing Victorian gown; here visitors would be clad in smart and spare Chanel-style clothes, joining the party to a George Gershwin soundtrack.

Surprises awaited around every turn; the classical protocols were nowhere to be seen, and little was familiar as a home. The kitchen, dining room, and living room were all open to one another, and rooms seamlessly ran from inside to outside, an enclosure morphing to an outdoor terrace in a few short steps. The horizontal strip windows framed the trees and grass outside, so that viewing the landscape was like watching a movie or looking at a painting in a museum. The bathroom, with a built-in chaise longue of checkered blue tile, was a Turkish bath. The handrails, white and tubular, recalled the ocean liners the architect so admired.

Though it was a white box with a band of dark windows, inside, Le Corbusier deployed the use of color that he had established at the Villa La Roche and La Petite Maison. The palette, based on the *polychromie* he had since formalized in a partnership with the wallpaper company Salubra, was of pulsating blood and the fresh hues of the prairie. These were applied selectively to walls and doors and panels, and never the same on adjacent surfaces. Color, he believed, modified space and activated interiors. The living room had pink and pale blue; Roger's bedroom had clear ochre; the master bedroom had light gray and wheelwright blue. Pastel yellow adorned the tiles, while the strip wood flooring was the natural color of oak. As a final touch he equipped the home with a system of small, elegant flood lamps, the precursor to track lighting, which in time would become ubiquitous in interior design.

Nothing about it would be easy. Building the Villa Savoye was not so much an act of construction as a perilous conjuring. Like a writer's manuscript, the blueprints were subject to constant revision, with many onsite adjustments and various decisions made on the fly, as difficult challenges presented themselves.[19] For the local government, the contractors, and the suppliers, this was unfamiliar territory in every regard. In issuing the equivalent of a building permit, nobody was quite sure what to write. Pierre wrote to the mayor of Poissy, informing him the house on the former farmland of the Château de Villiers wouldn't be aligned in traditional fashion along an existing road. It would have its own distinct way of approach. Nor would it rise up from the landscape in a conventional way. "We must free our minds of romantic, spidery construction," Le Corbusier wrote. Houses of liquid concrete "could be built in three days, like filling up a bottle. It comes out of its formwork like a piece of cast iron . . . no one will believe this; a house must take at least a year to build, they think, and surely cannot be a home without pointy dormers and attic bedrooms."[20]

As he imagined for his quick-construction Dom-ino houses, the Villa Savoye was cast onsite. The process was a combination of post and beam and laying of hundreds of clay bricks, concrete mixed with natural mortar imported from Switzerland, largely untried glazing and weatherproofing. There were issues with the wiring, the floors, the paint, the heating, the metalwork, and the joinery. The size of the window frames wasn't quite right. The shell rose up with simple spindly scaffolding all around. The budget rose, the delays extended seemingly every time it rained.

Yet when it was finished, the Villa Savoye would stand as his acropolis. It had been twenty years since the trip to Bulgaria, Turkey, and Greece, recording the simple forms and soothing colors of the Mediterranean and the elegant ruins of the Parthenon. He had propped himself up in hostel beds and drawn in his sketchbooks, and now it was here in front of him, splendid and striking and buzzing with the power of place.

Even before the clients would move in, Le Corbusier, convinced he had created something important, was hard at work at public relations. He invited two journals, *L'Architecture d'Aujourd'hui* and *L'Architecte,* to publish big spreads, the photographs depicting the pristine interiors, almost entirely free of furniture. The reception was seismic. The Villa Savoye was swiftly the most talked-about project in the world of architecture, a product so entirely fresh and new, it promised to alter the course of the profession for the rest of the twentieth century. The picture of the house would spread around the world, appear on magazine and book covers, the very definition of modern. Everything he had worked at for the previous twenty years – the theory, the artistry, the execution – came together on that meadow in Poissy. He had asked in *Vers une architecture:*

> From what is emotion born? From a certain relationship between definite elements: cylinders, an even floor, even walls. From a certain harmony with the things that make up the site. From a plastic system that spreads its effects over every part of the composition. From a unity of idea that reaches from the unity of the materials used in the unity of the general contour. Emotion is born of unity of aim....
>
> [C]lear statement is essential in a work of art. Clear statement, the giving of a living unity to the work, the giving it a fundamental attitude and a character: all is a pure creation of the mind.
>
> Architecture only exists when there is a poetic emotion.[21]

A cruise ship floating in air, a panoply of colors, a beach house on stilts, and, above all, a place of enjoyment, for living life. Sometime during the construction of the Villa Savoye, Le Corbusier finally concluded that a home so joyfully occupied was something he and Yvonne deserved to have as well. Amid the flurry of interest and commissions coming in, large and small – from Moscow to Algiers, Bogotá to Paris, the latter for the Cité de Refuge housing accommodations for the Salvation Army – there was another project in the sixteenth arrondissement that gave him his opening. The apartment building at 24 rue Nungesser et Coli, a few blocks from Roland Garros Stadium and the Bois de Boulogne, was an otherwise unremarkable act of urban infill. But on the top two floors, he would build a little villa of his own.

"Corbu has finally had enough of all the sarcastic remarks people make about it," Yvonne said, referring to the garret in Saint-Germain, "he wants to live in a Le Corbusier building."[22]

The new neighborhood was a big contrast to the Latin Quarter. Like La Chaux-de-Fonds, Paris was pushing itself to the outskirts. The area of Porte Molitor was once occupied by fortifications, but since the end of World War I it had been infused with sports facilities amid the Haussmann-perfected green spaces of the Bois de Boulogne. There was a big public pool, walking paths, and a botanical garden; the access to recreation and the light and air reminded Le Corbusier of his blueprints for the Plan Voisin. Development was picking up in the area, which was less than a mile from the spot where Raoul La Roche had situated his private art gallery and home. The Parc des Princes real estate company asked Le Corbusier and Pierre Jeanneret to fill in the gap between two apartment buildings at 24 rue Nungesser et Coli, just south of boulevard d'Auteuil, overlooking a soccer and rugby stadium.

The site didn't lend itself to a major aesthetic statement, and the building had to conform to turn-of-the-century building codes, but the atelier still managed to make a mark, with a facade of handsome dark glass and stone. Inside, the apartments, which were to be individually sold, were arranged with the style and precision of what he had envisioned for the Immeubles Villas.

The structural support of the building allowed him to design the units according to his five-point principle of the free plan.[23]

The top two floors, the penthouse unit, he kept for himself, to be outfitted with special care. "It was dangerous for me to go and live in a building of my own," he wrote, tongue in cheek, to his mother. "Really, it's magnificent. There's a view over the countryside with no sense of being perched up on the 7th and 8th floor"—thanks, of course, to his own architectural strategies, which made the penthouse duplex the most scrupulously designed living quarters for miles around.[24]

The rooms flowed into one another with ease. Overlooking the sports stadium and bathed in morning light, his private study and painting studio provided the critical space for him to work at home. He could sit at his simple desk, with its built-in pigeon-hole shelving, or wander over to an easel set up in the middle of a spacious studio. He deliberately left the party wall undressed, the masonry rough and exposed, foreshadowing a prerequisite feature in expensive real estate from New York City's Greenwich Village to blocks surrounding San Francisco's South Park.

A hallway dotted with built-in nooks for the display of primitive art led to the compact kitchen, dining room, and bedroom, with the platform bed raised up so he and Yvonne could enjoy the view out the windows without craning. On that side of the apartment building, the view to the Bois de Boulogne and Parc de Saint-Cloud was the equivalent of that from a tower at the edge of Central Park in Manhattan—of the city, but apart from it; a promontory overlooking comforting green. A simple spiral staircase provided access between the floors, to a guest bed and bath area, splashes of red and black amid the bright white. The rooftop terrace was a special observatory. He planted chamomile, mint, rosemary, lavender, thyme, and basil, and the flowers and herbs all thrived there. He would pad around his garden barefoot, smoking cigarettes in the open air and sunlight.

All the elements of the interior fit together in spare harmony. He would revel in his own handiwork, his own perfect client. And it was all in an up-and-coming neighborhood, with parks and gardens and cafés nearby, along with soccer and rugby, and tennis at Roland Garros. After he packed up the last of seventeen years' worth of papers and all his belongings from 20 rue Jacob, from the spring of 1934 onward, the domestic transformation was set permanently in place. Le Corbusier bought a dog, a wirehaired schnauzer given the name Pinceau, which he would walk in the adjacent park. With the move to the outskirts, he also began the ritual of the daily commute. Instead of walking to the atelier, he would take the metro – the No. 10 line went straight from Michel-Ange–Auteuil to Sèvres-Babylone, where he could emerge right at Le Bon Marché – or drive, making his way across the Seine and through Javel, the district home to bleach factories and André Citroën's assembly plant. When he was not traveling, the routine was sacrosanct: The mornings were for painting, and the arrival at the atelier would wait until the early afternoon. The penthouse at 24 rue Nungesser et Coli would be the couple's primary home for the rest of their lives.

Yvonne was far from overjoyed. She had no interest in leaving Saint-Germain-de-Prés, where she knew all the shopkeepers and the neighborhood, and shared none of her husband's enthusiasm for being a pioneer in a new part of town; why would anyone want to leave the heart of Paris? The interior of the penthouse left her equally cold, all bright and white. It hurt her eyes, all that clean, unoccupied space. Decor had become a special focus in the couple's long-standing practice of driving each other crazy. She would see a space and move to fill it with something – a doily, a knickknack, anything. His preference was to leave white space alone, or selectively place a primitive sculpture – a piece of Peruvian pottery, a tapestry by Léger. After seeing the rue Nungesser et Coli apartment for the first time, even before moving there, she had lamented to a friend, the Hungarian photographer Brassaï, "You can't imagine what it's like! A hospital, a dissecting lab! I'll never get used to it."[25]

The move was a battle she was destined to lose. The sixteenth arrondissement was the new lively part of town, he argued. There were new neighbors, right there in the building, and they were terrific. "The sky is radiant and for two weeks now we've been living in a miraculous new setting: a home that's heavenly, because everything is sky and light, space and simplicity," he wrote to his mother. "After grumbling on principle, Yvonne did what cats do: she went round and round in her new box and now she's purring. That means that broom in hand and polishing endlessly she's running her house with the jubilation of a conqueror. She won't say so, though, because she's as obstinate as a little donkey . . . she's got her own ideas and habits. We leave each other in peace. The apartment fits admirably with this form of wisdom."[26]

Over in Poissy, the situation could not be papered over quite so easily.

When the Savoyes saw the first sketches, their concern was that the project would surely go over budget. Le Corbusier came back with another pared-down set and a slightly different design to placate the clients. In the end, they wanted the original design—just with assurances of a lower cost. The fixation on the hundreds of thousands of francs they were spending may have left them unprepared to witness the final product, in all its shocking, radical beauty. Emerging into the hilltop clearing, they gasped. Pierre Savoye turned to his wife, who was consumed, taking it all in, and had just one question: Where is my wine collection supposed to go?[27]

While the elite of the architectural world was enchanted, the family seeking a country retreat wrestled with a variety of disappointments, some of them downright alarming. Eugénie Savoye, having moved in during the summer of 1930, put it succinctly: It was raining in her house.

The water came in through the entrance hall. The garage wall was absolutely soaking. The bathroom, too. The dampness was a particularly bad problem because their son, Roger, had respiratory problems. An added insult was that the rain made a terrible noise on the windows and surfaces of the Villa Savoye, keeping everybody up all night.[28]

The gradients didn't drain, and the bituminous waterproofing malfunctioned. The heating system didn't work properly; the wiring was faulty. Le Corbusier blamed the contractors, who laid the fault at the design. The exchange of letters became increasingly feisty, as the clients disagreed on everything from furnishings to the plantings outside. By 1937, Eugénie had had enough. "I was very surprised by your letter after numerous complaints," she wrote, after Le Corbusier had once again dodged the issues she had raised. "You have finally recognized that the house is not habitable," and the responsibility to make things right was his alone, after ten years of struggle. "I do not intend to get involved in this expense. Please make the building habitable at once. I hope that I will not have to resort to legal means."[29]

Pierre Savoye stepped in, intimately familiar with disputes and litigation as part of the insurance business. You seem to be able to send visitors to my house, he told the architect, but not respond to my letters. He demanded to see the plans, convinced it was not the contractor but the original design that was flawed, and began the steady process of threatening to sue the architectural firm.[30]

Dealing with complaints had settled into a familiar routine. At first, Le Corbusier would take the slightest criticism as a personal affront and provide a lawyerly point-by-point rebuttal, withering and often sarcastic. Frequently, clashes arose when inhabitants did not follow his choreography properly, in the use of windows, the planting of flowers, or the furnishing of interiors. He had a way of making the recipient of his admonitions feel silly and ignorant, backing off just enough at the end of a vituperative letter to make it seem like it was everybody else who was being petty and vicious. The response to Pierre Savoye was typical. "We wish to do our utmost to satisfy you and you should consider us friends of your house. I hope to remain a personal friend of yours, since our relationship has been built on trust," he wrote. "I am, and will always remain, the friend of my clients."[31]

But year after year, the vision of the country club life in the fashionable western suburbs dissipated. The Savoyes were hardly going to Poissy at all by the time the German soldiers were closing in. Another war had come, just as Pierre Savoye knew it would. As a final gesture, before the occupying army used the hilltop site as a depot, he buried his country house wine collection in the meadow in front of the floating white box.[32]

3 ▪ THE DEBUT

The skyline of lower Manhattan emerged through the mist as the SS *Normandie* glided by the Statue of Liberty, the great gift of France. It had been five days since the grand art deco luxury ocean liner had left Le Havre, time well occupied in a first-class cabin and an ornate dining room that recalled the Hall of Mirrors at Versailles. En route, Le Corbusier had readied himself, jotting down phrases in English on cocktail napkins, including a toast, "Here's looking at you."[1]

When the big ship berthed, the towering bow of black and red trim nosing into the busy docks at the Hudson River, Le Corbusier prepared to step out of quarantine and into the metropolis he had seen only in photographs. He had spread his gospel of architecture and urban planning in Europe, Russia, northern Africa, and South America, and finally he had come to the ultimate frontier, the temple of the New World, as he called it – the nation that had come to embody the very definition of the modern. In his conceit, the question was not whether he would be welcomed, but the extent of the adulation.

The trip had been arranged, after arduous negotiations over fees and travel accommodations, by the Museum of Modern Art, later rebranded as MoMA, his main benefactor. But what started as a lecture accompanying an exhibit at the museum became a multicity tour worthy of Frank Sinatra. He was scheduled to visit civic institutions, museums, and college campuses all through the Northeast and the Midwest. He was set to see the vestiges of Daniel Burnham's 1909 Plan of Chicago and a Ford auto assembly plant in Detroit. He would visit the Massachusetts Institute of Technology (MIT), Yale and Princeton Universities, and Vassar College. In total, he would deliver twenty-two talks in nearly as many cities.[2]

The gallop through the United States would begin and end in New York City, however, and the first stop was the modern art museum, then in modest digs before the construction of its current location in midtown Manhattan. The museum curated an exhibit celebrating the visiting architect's life work, including drawings, photographs, and models of the Villa Savoye and another recent proposal for Moscow, the Palace of the Soviets. The museum walls were painted a pastel pink—"Corbusean pink"—as a nod to the architect's *polychromie*.

It was all so giddy, so full of promise. Yet the first moments in the new republic were puzzling—and a foreshadowing. Dressed in an orange shirt, dark tie, and gray suit, he assumed he would be greeted by paparazzi, capturing his arrival as a celebrity with the New York skyline in the background. But the guide and interpreter sent by the museum, Robert Jacobs, appeared all alone. "Jacobs, where are the photographers?" Le Corbusier asked. Thinking fast, Jacobs took him to the upper deck where a press photographer was taking pictures of a group of chorus girls vamping along the gunwale and offered five dollars if he would take a few shots of the architect. Wish I could help you, the photographer said, but I've just run out of film. Jacobs whispered in his ear that for the love of God, he had to live with this man for the next two months, and could he please just pretend to take his picture. Le Corbusier posed with stiffened back and ceremony while the empty camera snapped. In the days ahead, as he scanned the newspapers, he would ask, Where's my photograph? His American guide could only sheepishly shrug.[3]

Le Corbusier's expectations were as outsized as the city that would soon surround him. The journey that began that October morning in 1935 was many years in the making. Crossing the Atlantic had long been a singular goal, begun when he was a young man in La Chaux-de-Fonds and first glimpsed in journals the dazzling work that was going on in America. The monumental infrastructure was poetic to him—the flatiron skyscrapers, the bridges vaulting the East River, Central Park, Grand Central Terminal, Pennsylvania Station, and the Hudson terminal in New York, and the stately towers erected by Louis Sullivan and Daniel Burnham in Chicago. His admiration and wonder grew for the nation's engineers, who were surging ahead in construction methods of skeletal steel frames, embracing the technological advances of the industrial age, and transforming the cityscape. The great experiment of urban America was an inspiration for all of Europe, but Le Corbusier seized on what was happening with special zeal. The grand scale of building, and the efficient means of production, inspired his City for Three Million People and Plan Voisin, and the more recent iteration of towers in the park, what he had begun calling the Ville Radieuse, or "Radiant City." A diorama at the L'Esprit Nouveau pavilion at the 1925 exposition in Paris was labeled *Si Paris S'Américanisait* (If Paris Americanized Itself).

At the time of Le Corbusier's visit, the city was rising up in spectacular fashion in midtown, sixty blocks and a dozen subway stops from the cluster of Gothic and wedding-cake-style towers in lower Manhattan. Those ornate buildings, most named for the titans of industry of the time, outdid each other, one after the other, for the record of tallest building. Framed with steel and clad in stone, they were topped by neo-Gothic crowns worthy of the Notre Dame cathedral. The Metropolitan Life Insurance Company Tower was bested by the Woolworth Building, and so on, until the skyscraper arms race moved to midtown. In the space between Thirty-Fourth Street and the base of Central Park at Fifty-Ninth Street, the new cathedrals soared skyward: the Chrysler Building, with its sweeping art deco spire; Rockefeller Center, designed by the American architect Raymond Hood for the Rockefellers, the family that was so dominant in shaping the landscape of New York City; and there, rising up from seemingly the dead center of the island of Manhattan, the Empire State Building.

When he first saw that angular and tapering tower, he just wanted to lie on his back right there on the sidewalk and gaze up, the top floors piercing the blue sky, the spire reaching to the clouds. Its fresh appearance was clear evidence of what the Americans could do if they put their minds to it. New York did not dither in erecting the world's tallest building. The architect, William F. Lamb, put together the plans in under two weeks, basing the design on his twenty-one-story headquarters for the R. J. Reynolds Tobacco Company in Winston-Salem, North Carolina. (The staff of the Empire State Building would send a Father's Day card every year to the staff of the tobacco company, in a tribute to the origins of their own skyscraper.)

The project had the full backing of the governor of New York and the mayor and businesses of the city, all convinced of the need for an economic development project in the wake of the 1929 stock market crash and in the early years of the Great Depression. Over the course of just four hundred days, limestone was hauled in from Indiana, ironworkers applied rivets at a furious pace, and seventeen million feet of telephone wires were installed in the fifty-eight-thousand-ton steel frame. The interior was equipped with art deco flourishes, and the antenna spire reached fifteen hundred feet. Receipts from visits to the observatory exceeded the rents from tenants in the early days; it was like being in an airplane up there. The dizzying heights soon also inspired a rash of suicides, the bodies crumpling the roofs of parked cars and limousines on the street far below. The Empire State Building glowed with energy and promise and a certain terrifying beauty. It would be the tallest building in the world for four decades.

Le Corbusier loved it but for one thing: It wasn't big enough.

As impressive as New York City was, Le Corbusier had come armed with a blistering critique. He was no more prepared to lavish praise on New York than he was to let Charlotte Perriand know he was impressed by her furniture design. America, he believed, was fumbling the opportunity for a true transformation into the modern world. Ambitions were being unnecessarily contained. The great cities were going about it all wrong. The builders and planners needed help – they needed *his* help.

The fundamental problem, as Le Corbusier saw it, was that the skyscrapers were too close together, built in a jumble, each driven by individual private interests, without a coherent unity. The modern city required more height and greater density. A truer arrangement of the *grattes-ciel,* "skyscrapers," was this: bigger, taller, and each occupying its own block, allowing more room between the buildings and bathing the structures in light and air. The greater spacing, in turn, would allow better circulation, with cars and trucks zipping along on wider streets and elevated roadways.

New York City's grid, which from the earliest settlement of lower Manhattan had been laid out by a commission beginning in 1811, was a laudable exercise in planning ahead, in anticipating the rapid increases in urban population. The planning commissioners had the right idea of establishing order, eliminating the shantytowns that were dotting the upper reaches of Central Park. But the grid, Le Corbusier believed, fell short as a matter of scale, the blocks too small, the street network not robust enough, the avenues insufficiently wide. Le Corbusier warned against development that was cheek by jowl, like what had already happened in lower Manhattan. Accommodating housing and commerce could not be left to the forces of Wall Street and real estate speculators. There needed to be much more planning, more order.

And while he admired the system of parkways being built by New York's master builder, Robert Moses, he was wary of suburban expansion. The parkway should not be a tool to flee the city, he argued. Free circulation paired with greater density would bring all the benefits of the suburbs to the center of the metropolis.

It was a nuanced message, and a challenge to articulate for the visitor from Paris. In a radio address delivered three days after his arrival at the top of the RCA Building in Rockefeller Center, he flattered audience members, telling them how handsome and beautiful they were as they sashayed down the boulevards. But America could do better, and indeed the world expected the United States to blaze trails, in contrast to the stodgy deliberativeness of Europe.

"This is architecture's hour," he told his radio audience. He went on to say, "New cities have always replaced old cities. But today it is possible for the city of modern times, the happy city, the radiant city, to be born. . . . America, in permanent evolution, and in possession of infinite material resources, and animated by an energy potential unique in the world, is surely the first country capable of achieving this task today, and with exceptional perfection. It is my deepest conviction that the ideas I am setting forth here . . . and which I am offering in the phrase 'Radiant City' will find in this country their natural ground."[4]

"The old order is changing; we are entering upon a new era," he wrote in a guest editorial essay in the *New York Times,* illustrated with a photograph of the rooftop terrace at Villa Savoye. The home, architecture, town planning – all must be revolutionized, an exercise "so tremendous that we can only regard it as the beginning of a new cycle in the history of the human race."[5] While the skyscrapers of New York and Chicago have captured the imagination of all of Europe, their fatal flaw was the willy-nilly nature of urban development. The American cities were "mighty storms, tornadoes, cataclysms . . . utterly devoid of harmony." New York City, he said, was a beautiful catastrophe.

The clear goal was to gain commissions, to redirect American urbanism to align with his principles. But as a marketing exercise, the visit faltered early on. At his very first press conference, at the Museum of Modern Art – perhaps because he was tired from the journey and overzealous to finally make his points, like a candidate who stays up all night preparing for the big debate – the champion of a new urban form ended up sounding like a bit of a crackpot, critiquing the wondrous metropolis in terms that were utterly lost in translation.

SKYSCRAPERS NOT BIG ENOUGH, LE CORBUSIER SAYS AT FIRST SIGHT, read the headline in the *New York Herald Tribune,* above a picture of the architect looking up through Coke-bottle glasses, owlish and goofy, even slightly depraved. He later claimed the flash surprised him and couldn't understand why the assembled photographers weren't interested in his studio portraits from back in France, which he offered to them for the bargain sum of five dollars each. "My God, you can't do that to the *New York Times*," said Sarah Newmeyer, the museum's publicity director. Le Corbusier pocketed the pictures, looking slightly injured.[6]

The accompanying article, by a young Joseph Alsop, an Ivy League–educated skeptic of modern architecture who would go on to become a noted national political columnist, described the visitor in unflattering terms and is thought to have coined the term "egghead" in the process. In the subheadline, Le Corbusier's "Radiant City" was translated as the "Town of Happy Light," like an absurd item on a Chinese takeout menu. With the dubious Alsop at the keyboard – who spoke perfect French, favored bow ties, and in later years wore round eyeglasses exactly like Le Corbusier's – the outmatched Parisian didn't stand a chance.

For every step forward, there were two back. Through the modern art museum, he had solicited *The New Yorker* to do a big profile on him, on the occasion of his visit; an unimpressed editor took a pass. At times, he strained to make cultural connections. Displaying the chaise longue of metal tubes and comfortable fabric, fundamentally designed not by him but by Charlotte Perriand, he claimed it was inspired by the "lounging cowboys with their feet on tables" he had seen in the movies.[7]

He was getting attention, just like at the L'Esprit Nouveau pavilion at the 1925 exposition in Paris. The challenge was to be taken seriously.

Undeterred, Le Corbusier carried on, determined to convince the power structure, if not the public, of a superior form of city building. That October, he met with the directors of the Port Authority and the housing authority, and dined with Nelson Aldrich Rockefeller and the architect Wallace K. Harrison, the trusted friend of the Rockefellers who had worked on Rockefeller Center under Raymond Hood.[8] Le Corbusier clarified his remarks about the city's skyscrapers, objecting to them being like "little needles crowded together," rather than monumental obelisks spaced well apart.[9]

From New York City, he would venture to the Northeast, to Yale, Harvard, and MIT, and south to Princeton and Philadelphia, then on to Chicago and Detroit. But first, there was a far more important rendezvous. His accommodations were a matter of some drama. Rejecting the museum staff's offer of a bedroom at the French Institute, he requested the Waldorf Astoria, which was unavailable. "I wish to be where I can see Broadway," he announced. His old friend, the painter Fernand Léger, was staying at the Park Central, a grande dame of a hotel on Seventh Avenue that Le Corbusier found somewhat mediocre – but was interested to learn that a Jewish gangster, Arnold Rothstein, had been gunned down there, giving the place a tinge of excitement. Once the lodging was settled, he moved on to more urgent matters. Moments after checking in, he contacted the red-haired, blue-eyed woman he had recently met in Switzerland. The heiress with the mansion in Darien, Connecticut, and a beachside cabin on Long Island Sound was his truest guide and companion in America.

Marguerite Harris was tall and athletic, comfortably wealthy, and restless. The daughter of Richard Tjader, a Swedish big-game hunter, explorer, and evangelist, she attended Bryn Mawr College and Columbia University and married Overton Harris, a successful New York attorney and later a judge, but the marriage disintegrated, ending in divorce in 1933. She befriended the socialist author Theodore Dreiser, who helped her found *Direction,* an edgy leftist journal that featured a Christmastime cover of a white present wrapped in a ribbon of barbed wire and dotted with bloodspots. In addition to being an editor, she was a budding novelist herself. She wasn't one to stay at home.

In her estrangement, she made an extended trip to Switzerland in 1932, taking her young son, Hilary, with her. They went on hikes, taking in the alpine air. Basing herself in Vevey, she came upon a striking rectangular box of a building on the shore of the lake one day. Thinking it might be a holiday cottage, she rang the bell at the Villa Le Lac. "Is this place, by any chance, for rent?" she asked of the white-haired owner, in slippers, who answered the door. Le Corbusier's mother politely explained that she lived there year-round, in the house built by her son. A month later Le Corbusier was there, on one of his regular visits back home, and was soon out on excursions with Harris, exploring the vineyards that sloped steeply above the lake and describing the house he would build for her someday.

After she returned to the United States, they maintained a secret correspondence, right up until those breezy October days when he arrived in New York. She was thrilled he was coming to America, and he eagerly accepted her invitation to be a chauffeur and interpreter. Driving into the city from the family's Victorian mansion in Darien, Harris took the architect to the top of the Empire State Building, the Chrysler Building, and the RCA Building, each an inspiring promontory. They took the subway to Wall Street and back up to jazz clubs in Harlem, and danced at the Savoy.[10] They climbed into Harris's black-and-tan Ford V-8, putting Hilary in the rumble seat, and traversed the glorious parkways that Robert Moses had built, the George Washington Bridge, and the Pulaski Skyway, an enchanting piece of infrastructure for Le Corbusier, raised up as it was on pilings that recalled his beloved pilotis. The roadway soared over the industrial plains and opened up to the skyline across the Hudson River. Romance and architecture, together again.

They repaired to Fairfield County in the evenings, and took a rowboat to a beach cabin the Harris family rented on Pratt Island, a spit of land off Darien on Long Island Sound. It had a fireplace and a deck overlooking the water. The sound was serene and blue and the beach was dotted with mussel shells. The architect stripped down and dove in at the first opportunity.

The college campus provided more of the welcoming reception Le Corbusier was anticipating. Striking out from New York, he delivered twenty-one lectures in thirty-four days, most under the title "Modern Architecture and City Planning," making the case for the Radiant City, his Plan Voisin modified into a repeatable template.[11] A silent film of the Villa Savoye was often shown, accompanied by the melodies of George Gershwin. He would sometimes refer to notecards but never read from prepared remarks, instead drawing on long sheets of tracing paper taped to blackboards, the PowerPoint presentation on the fly that he had perfected in South America. He would go through six rolls, nearly a third of a mile, of that paper, by his own calculations.[12]

One by one, he descended on the buttoned-down institutions of the Northeast, appearing at the Wadsworth Atheneum, Wesleyan University, and Yale in Connecticut, before moving on to Harvard and MIT. In Boston, he stayed at the Copley Plaza hotel, dined at the Harvard Club, and ventured out at night to hear Louis Armstrong play at a jazz club. By day he met with the city's architectural community, including a young man named I. M. Pei, at MIT at the time; Pei would go on to build the John Hancock Tower, a Corbusean glass slab that remains Boston's tallest skyscraper, and the John F. Kennedy Presidential Library and Museum. At Princeton University, he marveled at the Gothic campus and the towheaded football players in their leather helmets and pads, and bestowed such pearls as "Gentlemen, you never have more than one bottom to sit down on."[13] When an uninitiated guest asked him to explain his work at a dinner at the Bowdoin College president's house in Maine, he borrowed a woman's red lipstick, cleared away the dishes, and sketched out a little urban planning right there on the white tablecloth. And at Vassar, some

six hundred students thronged his lecture, needing no translator because they all understood French, much to his delight. The
young women rushed the stage at the end, taking pieces of his
tracing-paper storyboards as souvenirs. He accommodated each
and every autograph seeker, bantering with them about how he
was really a humble and modest man.

The tour was not without the skirmishes he encountered in
the first days in New York. At a dinner in Philadelphia, he proudly
invoked the American phrases he had learned, including "son of
a beetch," to the shock of those seated around him. In the days afterward, he exchanged vitriolic letters with a prominent art collector, Dr. Albert Barnes, who had been there and was not amused.
Barnes called him "Master Crow" and accused him of being
drunk on whisky. Le Corbusier's last missive was returned, with
the word *merde*, "shit," scribbled on the unopened envelope.[14]

Chicago, the birthplace of the skyscraper and land of big
plans, would surely turn out better.

"Make no little plans. They have no magic to stir men's blood."
The admonition, attributed to Daniel Burnham, author of the
1909 Plan of Chicago, reflected just the kind of argument Le Corbusier used in the Plan Voisin — that true modernization could
not come piecemeal. America's second city would not imple-
ment everything in the plan, and there was far too much reliance
on the Beaux-Arts style, but the clear-eyed investments in infrastructure — and the resulting increase in property values — confirmed the inherent values of vision and scale. The radiating
boulevards and double-decker viaducts were designed in anticipation of the dominance of the car; the big parks and open space
recognized the need to bring in light and air and to ease congestion and overcrowding. And the big plans, ultimately, were born
of destruction. The Great Chicago Fire of 1871 wiped the slate
clean, eerily similar to the conflagration in La Chaux-de-Fonds,
making way for an orderly reinvention.

Like the first skyscrapers, including the majestic Monadnock, the planning to Le Corbusier was merely a good start. Chicago was still allowing itself to be too much of a jumble at its core, and leapfrogging expansion to the suburbs north, west, and south was troubling. Here again, the triumph of capitalism left obvious social shortcomings, infamously chronicled by Upton Sinclair in *The Jungle,* of which Le Corbusier would have been aware. From the slaughterhouses of the stockyards to the violent territories of Prohibition-era gangsters, there was a seedy quality to the metropolis.

But there was glamour, too. Once again it was only the best for Le Corbusier, who secured a suite at the Drake Hotel, at the top of the Magnificent Mile overlooking Lake Shore Drive. The future king of England had stayed there, and Joe DiMaggio carved his and Marilyn Monroe's initials in the bar in the Cape Cod Room, where the red snapper soup was served in pewter tureens. The architect was fascinated by all the finery: the carpeted staircases and grand ballrooms, and the sugar cubes brought by room service, individually wrapped in paper. The practice of wrapping things in paper and plastic was of particular interest; in Paris, he would say, food was arrayed in unsanitary, though appetizing, fashion.

Chicago was also the hometown of the man Le Corbusier viewed as his American counterpart and rival, Frank Lloyd Wright. The visitor from Paris let it be known, through third parties, of his interest in a summit. But the author of the Prairie style and Broadacre City — a suburban version of the Radiant City — was not interested, making the excuse that Wisconsin, his base of operations at the time, was too far. Privately, Wright said that "Corbu's influence in this country is just terrible, and he has no business here. I don't want to have to shake his hand."[15]

Eero Saarinen, the Finnish industrial designer who would make his mark in America with the Gateway Arch in St. Louis and the TWA Flight Center at JFK airport in New York, had no such reservations, meeting with Le Corbusier at Cranbrook Academy of Art outside Detroit.[16] Saarinen's father taught at the school, where the students included the modernist furniture designers Charles and Ray Eames; Saarinen's own tulip chair would be fabulously successful, marketed through the Knoll company. The trip to Michigan featured another highlight: a visit to the Ford assembly plant at River Rouge, capable of churning out six thousands cars a day. There was much to learn from this kind of efficient production – man and machine, building machines – that could be applied to architecture and city building. "Everything is collaboration," Le Corbusier wrote later, "unity of purpose, a perfect convergence of the totality of gestures and ideas."[17]

On his last night in Chicago, he discreetly arranged to engage the services of a prostitute. On the morning of that curious American holiday of Thanksgiving, he cuddled with her in the fine white sheets. He was in the mood to clown; when the room service breakfast arrived, he put one of the silver warming covers on his head, a shiny silver helmet to go with his uniform of broad-striped pajamas. Still punch-drunk on the flight back to New York, he stuck a plastic fork in his glasses by his ear. He was an alien visitor on a strange planet.

The disappointment was already starting to well inside him. The political and business leadership failed to embrace new thinking. The Americans seemed unserious, focused only on making money. His sour assessment formed the basis for the book *When the Cathedrals Were White: A Journey to the Country of Timid People,* a withering critique published after his departure. There were too many cars and not enough trees. The people glorified the past instead of looking to the future, and otherwise let Hollywood numb their minds.

In time, he drew a picture of himself stepping across the Atlantic, with a hat and his trademark glasses, and smoking a pipe.

One foot was toeing off from the promising metropolis of New York City; the other was stepping down in Paris, beside the Eiffel Tower. The direction of that long stride signified his return; he had given what he could.

On the final days back in New York, he summoned Harris once again, detailing his availability – on one day, only after midnight – by telegram. This time ensconced at the Gotham Hotel, he turned to her as a sole salvation.

"I can't imagine what my New York and my USA would have been without you ... around you affection accumulates," he wrote on the stationery of the MS *Lafayette*, on the journey back to France. "Everything was beautiful and fine and right, and fitting and loving. Why shouldn't the heart have the right to love in places where things cause it to open up, lay itself bare, and receive its full dose of joy and well-being?"[18]

Good-bye, my darling, he wrote.

He had every intention of seeing her again. But the other side of the Atlantic awaited, along with his life at home – Charlotte and Pierre and the team at the atelier, eager to know of the commissions they believed he would surely be carrying with him; Yvonne and her afternoon pastis; and Pinceau, delighted to go for a walk with his master through the parks of the Bois de Boulogne. The beach shack on Long Island Sound and the nights in the jazz club went back into their compartment. Stepping down the gangway onto the riverfront promenade at Bordeaux, the switch was flipped.

More than a decade later, Le Corbusier was summoned to help design a new international headquarters for the United Nations. Even if this kindled hope of a triumphant return, his relationship with America would only get more complicated.

The League of Nations was faltering in Geneva, and the world leaders sought a new beginning in a new capital, a fresh start to redouble efforts to resolve conflicts and avoid war. It was time to move from Europe, and the question was posed: Where is the center of the world?[19] The United States seemed a logical destination. San Francisco was deemed by the Soviets to be too far from Moscow, and Philadelphia, briefly considered, seemed less compelling. The New York City region emerged as the best candidate, with sites considered in Westchester County in New York, Fairfield County in Connecticut, and Flushing Meadows in Queens, favored by Robert Moses on the grounds of the 1939 World's Fair. Moses was heavily promoting the site when the parcel at Forty-Second Street on the East River was thrust into play. The flamboyant real estate developer William Zeckendorf had bought up a total of eighteen acres of what was known as Blood Alley, a collection of slaughterhouses and meatpacking facilities, the equivalent of Chicago's stockyards. The cattle were brought in on barges, the East River ran red, and the stench was overpowering. On these blocks, from Forty-Second to Forty-Eighth Street, Zeckendorf envisioned a futuristic complex he called X City, packed with luxury apartments, office and retail space, parks, a concert hall, and a heliport. But Zeckendorf had a secret: The financing wasn't even close to being in place. In a deal consummated over cocktails at the Monte Carlo nightclub in Manhattan, where Zeckendorf was celebrating his anniversary, the land was transferred to the Rockefellers for $8.5 million.[20] The Rockefellers promptly donated the site as the future home of the United Nations – and in the process blocked a new city-within-the-city that could have competed with Rockefeller Center.

The question then was what the complex should look like, and the consensus answer was modern, tilting toward futuristic, suggestive of audacity and rationality and reason, a brave new world at last. It was also decided that, befitting an organization with so many dozens of member states, the headquarters compound – a secretariat or office building for administrative functions, a conference building, and a general assembly – must be designed by a committee with full international representation. The man enlisted to coordinate this process was Wallace K. Harrison – top architect and all-around fixer for the Rockefellers, related by marriage to the powerful family, and the man Le Corbusier had met on his previous trip to New York in 1935. He was a big man, dark and hooded and handsome in his own way, easily mistaken for Robert Moses, except for his easygoing and conciliatory manner. As a young man he was an office boy for a construction firm in Worcester, Massachusetts, then took night courses as a junior draftsman in Boston, before joining the firm of McKim, Mead & White in New York. With Raymond Hood, he was a major force behind the development of Rockefeller Center.

As director of planning – a job title chosen over project leader to convey a team effort – his first task was putting together the panel of architects. On a piece of legal paper, he jotted down nearly twenty men from different countries to be recruited, and at the top of the list was "France: Le Corbusier."[21] Having studied at the École des Beaux-Arts in Paris, he admired Le Corbusier and was sympathetic about the way Le Corbusier had been roughly treated in the 1927 design competition for the original headquarters of the League of Nations, the precursor of the United Nations, in Geneva. The team at 35 rue de Sèvres had labored day and night to produce plans for a modern complex on the shores of Lake Geneva, but the submission was disqualified over a technicality: The renderings were not drawn with China ink as required by the specifications. The real reason was that the chairman of the committee disliked modernism and favored a traditional design, which was ultimately built.[22]

Harrison was also well aware of Le Corbusier's reputation for being difficult but invited him to join the team nonetheless, along with Gyle Soilleux from Australia, Gaston Brunfaut from Belgium, Ernest Cormier from Canada, Liang Ssu-ch'eng from

China, Sven Markelius from Sweden, Howard Robertson from the United Kingdom, Julio Vilamajó from Uruguay, and Nikolai Bassov from the Soviet Union.

The misapprehension began from the start. Le Corbusier assumed he would be the leader of the team, while Harrison worked as the primary liaison with the city. He never seemed to grasp the idea that this extraordinary place would be designed with all the players on equal footing, any more than a great work of art could be painted by committee. The first convening of out-sized egos took place on Presidents' Day, February 17, 1947, on the twenty-seventh floor of the RKO Building. Harrison, in shirt and necktie, having tossed his suit jacket aside, and smoking an ever-present cigarette, set out the mandate: to "produce something that will be a symbol for peace and security. Let's go to work."[23]

Le Corbusier was the first to speak, knowing no other way.

"All of Manhattan is our concern," he said. The complex should be a monumental exclamation point, a dramatic statement like no other in the city, with the secretariat as an immense tower in a park. In his pocket notebook, he had already drawn a giant rectangular slab of glass and steel, a variation of an outsized office tower he had proposed for Algiers, as well as the Ministry of Education and Health building in Rio.[24] The building should be oriented east-west, on the banks of the East River, to take advantage of the power of the rising and setting sun; the general assembly would extend northward, horizontally, at the base of the big office building. The whole block should be form, pure and simple. A spectacle in unity. He sought immediate agreement on his basic arrangement. The team, of course, had other ideas.

Nikolai Bassov from the Soviet Union countered with a totally different vision for the general assembly; Liang Ssu-ch'eng from China agreed that the compound should be bathed in sunshine but suggested lower buildings arranged in gardens. For the next four months they deliberated. The assembled architects produced some three dozen different schemes, every inch of wall space occupied by pinned-up designs, and the room dotted with models hastily created by the junior draftsmen known as the back-room boys.

After many smoke-filled days, broken up by lunch at Del Pezzo, an Italian restaurant Le Corbusier favored on Forty-Seventh Street, the schemes were winnowed down to two basic concepts: the buildings close together, as Le Corbusier had proposed, or pulled apart. The latter was championed by a late addition to the team, though tardy only because the US government balked at his communist affiliations. Oscar Niemeyer was the rising star of Brazil, soon to be the author of the sweeping plazas and monumental government buildings of Brasília, the modern capital. Dashing and obsequious, he brought a Latin verve to modernism, eschewing the hard, straight line for "free-flowing, sensual curves. The curves that I find in the mountains of my country, in the sinuousness of its rivers, in the waves of the ocean, and on the body of the beloved woman."[25]

Niemeyer had met Le Corbusier in a café in Rio in 1936 and helped execute the Ministry of Education and Health building, completed in 1943. On the UN design team, he was deferential, but ultimately the apprentice gained confidence to challenge the master, putting his signature on Scheme 17, the main competition for Le Corbusier's Scheme 23. Alliances were formed, and Niemeyer drew support from those who had developed a growing dislike of Le Corbusier; some could hardly stand to be in the same room with him. Harrison was determined not to take a vote, which would result in winners and losers, and urged the team to arrive at a consensus.

Sensing that he needed to assure everyone that he was a team player, Le Corbusier made a statement at a press conference, attended by more than thirty reporters from *Time, Life,* and the *New York Times,* among others. He stood amid the cigarette smoke, dressed in his dark blazer and bow tie, blinking rapidly behind his round black glasses, and delivered the message: that this wasn't about one individual's ideas or one person's credit. The task at hand was too important for that. "We are united, we are a team," he told the gathering, who had heard the rumors about a bitter battle over the form of the compound and jotted down Le Corbusier's assurances through a translator. It was actually invigorating not to work alone. They were all there, "laying down the plans for a world architecture. We will all work anonymously."[26] Niemeyer, sensitive to the cold, stayed in his hotel room.

In his private journal, Le Corbusier sketched what he really thought—a beautiful nude at rest on one page, representing Scheme 23, followed by the body parts violently broken apart, his depiction of how the young Brazilian had betrayed him by separating the building locations at far corners. The two men took turns drawing up new designs on the wall, each with a fistful of pencils, until Harrison attempted the masterstroke of diplomacy: that the final scheme would be based on Le Corbusier's, but with incremental adjustments by Niemeyer.

The design team dispersed, and Harrison took over the construction of the project—which in the end was, essentially, Le Corbusier's original design: an upright slab oriented east-west, with a swoop-roofed general assembly building adjacent to the north. President Truman laid the cornerstone, and the complex was completed in 1952.

Despite Le Corbusier's statement to the press, it was about credit. The UN building was his idea, but he had been steadily excluded and marginalized. On a later visit, he had himself photographed at the base of the compound, holding in his hand a picture of his original design, with the UN building in the background, rendering and reality one and the same.

He could have done the same thing elsewhere: the cruciform towers of the Radiant City juxtaposed with public housing projects that were built in Manhattan, Queens, and the Bronx and, in time, St. Louis, Chicago, and across urban America. The towers rose up spaced well apart, just as he said they should be. He could have posed with a picture of the Villa Savoye in front of dozens of copycat modernist homes, white with horizontal ribbons of black windows, from Westchester to Los Angeles. Or stood before Boston City Hall and other concrete structures on pilotis in the downtowns of just about every American city, developed in the era of urban renewal in the decades to follow. But all of that was imitation, and he was not flattered. It would take another time and another place for him to conjure a building in America that was his alone.

4 ▪ THE OPPORTUNIST

In summers past, from the rooftop at 24 rue Nungesser et Coli, he could hear the roar of the crowds at Roland Garros, as the French Open stars René Lacoste and Henri Cochet triumphed on the red clay. Now, in the gathering darkness, the great tennis stadium was being readied as a prison camp.

Everything was different after the columns of German soldiers marched down the Champs-Élysées, the trumpeters on horseback, the city festooned with bloodred, black, and white Nazi swastika banners. The occupation had begun; the shops and cafés shuttered, and the nation reeled at how a military strategy could have gone so terribly wrong. The Maginot Line – the thick band of bunkers, lookout towers, bell-shaped turrets, and other weapons installations running for hundreds of miles along the border with Germany between Switzerland and Belgium – had cost billions. It was supposed to stop another Lost Generation. The upstart young general Charles de Gaulle had warned against this strategy of defense, pleading for investments instead in mobile, mechanized warfare, in tanks and planes. But the graying generals of France were busy fighting the last war. The shock and awe came in the speed of it all – in simply going around the fortifications, through the Ardennes and the low country of Belgium, the Germans took just six weeks to complete the invasion. Across the countryside, tens of thousands of people had put their belongings on their backs or packed in cars, scrambling ahead of the advancing army. Instead of manning the pillboxes and fending off the invasion, the retreating troops spent the final hours destroying the remaining artillery they were forced to leave behind at the massive evacuation at Dunkirk. The tops of the cannon cylinders that were busted apart fell away like a banana peel.

Hitler had choreographed the humiliation well, culminating in the surrender ceremonies in the very same railcar where the First Armistice of Compiègne with Germany had been signed more than twenty years before. The dazed citizens of the proud republic wondered if there would be a France ever again.

As the world disintegrated all around, the penthouse apartment in Boulogne-Billancourt provided a safe enough haven. The building had a fine bomb shelter. Yvonne had done some redecorating and husbanded what the couple knew would be the last of diminishing food supplies. But like so many of their neighbors, the occupation signaled that it was time to leave. The architect closed the studio at 35 rue de Sèvres, put his surging career on pause, and quit the capital for a village in the Pyrenees. His cousin Pierre joined them there, in the little town of Ozon, far in the south near the border with Spain, and they rented side-by-side cottages. But the question of what to do next had never before been so unsettled. He had always had a plan, and it felt unnatural not to have one.

He had read how de Gaulle had fled for London, vowing to return and calling on all patriots who could to get to Britain to fight on. In the months that followed the fall of France in June 1940, though, the summoning of his fellow countrymen was improbable. Though many would join the infamous Resistance, most were sheltering in place, hoping to proceed with their lives as best they could, and were taking their cues from Marshal Henri-Philippe Pétain. The revered hero of World War I was working on a deal with the Germans to spare the bulk of the country from the destruction of war – an agreement for splitting the country in two, the north occupied by Germany, the rest administered by Frenchmen who pledged a full cooperation with the Nazi regime. That was the new reality, and Le Corbusier decided he would not run, or wait out the war, but rather seek to join the extraordinary arrangement, this different kind of surrender. The new government, as he saw it, would be intent on restoring stability and could use his help rebuilding the cities and providing low-cost housing, his specialties. It was a matter of patriotic duty. He would go to Vichy.

The spa town of Vichy, some five hundred miles south of Paris, had been a destination for taking the waters since Roman times. Now the leaders of unoccupied France were assembling a new capital there. Pétain, one of the generals who had insisted on the Maginot Line, led the way. All of France had seen the photograph of him shaking hands with Hitler at the summit at Montoire-sur-le Loir, his cylindrical French military cap pulled down close to his eyes, which met the gaze of the Führer in his double-breasted overcoat badged with an iron cross.

"It is with honor, and in order to maintain French unity," Pétain had said, ". . . to create the European new order, I today enter the road of collaboration."[1]

From a base of operations in a suite of rooms at the Hôtel du Parc, the best of the luxury properties in the quaint village, Pétain dissolved the last vestiges of democracy and gave himself unbridled powers. France's defeat, he argued, was not so much due to the Maginot Line as to moral weakness. France had been sidetracked, its ethos diluted. The new leader called for a return to basic values of work, family, and country, to grow strong again in a new order. The alliance with Germany would be a return to roots, to tribal traditions centuries old between the two countries; the friends of the twentieth century were now not to be trusted. The conquest of Britain was assumed to be inevitable, mere months away. As Hitler prepared to invade the Soviet Union, Pétain also stepped up an anticommunist crusade, targeting leftists who had been a political force in France for decades. And a special enthusiasm was reserved for aiding Germany in persecuting Jews, with legislation limiting ownership of businesses, confiscating property, and restricting movement, the first steps toward rounding up men, women, and children to ship them to concentration camps. The Vichy regime ultimately was as aggressive as the Germans in the purge; no mission better articulated the necessary purification of the country. Pétain and his cabinet quickly realized how easy it was to blame others for France's demise, to build popular support, confirm the new regime's authority, and assure the victors they were thinking in lockstep.

The team assembling in Vichy was a Machiavellian bunch with malleable loyalties. But led by the triumvirate of Pétain – who maintained respect and credibility among his countrymen – Prime Minister Pierre Laval, and Admiral François Darlan, the Vichy government plunged into the business of collaboration with zeal. While Darlan talked convincingly of a "greater Germany" stretching from Budapest to Brittany, he secretly harbored a plan to make a deal with the Allies after the invasion of North Africa years later. It was Laval whom the Germans trusted – and whom the French people loathed and feared. He coordinated the export of "volunteer" French workers to Germany and oversaw the deportation of Jews. And together with another stalwart fascist, Joseph Darnand, Laval was the official leader of the Vichy police force, the dreaded Milice, whose flinty members sported blue uniform coats, brown shirts, and wide dark berets, worn sharply angled down on one side. Their tactics of torture, round-ups, and summary executions made them more feared, by many, than the Gestapo and SS.[2]

It was this baleful milieu in the resort town in the center of France, amid the suspicious glances and the leather-holstered pistols and cocked berets, that Le Corbusier sought to join.

He made no public pronouncements of explicit support, but privately, he seemed to have convinced himself that an acceptable, and indeed promising, new order was at hand.

"If he is sincere in his promises, Hitler can crown his life with a magnificent work: the remaking of Europe," he wrote to his mother. He added, "Personally I believe the outcome could be favorable . . . if the problem consists of assigning each nation its role, getting rid of the banks, solving real – realistic – tasks, then the prognosis is good. It would mean the end of speeches from the tribunal, of endless meetings of committees, of parliamentary eloquence and sterility."[3]

The promise of real action in the place of bureaucratic dithering was especially appealing. Ever since the debut of the Plan Voisin and its later iterations, the high-density but lower-slung apartment buildings of the Ville Radieuse, he had struggled to win government support of his theories for large-scale urban re-development and housing design – not just in France, but anywhere. Brazil, in the end, had been a bust; only one building, the Ministry of Education and Culture, would be completed in downtown Rio. His proposals for apartment blocks overlooking the beaches never materialized. His advice on properly planning cities in America had similarly been ignored.

In Vichy, there would be a fresh start. It was a moment that needed clear direction and a mission: to rebound from the de-struction of the German invasion, to provide immediate shelter for the homeless and refugees, and, all the while, to plan for the future. The Pétain administration was merely the vehicle for finally putting his ideas in place; he just had to get in as a top adviser on housing and urban affairs. Then he could start orchestrating human settlement from a real position of power.

Though the new government would surely see the value of his counsel, he knew he would have to insinuate himself in an artful manner. Like anyone angling to be appointed a cabinet secretary, he needed not just a résumé but connections. The networking he engaged in, however, brought him squarely into the realm of right-wing French politics, xenophobia, and racial supremacy.

He built up relationships any way he could. The playwright Jean Giraudoux, who agreed to write an introduction to one of the architect's books, had become a propaganda specialist in support of Germany and retired to Vichy, carrying with him his obsessions with traditional marriage, the dangers of immigration, and racial purity. France, as he saw it, needed a minister of race to weed out the immigrants who had been "invading" the country and focus attention on proper breeding.[4] Dr. Alexis Carrel, who also became a major player in Vichy, had many of the same ideas, promoting eugenics and euthanasia. Le Corbusier came to know him literally by accident. He had been out for a swim off Saint-Tropez when a motorboat struck him and its propellers sliced open his right thigh. After being sewn up, he was told about a healing solution invented by the Nobel Prize–winning scientist and began a treatment regimen. The experience was a natural conversation starter.

Introduction led to introduction; the architect pursued his bid in an inscrutably personal way. When he finally met François Darlan, the small talk came around to the science of breeding dogs. The admiral's own dog was in heat for the first time, and Le Corbusier offered his beloved schnauzer, Pinceau, as a suitor. The match was never consummated; neither Pinceau nor the bitch was the slightest bit interested.[5] But he was gaining trust – to an extent. One of the first sticking points in becoming part of the new government had to do with his own issues of purity and allegiance. He was, after all, Swiss. Never mind that he had become a French citizen in 1930, spoke perfect French as his native language, and had lived full-time in Paris since 1917. One could never be too careful in Vichy – or feel totally secure.

He made the first arduous trips by car from the Pyrenees to Vichy, only occasionally subjecting Yvonne to being there. He took a room at the Queens Hotel and waited to be summoned, not knowing how long he would be there. He could not be blamed for feeling spied on when the care packages from his mother arrived from Switzerland. But his patience was rewarded. He finally met with Pétain and was appointed the equivalent of a cabinet secretary overseeing habitation and urbanism. At long last, Le Corbusier was poised to be the master builder of the new France. His initiatives began with the *constructions murondins,* neat shotgun shacks made of logs and tin roofs that served as temporary housing for refugees, and a sweeping new cityscape for Algiers in North Africa, which continued to be under French control. In Algiers he proposed continuous ribbons of curving apartment buildings served by an elevated freeway, and a huge tower, its facade a jigsaw puzzle of various-sized windows equipped with brise-soleil, his system of concrete windows and balconies designed to block the hot sun but let in cooling breezes. There were many other blueprints he hoped to roll out for the approval of the leaders of the unoccupied zone.

Eventually, when it was clear he'd be staying, Le Corbusier brought Yvonne into town, upgraded to a better hotel room, and started taking in a paycheck. Yvonne's health was deteriorating – she was dogged by everything from a blocked tear duct to liver disease, and was undergoing violent mood swings because of menopause. But her husband was determined to make the most of this new life. Best of all, his mother was supportive, happy that her son had navigated the difficulties of the horrible war; she wrote approving letters that he had long craved. Others were not so impressed. His faithful and hardworking cousin Pierre stayed in the Pyrenees to wait things out. Before the war, he and Charlotte Perriand had set a different course, aligning themselves with the political left. In Paris they had joined Les Jeunes (the Young Ones), an organization of communists and socialists, and convinced Le Corbusier to work with the group to put on the Pavillon des Temps Nouveaux at the Paris World's Fair in 1937. After fleeing Paris and moving to Ozon, Pierre relocated to Grenoble, utterly opposed to German domination. Le Corbusier's choice was so unfathomable that those closest to him could not speak of it. In a letter addressed to Le Corbusier's hotel in the picturesque riverside town, Pierre wrote that he didn't know where in the world his cousin was, but surely, he was not in Vichy. For Charlotte as well, the rupture would last the rest of their lives.[6]

Marie Jeanneret knew better. She was not surprised that her son would insert himself among powerful men. His dreams of reshaping human settlement – of nothing less than reordering society – had long been grounded in political realities. His impulses were, fundamentally, nonideological. He pursued those in power as a way to build. Whoever they might be.

More than a decade earlier, he had lectured for the Redressement Français, a neofascist group. In 1934, Benito Mussolini invited him to make presentations in Rome, Milan, and Venice. He came close to getting an audience with Il Duce, and was prepared to flatter and cajole the dictator to allow him to build his urban design schemes in Italy.[7] Another collaboration, an urban design scheme for Addis Ababa, the capital of Italian-controlled Ethiopia, was done with Giuseppe Bottai, head of the Italian Fascist Party.

Joseph Stalin, who like Le Corbusier had changed his name — the mustachioed dictator drew from the Russian word for steel — was general secretary of the Communist Party in the Soviet Union when the invitation arrived at 35 rue de Sèvres to enter a competition for a major government complex in Moscow. The Centrosoyus would need to hold some thirty-five hundred employees in the Central Union of Consumer Cooperatives, the social condenser that Stalin was envisioning. The atelier jumped at the chance to build in Moscow. Le Corbusier beat out his former mentor Peter Behrens in the first round of competition for the commission, and his remaining competitors conceded that the job should clearly go to him. His proposal was for a massive yet elegant complex, a combination of straight lines and gentle curves, a maze of interior ramps through seven floors, curving horizontal windows in staccato succession, and a ground level freed by pilotis. Observing the movement of the people on the streets, he fully believed his building would not just transform the site but the entire neighborhood.

When he traveled to Moscow he was the toast of Red Square. He was photographed at every turn, fitting right in with the chain-smoking Soviet architects he would team up with, clad in tweed and wide-lapelled leather trench coats. He had pictures taken of him and the burly Russian workers pouring concrete into forms. Architecture in the Soviet Union, dominated by the constructivist movement — art in service of the revolution — was a brutal business at the time. As in virtually every other aspect of Soviet society, there wasn't much room for different ideas. But Le Corbusier was welcomed with open arms. "Surprise, surprise," he wrote to Marie after one of his more productive visits.

"I'm proclaimed the great father – the father, no less! And signs of affection and esteem endlessly, endlessly, for the last 10 days."[8]

He would be called a communist and a lackey of capitalism, a socialist and a fascist. But the truth was, he would work for anybody. In the name of architecture, he was a brazen opportunist. His critics would detect a genuine fondness for fascism, with its cold functionality and inherent promise for getting things done; many would find it hard to believe that he could set aside his own moral compass to affiliate with such odious regimes. Yet his powers of compartmentalization were easily underestimated. Always, what he was chasing was the commission.

Charm and beautiful renderings didn't always carry the day. Over the years, Le Corbusier came to understand that governments, authoritarian or otherwise, needed to be convinced of the merits of modernism. The idea of a political organization, a banding together of like-minded modernists, took hold.

Like much in Le Corbusier's career, the founding of the Congrès International d'Architecture Moderne (CIAM) was born of spite. His motivation could be traced to the experience that ultimately made him hesitate before joining the UN project in New York – the rejection, in 1927, of his proposal for the League of Nations headquarters in Geneva. His was 1 of 337 submissions in the competition for the organization, formed after World War I to foster international diplomacy. It was the perfect commission to symbolize the postwar promise of the twentieth century, and Le Corbusier and Pierre drew up a complex of sleek, low-slung buildings that mirrored the ridge line of the mountains behind. The idea was compelling, that modern architecture would make a statement for the fledgling institution. But a neoclassical cabal prevailed, awarding the commission to prominent Beaux-Arts architects who merely aped historical forms with unremarkable results.⁹ The disqualification of his submission on a technicality – the preposterous charge that the drawings weren't in the proper kind of ink – only confirmed what he would later call the "unscrupulous intrigue" of the experience. He cajoled and threatened and considered legal options, but he had been outmaneuvered.¹⁰

The defeat in Geneva stung – he felt at the time that if his project was embraced, it could be a real turning point, for the atelier and all of modern architecture. He promised himself he would never fail like that again – and that others should not suffer the same fate. Modernism needed a lobbying arm, he argued, to articulate the basic principles of the movement and to be taken seriously. But this could be no ordinary professional association and nothing like a chamber of commerce. From the beginning the goal was to create a democratic convening, built for the exchange of ideas. It was quite intentional that Le Corbusier favored calling it a congress.

Banding together was a natural inclination in the modern movement; the break with the past was so radical that the ideas required clear articulation. The Bauhaus, powered by Walter Gropius, Ludwig Mies van der Rohe, and others, had been an important driving force. But the Bauhaus, set in three German cities – Dessau, Weimar, and Berlin – was officially a school. Le Corbusier sought to create something even more powerful and more politically oriented: designed to influence policy decisions being made in real time, to secure modern architecture's place in global politics. Its mission would be nothing less than a social transformation aimed at municipal governments, through housing, commercial development, and public institutions.

With his schedule so congested, and in unfamiliar territory in terms of working with others, Le Corbusier turned to an ally, the Swiss art historian and architecture critic Sigfried Giedion, to be the group's first administrative leader. In Paris, he met with a crucial benefactor, who was eager to host the maiden meeting. Hélène de Mandrot was from one of the old aristocratic families in Geneva and had dedicated herself to modern art and architecture; she had commissioned Le Corbusier to build the Villa Mandrot outside Marseille, a single-story collection of cubes in stone and glass, set into a hillside. De Mandrot owned the land that was the site of the League of Nations, and she was outraged by the way Le Corbusier had been treated. CIAM could meet for the first time, she offered, at her estate in Switzerland. In June 1928, twenty-eight architects, including Giedion, Karl Moser, Ernst May, and other like-minded modernists, descended on the Château de La Sarraz, a castle with thick, towering spires north of Lake Geneva. Walter Gropius and Alvar Aalto would join later. The pristine grounds at the château accommodated a crazy scene. The architects arrived in fedoras and bowler hats, trench coats and neckties, but inside for a themed evening party, they dressed as marching musicians, with brass-buttoned waistcoats topped by tasseled epaulettes and plumed shakos. Le Corbusier hoisted a big snare drum. They were leaders of the band.

As the group got around to setting out an agenda, a clearer picture formed: to advocate the idea of modern architecture; to introduce the movement into technical, economic, and social circles; and to get down to the business of solving architectural problems, redevelopment, and affordable housing, whether in industrialized capitalist or communist societies.[11] Le Corbusier was once again the visual recorder, filling the long strips of newsprint he favored for his lectures with diagrams, flow charts, and talking points.

There would be ten more meetings of CIAM in the years that followed. Le Corbusier injected a flair for the theatrical to keep the energy going. The fourth gathering of CIAM was held on board the SS *Patris,* steaming from Marseille to Athens in July 1933.[12] The group agreed on the need for a guiding constitution, based on the analysis of data and three dozen case studies of twentieth-century cities, but at its core, what was proclaimed as CIAM's Charter of Athens was straight out of Le Corbusier's schemes for the Ville Radieuse, the Radiant City: massive housing districts with high towers spaced widely apart, amid large green parks, with wide commuting corridors to accommodate vehicular traffic. The CIAM manifesto became a blueprint for urban renewal, asserting blithely that the existing fabric of the city may be preserved only when true historic value could be determined and did not sentence the inhabitants of the city to unhealthy living conditions.[13]

Le Corbusier's view was that the congress was necessary to get things done as a group, when the individual architect could not prevail. But it was a raucous group that would seldom agree on anything easily. Le Corbusier was pleased that the young man from Barcelona who briefly joined the atelier at 35 rue de Sèvres – Josep Lluís Sert – emerged as an organizing force for the discussions, juggling disparate views and nudging the group toward consensus. Still, CIAM and the Charter of Athens would never be the silver bullet he had hoped for. Modernism continued to fight its way in from the fringe, and projects were routinely being rejected.

His own bitter experience with the League of Nations was repeated in Moscow, even after he had been welcomed with such adulation. The Palace of the Soviets, a proposed complex even grander than the Centrosoyus, the government center Le Corbusier had successfully completed, was a sprawling flourish of architecture with a parabolic arch, thick but delicate cables, and a series of exposed supports that looked like modern versions of a cathedral's flying buttresses. He was in the competition right up until the end, producing a detailed model and construction schedule, when Stalin stepped in and unilaterally chose two Soviet architects with a neoclassical design. There were some things – many things – that no professional organization could overcome.

There was progress, especially in America. After World War II, the CIAM program was the go-to template for many city governments. Master builders such as New York's Robert Moses eagerly adopted the ideas as they attempted to reinvent the American city, increasingly threatened by the decanting of businesses and people to the suburbs. But Le Corbusier stopped attending the organization he had founded, even before the decision was made that a thirty-year run was good enough, and the group disbanded as readily as it had come together. His own abandonment was based on a smaller-minded objection. The members had begun insisting that the sessions be conducted in English, rather than in French.

The tenets of CIAM were embraced by his friends in Vichy. The introduction that Giraudoux had written was for *La charte d'Athènes* (*The Athens Charter*), Le Corbusier's book version of the proceedings of the CIAM's fourth congress. And at first, it looked like Le Corbusier and all the principles of CIAM would be welcomed by the regime. The architect attended concerts and athletic events, and walked along the shaded streets of the spa town, waiting for the new government to settle in. But as it quickly became clear, there was too much chaos – shifting alliances and defections and internecine warfare that virtually immobilized Vichy, at least for his purposes. For all his efforts, his actual role remained unclear. Getting authorization to do anything was impossible; everything was taking much longer than he ever expected. All the while, Yvonne was growing increasingly unhappy and frail. The resort town where visitors came to rejuvenate and be cured seemed to be punishing his faithful wife.

Less than two years after his arrival – having never become the chief planner of the new France – he made the decision to return to occupied Paris for the first time. The deprivations there were shocking, with little fuel for heat and long lines for food. The care packages from Switzerland became crucial, and Le Corbusier gave his mother specific instructions to camouflage their contents so they wouldn't be stolen. But it felt right to be back.

By the summer of 1943, he had relocated for good. In October, he reopened the atelier at 35 rue de Sèvres and hired two employees – one of whom, a young Polish assistant named Jerzy Sołtan, would stick with him for years to come. It was not at all clear where the work would come from; there was an urban design scheme he had been working on for Buenos Aires, but the project in Algiers had been all but abandoned. When the skeleton staff emerged from the unheated atelier at night, they passed the glowing lights of the Hôtel Lutetia, where the German officers had set up shop for drugs and prostitution.[14] Around the corner was the jail, where Parisians were routinely locked up for violating curfew or not having papers in order, many never to be seen again.

As the Allies prepared for the Normandy invasion, it was increasingly clear to Le Corbusier that he should disentangle himself from Vichy. But he was not above some last gasps of collaboration. He talked with Charles Trochu, secretary-general of the ultra-right National Front and an important figure in the municipal government of German-occupied Paris, about being named to a committee on housing in the occupied zone.[15] And when Hitler's favorite sculptor, Arno Breker, invited him to discuss Germany's plans for functional architecture, he accepted, not least because of the choice of rendezvous.[16] They agreed to meet at Café Josephine, a landmark destination on rue du Cherche-Midi, famous for its soufflés doused with Grand Marnier and *millefeuille de pigeon*. Le Corbusier wanted to be particularly discreet, back in his hometown; the chef opened the doors at lunchtime when he otherwise would have been closed.[17] Breker had kind words for Le Corbusier and his plans to open up urban areas, and the two men chatted about the use of concrete, steel, and glass. The architect, although a bit more skittish, made known his disapproval of the grandiose and colossal works of the Third Reich thus far. They parted and promised to keep in touch, and Breker thanked him for the conversation.[18]

In truth, Le Corbusier didn't much care if they ever reconnected. He was already in the process of switching sides yet again.

Founding yet another new organization, an offshoot of CIAM he called the Association des Constructeurs pour la Rénovation Architecturale (ASCORAL), he started laying the groundwork for advising on postwar reconstruction – but this time for the French government, following liberation by the British and Americans. That long-awaited day came for Paris in August 1944, as the tanks rolled through and the GIs were showered with kisses and flowers. Without skipping a beat, Le Corbusier sought an audience with Raoul Dautry, the freshly minted liberation minister of reconstruction and urbanism, and told him about ASCORAL and how he was at the ready to assist with France's rebuilding.

It took a lot of nerve, but he had already put Vichy behind him and moved on to this new path. It was a matter of survival. Plenty of his countrymen had stayed on the fence, waiting for fortune to favor one side or the other – the *attentistes,* those who got by as best as they could, waiting the war out, trying not to offend.[19] Others had made accommodations they were not proud of but were necessary, as they lost weight while portly German officers plundered the department store shelves and bistros: *il faut vivre,* as many Parisiens recognized – it was necessary to live. There was some forgiveness for that – but not for those who actively collaborated, as Le Corbusier had done. A special fury was reserved for those who had aided and abetted.

When General Patton was on the outskirts, it was not a good time to be in a German uniform. The Resistance fighters were emboldened to step up their assassinations, hurrying the occupiers to flee as quickly as possible. After the German general in charge of Paris surrendered and disobeyed Hitler's orders to lay waste to the city, and Charles de Gaulle made his triumphant return, marching down the Champs-Élysées, the focus turned to collaborators. At that point, the rage against the occupiers was nothing compared to the hate unleashed against those who had betrayed France. Anyone associated with the Vichy regime, and especially members of the Milice police force, was caught in the dragnet; most received a bullet in the head, sometimes after a brief "popular trial." Frenchwomen who had engaged in "horizontal collaboration" had their heads shaved and were paraded through the streets. Pétain was sentenced to death, and Laval was shot.

With his former friends being executed, Le Corbusier settled on a game plan. He would carry on as if he had been horrified by what had transpired under the Vichy regime. Incredibly, he would seek to blend in with the heroes de Gaulle was honoring, the men and women of the Resistance, who routinely risked their lives over the previous four years and carried suicide pills to evade torture.

But yet again it was necessary to look toward the future. The reconstruction of France, with so many homeless, the landscape scarred and destroyed, was what was important. The cities had been reduced to rubble. In one, Saint-Dié-des-Vosges in eastern France, the retreating Germans bombed and burned the city almost completely to the ground. Le Corbusier alone could stitch the place back together, with his ideas for human settlement in giant apartment buildings spaced well apart and served by wide roadways. He was almost giddy about the blank slate that had been created. "Saint-Dié was systematically destroyed in three days," he wrote to his mother. "A splendid problem."[20]

Crafting cityscapes out of destruction went back to Le Corbusier's youth. While a student at the École d'Art, he had proposed a reconstruction of the Italian town of Messina after a devastating earthquake and tsunami in 1908. He watched in wonder as a fire swept through Istanbul during his visit there, marveling at the destructive power of the conflagration. And he well knew the history of his hometown, La Chaux-de-Fonds, rebuilt in orderly and uniform fashion after the crazy-quilt medieval settlement had been wiped clean by fire.

Rebuilding was how he could serve his country. He had gained the confidence of Raoul Dautry, the reconstruction czar, and was asked to present a plan for the rebuilding of Saint-Dié. Equally important, he was appointed chairman of the Mission on Architecture and Urbanism, a fact-finding initiative launched by the Ministry of Foreign Affairs to examine how other countries were handling city building.[21]

Having such a significant position in the new administration required a meeting with de Gaulle himself. Le Corbusier had just returned from visiting his mother in Switzerland, when he was summoned to meet the tall, prickly general in the town of La Rochelle, where he was setting up the postwar regime. After being kept waiting for what seemed like a long time, the two men met and shook hands. And that was it.[22] There was much unspoken. For Le Corbusier, it was a closing of the chapter on Vichy. It was less clear why de Gaulle welcomed him as part of the administration. He surely knew what Le Corbusier had attempted to do in Vichy, but may have looked beyond it. He may have liked Le Corbusier's energy and, above all, his ideas. Decent housing for the French people living in recovering cities was a top priority. De Gaulle, patriotic beyond reproach, was also a pragmatist. He needed results.

The new opportunity presented itself, and Le Corbusier went to work. There was a problem to be solved, cities to be rebuilt, people in desperate need of housing that should be organized with maximum efficiency. All he needed to do was reinvent himself one more time.

5 ▪ THE COMEBACK

They walked across a forest floor of construction debris, Le Corbusier and Pablo Picasso, past thick triangular concrete supports holding up the long building overhead – a huge structure that despite its mass seemed to be floating on air. The architect and the artist both wore white shirts unbuttoned nearly to their belt buckles.

They had become friends after meeting in Paris some three decades earlier, though relations had frayed over the years. In typical fashion, Le Corbusier had first embraced the painter's innovations, joined his slipstream of fame, and then turned against him, deeming his work insufficient, timid, and bourgeois. It was not lost on Picasso that Le Corbusier's 1918 manifesto was titled *Après le cubisme*. The painter, in turn, was increasingly dismissive of the forms being produced by the atelier at 35 rue de Sèvres. He went out of his way to mock a one-hundred-thousand-seat stadium Le Corbusier had proposed as an absurdity, a cup without a saucer. But on that warm day in September 1952, all was forgiven. Picasso had heard about the breakthrough project in

Marseille – an entirely new vision for how people could live in cities. Le Corbusier called it Unité d'Habitation, and it sounded like an experiment Picasso needed to see. He got in touch by way of Josep Lluís Sert, the Barcelona architect who had joined the atelier some two decades earlier, and asked to come from Spain for a private tour. The sooner the better, Le Corbusier swiftly replied. The visit did not disappoint.

Fifteen minutes south of downtown Marseille, on the shelf of a slope above the Mediterranean coastline, the house of man had risen up: a giant rectangular slab, set at a slight angle as if to absorb every possible breeze and ray of sun. If the cruciform towers of the Plan Voisin had been shocking for their height, Unité d'Habitation was density turned on its side. Hulking and horizontal, it was 180 feet tall and 450 feet long, though a mere 70 feet from facade to facade.

The entire structure was perched upon Le Corbusier's signature pilotis, though not the simple circular kind he used at Villa Savoye, which allowed the clients to drive underneath the home and park in the carport. These were elephant legs, though incredibly, equally graceful, holding up seventeen stories of living space. The technique allowed circulation underneath the building in every direction, to the twelve acres of landscaped parkland all around, the playing fields and playgrounds and walking paths that formed the pastoral plenum.

The entourage – which included the project team, the construction workers, and, in a rare appearance, Yvonne – moved under the vast building. The pilotis formed an allée, like tree branches arching over a roadway, meeting the base of the building at their tops, a cathedral ceiling of panels that looked like a hardwood parquet floor. But it was reinforced concrete – *béton brut* – that most faithful of materials, as Le Corbusier had gotten into the habit of saying. It was chosen as the building material partly because steel was in short supply and partly because the mix of sand, stone, and water allowed him to sculpt his creation, an art perfected from his days learning the secrets of the medium in the studio of the Perret brothers.

They moved into the lobby and the banks of elevators, in the only part of the building that touched the ground, and ascended to inspect the apartments.[1] There were 337 of them and twenty-three different types, from bachelor to family size, enough to house sixteen hundred people. They were narrow, averaging twelve feet wide, but each had two floors, with a loft, reached by an elegant set of interior stairs, overlooking the signature double-height space.

To pack in as much density as possible, Le Corbusier organized each unit like pieces of a jigsaw puzzle. The entrances were along corridors on every other floor; to the left and right of these interior, midair streets, the residents would walk into a smaller space, typically containing the kitchen and dining room, and then either walk down or up to what real estate agents would later call the "floor-through"— the living area that extended all the way across. They were stacked in interlocking pairs, alternating and fitting together compactly and efficiently, one after the other. When the team at 35 rue de Sèvres built the model, they crafted the long living units as individual pieces, then inserted each one into the skeletal frame, like bottles in a wine rack.[2]

The use of space in the overall configuration of the building was fully optimized, but Le Corbusier was just getting started. The interiors were the ultimate act of efficiency, conjuring a sense of space where there was very little. Letting in light and air was the first step. Each apartment opened up to the mountains and the Mediterranean. At one end, the floor-to-ceiling picture windows of twenty rectangular panes in thin black frames offered a view to the world outside, like an observation deck. At the other end, compact balconies were places of special respite, allowing residents to be outdoors right outside their homes. The short walls of the loggias were checkerboards of concrete, throwing dappled light, like sunshine through a trellis, onto a space accommodating reclining chairs and a shelf for potted plants. The sun would rise over Marseille harbor in the morning and set over the mountains behind the complex by cocktail hour.

It was the interiors Le Corbusier was most proud of. He had turned close quarters into a feeling of spaciousness and luxury by abandoning a traditional layout. Dividing up the slender apartments into little rooms separated by fixed walls was a surefire recipe for claustrophobia. Instead there was continuous space, with one area flowing seamlessly into the other – the kitchen open to the dining area, the living room open to the bathroom. The banishment of fixed walls extended even to the bedrooms. The entryway to such private spaces were sliding pocket doors on rollers, left open for most of the day, and slid quietly shut for privacy. An added touch was that these sliding doors were coated with chalkboard, allowing parents to jot down to-do lists and children to doodle with impunity.

Storage was built-in and organized for maximum efficiency and minimal clutter. Highly organized closets, seemingly blended right into walls, replaced bulky wardrobes; clean-lined bureaus took the place of bowed, fussy chests. The shelves for books and pieces of art were carved into the perimeter wall. The wooden kitchen cupboards, equipped with sliding panels, were suspended over stainless steel counters, a four-plate electric range, and double sink with garbage disposal; also above all that workspace was one slanting space with hooks, reserved for most frequently used pots or frying pans.

If every function the families that would move there would need had been anticipated, it was thanks to the help of an old friend. Charlotte Perriand, who had gone her own way after Le Corbusier's entreaties to Vichy, read the architect's plaintive letters asking her to help fine-tune the interior layouts in the project and, against her better judgment, agreed to consult on the ideal choreography of the kitchen. She had only gotten better at figuring out the preferred movements of a hostess – being able to turn from the stove and place hot plates on a breakfast bar, for example, in an acknowledgment of how both family members and guests invariably gathered around the hearth. The kitchens in Unité d'Habitation were only six and a half feet square, but the succinct size facilitated every movement, from cooking to cleaning up. Every function was placed at just the right height and location, from the fold-down diaper-changing stations to the compact storage areas arrayed on the sinks.

The furnishings also benefitted from Perriand's magic touch: the simple chairs of thatched rattan and blond wood, floor lamps and lights sprouting out from the walls, and low-set coffee tables made of round wood on three simple wooden supports. Throw rugs and little chairs for young ones completed the ensemble, amid the perfect junctures of polished oak and rock-hard concrete, ceilings and walls of pure white.

And yet there was color – splashes of color everywhere – on the doors, on the soffits that covered utilities, and on the mailboxes in the hallway. The banisters were red, the water pipes yellow. On the outside, the use of color was even more striking. The balconies and windows of the apartments – the sides of these boxes were painted red and blue and yellow. The exterior was dotted by dozens of colorful squares at the brise soleil of each apartment window, reminiscent of Piet Mondrian's *Broadway Boogie Woogie*.

This place, Le Corbusier told his visitors, would be a happy hive. On the seventh level, he created an interior Main Street, a little village within the building, with a barbershop, laundry, medical facilities, pharmacy, post office, hotel, and restaurant and bar. There would be a butcher, a baker, and a fishmonger, all consolidated in another first – an elevated supermarket right there in the building. In the days following the opening, the Frenchwomen were dumbfounded, as the items typically requested from individual shopkeepers were already available on shelves. In time, instructions had to be spelled out in big letters on the walls to encourage the use of equally novel shopping carts, the chariots of the self-service bounty.

Going to the movies? Also right there in the building. Screenings of the Katharine Hepburn–Humphrey Bogart hit *The African Queen* were set to be on the agenda at the cinema club. School for the kids? A kindergarten was built on the rooftop, which also served as a playground and had a climbing wall. The rooftop complemented the Main Street in glorious fashion. High atop the apartment building, amenities for children and adults seemed to float among the clouds: a shallow splash pool, a garden terrace framed by tropical plants, built-in concrete tables and chairs for picnics. The view was extraordinary. There was Ping-Pong and basketball. There was an open area for calisthenics, a gym, a volleyball court, and a running track. It was a full-service recreation area. People had the option of taking the elevators down to the twelve-acre park at the base. But they didn't need to; they could get all the fresh air and exercise and communal gathering spaces they desired simply by taking elevators to the roof.

From top to bottom, Unité d'Habitation was the ocean liner on land Le Corbusier had envisioned on his trips to South America and beyond. The roof was akin to a top deck, with a swimming pool and shuffleboard. The apartments had all the luxurious efficiency of the staterooms where he spent dreamy nights with Josephine Baker. Though earthbound, nobody ever had to leave the compound. At night the checkered glow of windows was reminiscent of the strips of portals on a seagoing journey, and the sculpted ventilation towers looked like a steamship's smokestacks.

Picasso was impressed with the work in progress, the brush-strokes of architecture, as he made plain when they gathered for drinks and snacks after the tour. Yvonne was delighted, looking resplendent in a scarf and floral-print blouse, despite her worsening health.

And Le Corbusier was beaming. Picasso's approval was a special endorsement; the two men seemed equally exhilarated at the prospect of pushing into new frontiers and executing the disruption with precision and flair. The Spaniard, similarly adventurous, was a fellow specialist in reinvention. "Picasso does his work. The result is greatness. . . . He works, calls everything into question, searches for new answers. He's a creator in the biggest sense of the word . . . ," Le Corbusier said of the man he had led around the building. "There's a man who has never stopped."[3]

In the happy hive, the darkness of Vichy put behind him, he might just as well have been talking about himself.

Like virtually all of Le Corbusier's major projects, the vertical city did not unfold cleanly. Unité d'Habitation was the product of nearly three decades of struggle.

After the Plan Voisin, in 1925, was greeted with such an up-roar, he repackaged his vision for the city of the future and called it Ville Radieuse. The high towers were replaced by horizontal slabs that could be configured to the landscape, depending on local conditions, as long as the buildings were spaced well apart and set in the common denominator of open space. The basic template informed the grand city schemes of long, massive strips of apartment buildings in his proposals for Buenos Aires and Rio and Bogotá and Algiers.

The big plans were the ultimate act in planning for the future. He was convinced that cities would grow rapidly and that the metropolis needed to keep up with the huge numbers of migrants flowing in. The vast destruction of World War II created a different kind of urgency: housing the homeless – an estimated four million in France alone – and rebuilding from the rubble. The beauty of his formula, Le Corbusier argued, was that it accommodated both long-range and near-term needs. The Radiant City could be assembled at low cost. It was speedy and repeatable. Build one Unité d'Habitation apartment building, then another, and form a cluster, and in time the result was the instant, but lasting, city.

He had proposed the first version of Unité d'Habitation at Saint-Dié – the "splendid problem" of the bombed-out city center, with twenty thousand people left homeless. There, Le Corbusier had proposed eight versions of the apartment building that was under construction in Marseille. But after initial support for what he called a "symphony of nature [and] geometry," the weary citizenry rejected the vision, saying, as he recalled, "Do you expect us to live in these barracks?"[4]

Saint-Dié, a detailed master plan of buildings, plazas, and roadways that he poured his heart into, was a disappointment, but giving up was out of the question. He had utter faith in the concept. Given the chance, he said, Unité d'Habitation could utterly replace the traditional town, providing housing for twenty-five hundred in each building. He just needed another city to build the prototype. The blessing came when Raoul Dautry, the French minister of reconstruction Le Corbusier had approached at the time of the liberation of Paris, asked about the feasibility of a pilot project in Marseille. While he carried on as if he wouldn't deign to do the project unless he got special powers and fast-track status, he was thrilled to get the commission, which had the full backing of Charles de Gaulle. He would start with one, and the world would see the wisdom.

It would be one of Le Corbusier's biggest fans, Eugène Claudius-Petit, who would see the project through. Claudius-Petit, who had fought in the Resistance, took over duties coordinating reconstruction and housing, and was amenable to new ideas in architecture; as mayor of Firminy years later, he invited Le Corbusier to engineer a modernist makeover of the town center. He sought to provide for those who had nothing, and the Marseille project seemed to him first and foremost an affordable housing project. The apartments of Unité d'Habitation were to be made available for a low rent.

The blowback on the concept was swift and colorful. Although the features of modern living, from the efficiency kitchens to the tidy balconies, would soon become standard issue for city living, they were jarringly new at the end of the 1940s. For many, having a toilet of one's own, as part of an apartment, was a novelty. Nobody shopped in supermarkets, let alone a shopping center on the seventh floor of a giant apartment building. Packing all these functions into one building seemed strange and dangerous.

UNE VILLE RADIEUSE, ANNOUNCE THE "BUILDERS," blared one headline, with the word "builders" in quotes for an extra touch of sarcasm. More like a barracks, suggested the subheadline. The city of Le Corbusier, read another, is an immense "cemetery cage."[5] The Marseille project was soon being referred to as a rabbit warren and nuthouse – the Maison du Fada – a place where the inhabitants would go insane, living in such close quarters, and confined to one building all day and night. France's leading preservation society condemned the building, and a major hardware supplier announced its refusal to provide door locks or hinges, concerned that being associated with the project would be disastrous for its reputation.[6] Even officials in Marseille piled on. The health authorities were concerned such tightly packed conditions would breed unknowable disease.

Drawing energy, as always, from being criticized, Le Corbusier prepared his ripostes, asking a recently hired assistant, André Wogenscky, to organize a press conference. The design elements, he explained, actually made living in density a smooth and seamless proposition. He had inserted lead sheets in the walls separating the units for noise insulation, for example. The amenities, as well, could not help but to foster a sense of community. Not only will there be no quarrels between neighbors, he said, there will be no divorces.[7] He accurately predicted that the residents would form an association, following the human impulse to band together, facilitate friendships, and organize activities. Le Corbusier called it a "moral administration"; essentially, it was an early version of the co-op.[8] Community was what he was banking on – the way an infant gets swept up by others while mom finishes dinner, or a stranger helps someone struggling with his or her luggage. The acts of kindness that happened in the city streets and in cafés all over would promulgate within the halls of the big apartment building.

The quest for decent housing had been confined to the makeshift accommodations of well-worn nineteenth-century buildings because that was what was available. Once there was the option of a new way of living, Le Corbusier was sure, it would be embraced and become the new standard. The people just didn't know what they wanted yet.

There was something else the critics didn't understand. Unité d'Habitation was based on a scientific model for how humans function in physical space. Ever since the end of the war, Le Corbusier had been developing a guidebook for building. He called it the Modular.

Mathematics, which Le Corbusier called the "daughter of the universe," was a fascination from when he was a young man. The reading curriculum he had designed for himself brought him into the far reaches of the subject, where math blended with philosophy, art, and biology, and the progression of integers took on a mystical quality. Harmony and proportion could be traced to

basic truths found in numbers and equations, from the Pythag-
orean theorem to the Fibonacci sequence – the latter a recognition, adopted from Sanskrit oral tradition, of the patterns seen
in the curve of a nautilus shell or the branching of a tree. Above
all, there was the golden ratio, a rectangle divided up into the
perfect proportions of a square within, combined with another
rectangular on its side, that had been a guiding principle for centuries. This basic form could be seen in the statues adorning the
Parthenon, the facade of Notre Dame, the face of the *Mona Lisa,*
a Stradivarius violin – and, in the years to come, the credit card,
the flat-screen TV, and the iPhone.[9]

Le Corbusier had long thought of integrating the golden ratio
into a formal system for architecture, to ensure not only that aesthetic appearance would evoke a fundamental response, but also
that the doors, windows, rooms, and interior configurations were
all designed to accommodate basic human movement. Leonardo
da Vinci's *Vitruvian Man,* famously portrayed spread-eagled in
a perfect circle, was a good start. Another son of Florence, the
Renaissance cathedral builder Leon Battista Alberti, had also
established how the proportions of the human body could be
transferred to buildings. But a universal system of measurement
for architecture was still not in place. And as any builder doing
international work would lament, there was not one system but
two. The Anglo-Saxon system of pounds and inches had human
origins, going back to the time of *Beowulf* and beyond: the extended thumb became the inch; a man's foot, the foot; a man's
pace, the yard. Yet it was primitive. Weight was measured literally as a matter of stones.

The alternative, the metric system, had more planetary roots.
First developed by a church vicar in Lyon in the late seventeenth
century, the decimal system of measurement was based on the
length of one minute of the arc of a great circle of Earth and the
ground covered by a swinging pendulum. In the French Revolu-

tion, a formal and fully scientific system of weights and measures was decreed, based on a fraction – one-forty-millionth of the meridian, the great longitudinal circle of the planet Earth.

For practical purposes, as the world was beginning to get flat in the middle of the twentieth century, the use of two different systems was bothersome. But the real problem, as Le Corbusier saw it, was the lack of a common language for a bigger goal. Everything designed by man should serve man, so that people could walk through doorways without bumping their heads, reach a sink to wash their hands, and recline without their legs and feet overrunning settees. The protocol for ensuring all of that should thus not be based on a ring around Earth or the swing of a pendulum; it should begin and end with a man – the Modular Man.

Le Corbusier's improvement on Leonardo was a male figure with one arm raised above his head, 2.62 meters (approximately 8 feet 7 inches) from his feet to the hand held aloft. The standard head-to-toe height was 1.83 meters (approximately 6 feet) – originally a bit shorter, but adjusted upward to take into account bigger Americans. (Le Corbusier himself was 1.75 meters tall, just under 5 feet 9 inches.) It was during the tumultuous year of 1943 that he sketched the first versions of the Modular Man, a naked figure with an oversized hand, like a waiter holding a platter. He drew it on leftover stationery from his old magazine of the 1920s, *L'Esprit Nouveau*.[10] Later he added a red and blue measuring tape alongside the figure, spiraling up at regular intervals of measurement, which in turn could be applied to creating spaces for the Modular Man to function in. The basic area of movement within a space was 3.66 meters (12 feet).

Though he was a prolific writer throughout his career, the book he published on the Modular, in 1948, was exceptional in that it was both a philosophical treatise on the virtues of golden mean–based proportionality and a practical handbook for architects everywhere. He immediately wrote a second book, in 1955, expanding on the system he had invented and actively promoted it at venues such as the Milan Triennale Design Museum. His intention was that anyone could use the blueprint – and that anyone could make suggestions about how the system could be improved. "The ground is open to all comers, the doors are opened wide, and anyone may have the power to blaze a surer, straighter trail than mine."[11] A half century before the wisdom of the crowd, he was basically proposing that the Modular software be open source.

He applied it all at Unité d'Habitation – every set of stairs, every room, the placement of the counters in the kitchen, the width of the corridors. Every space accommodated the Modular Man, and he carved the figure in the cement outside the front lobby to drive home the point. The Modular would be inherent in all his architecture from then on.

The new system of measurement and the array of mathematical calculations behind Unité d'Habitation might have been lost on many in Marseille. But one man who did get it was the genius of the century, across the Atlantic. Le Corbusier had met Albert Einstein in 1946, traveling down to Princeton on a break from the tense work on the UN building in New York City. The two men – the architect in checked blue shirt and bow tie, double-breasted blue blazer with pocket square, and pressed gray pants; Einstein in rumpled khakis and sweatshirt, one collar in, one collar out – talked about many things, and Le Corbusier recounted the deprivations of the war. Einstein was interested in the new measurement system and Le Corbusier gamely tried to lay out equations with pencil and paper. The brilliant mathematician grasped it all instantly. "It's a set of proportions that makes the bad difficult and the good easy," he had said. Le Corbusier thrived on the endorsement and was elated to be friends with him. Scientists, he said, did truly important work, work that rearranged the meaning of life. Architects were merely "soldiers on the battlefield."[12]

The invitation for the opening ceremonies on October 14, 1952, showed interlocking ovals and just the date, in simple sans serif font, as if to suggest the beginning of a new era, modern and streamlined.

Almost exactly five years since the first pile driver bore into the loamy steppe off boulevard Michelet, the apartment building was poised to be the model of construction techniques, the use of materials, the control of sound, light, and ventilation, and, above all, super efficient housing for the expanding city. Le Corbusier, speaking at the inauguration, was pleased with the technical accomplishments, if not every execution of his instructions. But what he was most proud of was how he was able to provide a place people could enjoy in silence and solitude, facing the sun and all the greenery, sheltered in homes that were the perfect receptacle for the family.[13]

Most of the families moving in were thrilled to have housing, and were ready and willing to engage in the new way of living that Le Corbusier had created for them. But inevitably, some inhabitants complained – and it was in ways that struck at the heart of the design. Some deemed the living quarters too cramped and bemoaned the fact that each bedroom and bathroom lacked its own window. They brought in cots and set them up astride the built-in furniture. They fretted over the lack of wine storage. Climate control was another problem; despite the best intentions of the brise-soleil system, some units were baked by the Mediterranean sun, and residents were forced to jury-rig the openings with sheets in a desperate bid for shade. The ventilation system was subpar as well, subjecting the apartments to billowing steam and smoke and smells emanating from the kitchen. The archi-

tect's scripted protocols seemed to clash with how families actually lived.

The other secret about the project was that as an exercise in
affordable housing, the promise of lowering costs never materialized. Unité d'Habitation was supposed to cost $1 million, but
in the end the budget tripled, amid great convulsions of changed
orders and scheduling issues, design tweaks, and complications
with building materials. The subsidies flowed from the French
government and the municipality for the pilot project, but if others attempted to replicate the building with any kind of self-
sustaining financing, it would never pencil out. It would be a
very expensive enterprise.

Le Corbusier would have none of it. The pencil pushers had
to understand that this was the maiden project, with some kinks
to be worked out – though none of them his own fault. Every design component was critical to the success of the building. The
grumbling residents, meanwhile, were getting hung up on small
details. Why would anybody want a window in the bathroom,
when they were in there mostly first thing in the morning and at
night? As long as it was good food being prepared, he asked, what
was wrong with smelling that? And if people were unhappy, they
could go live somewhere else.

Le Corbusier was already building more versions of Unité
d'Habitation. The same year as the Marseille ribbon-cutting,
he traveled to Nantes, 250 miles southwest of Paris on the Brittany coast, to attend the inauguration of what the locals would
call the Maison Radieuse. Like Marseille, it was a giant rectangular structure on massive triangular pilotis, with seventeen
levels and just under three hundred apartments, set in a park.
The concept was greeted with some reticence because it was so
radical – word spread fast about the crazy idea of families living
in compact apartments like the rooms of an ocean liner – but on

the whole, the people seemed to be more grateful for the housing there. Le Corbusier choked up when he saw his second completed masterpiece, and the grateful residents applauded.

The Normandy invasion had occurred well to the north, but Nantes had been hit hard during the final years of World War II. The American forces subjected the entire area, including a submarine base at the delta of the Loire River, to heavy bombing. Unité d'Habitation was proposed as a model project for reconstruction – but like Saint-Dié, Nantes said no. It was up to a young lawyer dedicated to the idea of affordable housing to rescue the project and steer it toward its ultimate location, in Rezé, just south of the Loire. Gabriel Chéreau ran La Maison Familiale, the equivalent of a community development corporation, and was a huge fan of Le Corbusier. His organization had been working on social issues since 1911, and new concepts in experimental design were welcome for making the best use of urban land.[14]

There was one caveat. The Nantes-Rezé project could not have any of the cost overruns that plagued Unité d'Habitation in Marseille, and the architect was forced to find ways to cut costs. There would be no Main Street with any stores within the building, and only a small playground and open areas on the roof, though a kindergarten was built there as well. Called the École Maternelle Publique Le Corbusier, it would become the only school in France in a private building, and so beloved that residents would fight to keep it open for years to come.

Maison Radieuse included twenty-six studio apartments for single people, but it was the duplexes designed for families where Le Corbusier seemed to delight, equipping them with clever new touches: a shower door shaped like a big oval to keep the water from spraying out; a hatch in the kitchen that opened out to the corridor for milk and bread; and slots in the middle of the stair treads so crawling toddlers could grab on with their little hands. For a man who never had any children of his own – and indeed expressed horror in having them complicate his life – he had anticipated many needs of young families. At the base, kids took to the wide-open spaces of the park with abandon, riding bicycles around and underneath the giant building raised up on its pilotis. They fed the ducks in the man-made pond, which was spanned by a concrete bridge. He carved a Modular Man on the facade of the Nantes-Rezé project, too.

The Unité d'Habitation in Brittany was destined, though, to be another outlier. Only one would be built, standing all alone. The massive building seemed out of place, as if it should have been in the middle of a city, instead of in a low-slung suburb. In the years to come, one-story homes with driveways and garages would be built all around it, the articulation of a different kind of dream.

The apartment buildings of the Ville Radieuse would continue. After Nantes-Rezé, work was completed on another version, in Berlin, in 1957. And another, in Briey, in 1963. The final Unité d'Habitation would open in Firminy, in 1965. Each of them would stand alone. He had envisioned clusters of the big apartment buildings, steadily replacing the city, neighborhood by neighborhood. Years later, the idea of multiple dense buildings would take off, with stripped-down copies of Unité d'Habitation multiplying across Europe and proliferating in public housing projects, ultimately in New York City, Philadelphia, Chicago, and St. Louis. He would not live to see how the concept was so fully embraced.

Even if they were single-model projects, Unité d'Habitation was a triumph. He had addressed a fundamental challenge: the need for density. The demand for housing was so great, he sought to furnish abundant supply. But it had to be functional and feel good. That is where design came in – not only with all the features in the individual apartments, but also the composition of the building as a whole and, most important of all, the way it was built. During construction in Marseille, when he saw the sinks lined up in a long row, ready for installation, he was filled with joy. If everything could be mass-produced, prefabricated, and assembled onsite, the beauty and convenience of his scheme for modern living could be delivered to the masses, a confluence of popularity and good taste.

He had taken on a problem and had fun providing solutions. It had been the most formidable of problems, the millions in need of housing after a ruinous war. And he had faced down the worst kind of professional dilemma – the potentially career-ending foray to Vichy. He not only wriggled free of the consequences of his collaboration; he was lauded for creating a contemporary acropolis, a maestro who had composed a Tchaikovsky symphony of a building. Instead of being ostracized, he was being interviewed on radio and television and filming a movie about the building. A few years after the ribbon-cutting, he landed on the cover of *Time*.

The *Time* feature, published in 1961, was thorough, noting he was moody and difficult and resentful, holding on to grudges and with a penchant for firing his staff. The magazine had been tracking Le Corbusier and Unité d'Habitation since 1947, and in earlier articles noted the "cramped" quarters and included several odd and possibly dubiously translated quotes that made him appear unhinged ("shall we burn down the Louvre?").[15] But the American journalists seemed to have come around to giving Le Corbusier his due. He was called a modern-day Leonardo da Vinci, responsible for the architectural equivalent of Sputnik, and, simply, the world's greatest architect.[16]

The atelier at 35 rue de Sèvres was buzzing again, with a raft of new hires who were more dedicated and loyal to the master than ever before. Commissions were coming in on a weekly basis. Unité d'Habitation, conceived in the tumult of the end of the war, was at the center of the extraordinary comeback. It was his greatest idea yet. "Any architect who does not find this building beautiful," said the fellow modernist pioneer Walter Gropius, "had better lay down his pencil."[17]

There he was, on the cover of the weekly newsmagazine, eyes sparkling behind his trademark black round glasses, wearing a bow tie, a picture of the Modular Man beside his visage and the colorful geometry of the Unité d'Habitation behind him. This was truly the kind of news to share with one's mother. He was on the cover of *Time*.

6 ▪ THE GETAWAY

The work on the apartment building in Marseille at the dawn of the 1950s brought him to his favorite place in the world. The South of France spoke to him like it was in his genes.

"Over the years I have become a man of the world, crossing continents as if they were fields. I have only one deep attachment: the Mediterranean . . . the queen of forms and of light," he once said. "In all things I feel myself to be Mediterranean: my sources, my diversions, they too must be found in the sea I have never stopped loving. Mountains I was doubtless repelled by in my youth – my father was too fond of them. They are always present. Heavy, stifling. And how monotonous! The sea is movement, endless horizon."[1]

So in the matter of where to go for vacation, there was little doubt he would end up at the Côte d'Azur.

Time off had become a critical component of his life. Though he lived for his work, it was exhausting. Some days at the atelier, when the afternoon dragged on, he would give up, toss a pencil or piece of charcoal on the drafting table, and say, "It's a hard thing, architecture," before heading to the exit. The tangles with bureaucrats, answering the critics, all the while showing nothing but his trademark unwavering confidence, even as he constantly fended off self-doubt – it would sap the energy of any man. The need for a retreat, to recharge, had become obvious.

His Calvinist roots would never permit anything too luxurious. What he longed for was simple – a place where the big decisions were what to have for lunch and when to go for a swim. Where there were no appointments and conversations had no hard stop, and he could trade in the three-piece suits for a pair of comfortable swim trunks. For the hard-charging professional who most other days of the year was devoted to being the world's best-known architect, that getaway was 140 miles to the east of Unité d'Habitation in Marseille, on the border with Italy, at the village of Roquebrune-Cap-Martin.

Like many summer retreats, it was a place that the uninitiated would have difficulty finding at all. The narrow roadway clung to the hillside, switching back relentlessly on the approach to town. Over the stone guardrails, the villa rooftops appeared, the Mediterranean farther below. The journey from Monaco was both romantic and perilous – the traveler literally on the edge. It was a stage set for car chases in the movies, and the scene of the fatal real-life accident in which Princess Grace crashed her Rover P6. Roquebrune-Cap-Martin was arranged in a stack, with a castle and the medieval village up above, while the railway line ran close to the pebble beach down at the sea, everything serviced by switchbacks and serpentine pathways and zigzagging steps. The sea breeze swirled around the hillsides, covered in lollipop cactus, yucca, and palms, and stirred up the smell of lemon, eucalyptus, and jasmine. It was a fantasy of nature, encyclopedic in its diversity. The smallest things seemed to have a story, like how the seeds in the fig-like fruit of the carob tree were the basis of the gem-weighing measure the carat.

A trading post on the Roman road, Roquebrune-Cap-Martin had long been a world apart. The Grimaldi clan from Italy built the castle high on a redoubt in the tenth century; the fishing village, closer to the water, was so sequestered it became an oasis from the black plague throughout the Middle Ages. As a destination it remained happily in the shadow of its infamous neighbor, Monaco, which in Le Corbusier's time was well on its way to becoming a mecca for the superrich. Yachts were already cluttering the tiny harbor, Porsches and Lamborghinis plied the narrow streets, and two-bedroom apartments sold fast, despite the fact that they cost more than an entire country estate. Soon there would be more millionaires packed into the dense city, smaller than New York City's Central Park, than anywhere in the world, exempt from taxes and seemingly from the laws of nature, Monaco having the highest life expectancy in the world.[2] The Monte Carlo Casino and the annual Grand Prix race only added to the glamour. Monaco was meringue and limoncello cocktails at the Hôtel de Paris, Rolex watches and the polished high-stakes chips at baccarat tables. By comparison, Roquebrune-Cap-Martin was the sleepy town down the road, the place for a simple meal and a good night's sleep. It was gorgeous.

Le Corbusier might have been reminded of Amagansett on Long Island, where he stayed during trips to New York as the guest of his friend, the Italian sculptor Constantino Nivola, and made sculptures in the sand. The village out of the spotlight made Roquebrune-Cap-Martin favored by film stars. Lauren Bacall, Jane Fonda, Brigitte Bardot, Kirk Douglas, and Nat King Cole all sought out Le Pirate on avenue Winston Churchill, a tumbledown *boîte* serving sea bass and flutes of champagne with cassis. The host was the shirtless pirate himself, Charles Viale, well known for putting a few extra drinks on the tabs of the wealthy, covering drinks ordered by locals.[3] At the Hôtel Le Roquebrune, Sean Connery stopped by to play the piano, Frank Sinatra and

Gregory Peck munched on crudités, and Cary Grant was so impressed with the hotel's chocolate soufflé during a lunch there with Alfred Hitchcock, he telephoned from the set of *To Catch a Thief* in nearby Nice to get step-by-step instructions to make it at home.[4]

One of Roquebrune-Cap-Martin's most famous residents perfectly channeled the understated class of the place. Coco Chanel lived at La Pausa, meaning "restful pause," a villa on a shelf of land that the aristocratic families of Monaco used to use as hunting grounds. The sprawling estate, the gift of a smitten English duke, was perched high above, on the way to the town's steeply sloping cemetery. Chanel was the kind of entrepreneur Le Corbusier could identify with. They traveled in the same circles in Paris in the 1920s; she was pushing the boundaries in fashion just as he was doing the same with architecture – simplifying lines, dispatching with frills, and using stretchy fabric from men's underwear to create a boyish yet dignified look. Her little black dress would become a widely copied icon, just like Villa Savoye. And there was one other thing that Chanel and Le Corbusier had in common: collaboration with the Nazis. During the occupation, she appealed to Nazi occupiers to cut off a Jewish family's control of her empire. (It was later revealed that she worked with SS spies.) She would similarly try to expunge those details from the story of her life, just as Le Corbusier downplayed his engagement with Vichy.

The path that led her to Roquebrune-Cap-Martin began when she met Hugh Grosvenor, the Duke of Westminster, in Monaco. Of all the things he lavished on her, including a flat in Mayfair in downtown London, the gesture she most welcomed was the gift of the plot of land for La Pausa. She plunged into the design of the four-level, ten-thousand-square-foot mansion, working with the architect Robert Streitz, and inspired throughout by the austere orphanage where she spent her youth: white walls with black trim for multipaned picture windows, a central staircase of stone, neutral colors, and rustic Provençal furnishings. But it was as luxurious as her outfits. The terrace let out on extraordinary views, the pool, and the gardens of lavender, rosemary, and olives; ultimately, a fragrance in the Chanel line of perfumes was named for La Pausa. There were separate bedrooms for her and the duke, and shortly after completion of the estate, they went their separate ways. In one of the most famous marriage refusals of all time, she told him there have been several duchesses of Westminster, but there is only one Chanel.[5]

She carried on for years as the solo hostess of the Riviera estate, entertaining movie stars and other royalty. Over the years Greta Garbo, Noël Coward, and Rose Kennedy paraded through, and Winston Churchill stayed there to finish his series on the history of English-speaking people.

La Pausa was one way to live in Roquebrune-Cap-Martin. Another woman, another self-starting entrepreneur, would take a much different approach.

From the time Eileen Gray starting hacking her way through the broad-leaved banana trees well down the hill from La Pausa, close to the water, she was determined to create no ordinary shelter. It was through Gray that Le Corbusier would discover summertime at Roquebrune-Cap-Martin. Neither could have known that the villa she would design would become the scene of a triangle of relationships supercharged by ego, sex, and professional jealousy.

A painter's daughter schooled in London, Gray had convinced her wealthy mother to install her in Paris, where she established herself in art deco interior design and furniture. She crafted undulating armchairs — one she called the "dragon" chair, with armrests flowing up from the floor like a sea monster — and expanding side tables and lacquered folding screens that would endure, and be widely copied, for decades to come. She immersed herself so much in her work that she damaged her hands working with lacquer. Her wildly successful gallery brimmed with exotic woods, cork, fur, and ivory, and, as she embraced modernism, aluminum and steel, for industrial lamps, a sofa of curving white marshmallow cushions set in a base of metal tubes, and a chest of drawers made of neat cubes.

A handsome brunette, she would just as soon retreat behind peacock feathers as pose for photographs among them. She was quiet and introspective and enigmatic, a bisexual immersed in the lesbian scene in Paris in the 1920s. While dating Marie-Louise Damien, better known as Damia, the Gitanes-smoking singer who preceded Edith Piaf, she met a dashing Romanian, Jean Badovici, an architect and architecture critic, editor in chief of the avant-garde architectural publication *L'Architecture Vivante,* and one of Le Corbusier's greatest promoters. Badovici splashed some drops of benediction Gray's way, in an essay in an avant-garde Dutch art magazine that devoted an issue to her designs.[6] Other motives were clearly at work. Dark and lean, a serial philanderer who had also charmed Charlotte Perriand, Badovici convinced Gray to build him a modernist villa somewhere on the French Riviera, so the two of them could run off together and luxuriate by the sea.

Gray had come down on her own and done the reconnaissance, settling on a strip of hillside in Roquebrune-Cap-Martin, just east of the train station and the beach. She loved the fact that it could only be reached on foot. The Rolls-Royces pulling up to the gates at La Pausa couldn't get near this spot. The sea was so close it seemed like one could dive in from the front yard; to the west was the town beach and, farther down, the outcroppings of Monaco. The site, she concluded, would lend itself well to a simple white box set into the hillside, with a landscaped terrace in front and a set of stone stairs leading to the sea. Three years in the making, the house she created was like a down-sized, beachside version of the Villa Savoye, which was nearing completion at about the same time. She was well aware of Le Corbusier, having met him at the Salon d'Automne in Paris. The architect had praised her innovative designs. But she felt his purist approach to architecture, its functional orientation, was too hard-edged. "A house is *not* a machine to live in," she said, a pointed retort to Le Corbusier's catchphrase. "It is the shell of man – his extension, his release, his spiritual emanation."[7] Her creation at Roquebrune-Cap-Martin was gentle and sensual, though framed with the same clean lines. She studied the way sunlight bore down on the hillside and put everything in place accordingly, from the tiled solarium to the floor-to-ceiling windows. The central staircase spiraled to a skylight that twirled like a nautilus shell. White walls were set against splashes of color, while delicate ribbons of metal ran as handrails or were part of the furniture, all Gray's own. It was a sleek and playful perch, equally comfortable inside and out, from the living room with its monochromatic throw rugs to the stone terraces overlooking the sea. Forgoing a romantic name for this vacation home, the lovers called it simply Villa E-1027 – the E for Eileen, the 10 for J (the tenth letter of the alphabet) to honor Jean, the 2 for the B in Badovici, and the 7 for the G in Gray.

The building stood firm, but the romance did not. By the time of completion, Gray and Badovici were on the way to breaking up, and the couple spent little time together there. One day in 1930, while on a solo trip, Badovici invited Le Corbusier and Yvonne. Walking into Villa E-1027, seeing the pure white walls and the interior furnishings so similar to his own designs, was a strange but exhilarating experience. This was a house he could have built. When he gazed out the horizontal windows to the Mediterranean, everything seemed right with the world. Yvonne was happy to be near her birthplace of Monaco; Le Corbusier could see himself coming to this quaint seaside village again and again. Badovici welcomed them to stay there as much as they liked. Soon Le Corbusier thought of the place as his own, to such an extent that he would mark the territory in extraordinary fashion — naked, with a paintbrush — and establish himself as one of Roquebrune-Cap-Martin's most infamous summer residents.

The notion of a summer getaway had been percolating in Le Corbusier's mind since before he started his architecture firm. From his earliest days as a permanent resident of Paris, he felt the need to get out of town, particularly in the month of August, when it seemed like the entire population vacated the city.

Plotting the retreat, like nearly everything in his life, was a matter of careful thought. For many, anywhere in the country would do fine. But the son of Switzerland wasn't so much interested in the forest and the mountains, where his father had dragged him and his brother so many times for alpine hikes. What he wanted was to be near water.

Destinations came by word of mouth, and that was the case with Le Piquey, a town designed for the summertime holiday excursion, on a bay on the coast of Brittany. His sculptor friend Jacques Lipchitz had rented a cabin there, and the architect found the area to be a perfect respite from the city.[8] It was serene and rustic, with scrub pine forests that smelled of resin leading to the long beaches of pristine sand dunes. The sun baked everything deliciously, moderated by a constant breeze off the Atlantic; he reveled in the heat, bragging about it to his family and pitying them for being stuck in the cold of Switzerland. He felt the sand between his toes and his clothes felt clean just by being there. He and Yvonne slipped into bathing suits and hung around with no agenda, other than to be somewhat mindless and playful. It was on the beach there that he was photographed in a ludicrous boxing pose with his cousin Pierre, smoking a pipe. His beach reading was the tide charts, and he became fascinated by the patterns in the sand, the seashells, and the gnarly sculpture of the driftwood that washed up on the shore. The sweeping beaches and the endless horizons were the desired antidote to "deadly" Paris.[9]

Le Piquey was also where Le Corbusier learned to swim. He realized how much he enjoyed gliding through the water, testing himself on how far and how quickly he could go, and dutifully recorded the achievements to his mother in Vevey. After the regular visits to Le Piquey, he swam whenever he could for the rest of his life.

There was one other destination that he and Yvonne occasionally frequented: the hilltop town of Vézelay in Burgundy. Badovici had a house there and, with Gray, had been doing some restoration work in the village, the site of an imposing Romanesque church, the Basilica of Saint Mary Magdalene, at the center. A monastery had been envisioned there as early as the ninth century, and it had become a stop on the Christian pilgrimage route. The village on the top of the hill was cozy and cluttered, and Le Corbusier enjoyed walking his dog, Pinceau, along its streets. He installed Yvonne there when he was doing business in Vichy. But it was entirely landlocked, being near the geographic center of France. There was a river at the bottom of an old stairway, and one day when he was out on a walk with an art student he had befriended — and later hired to work at the atelier — he had stripped down and jumped in, unable to restrain his need to swim. The student did the same and showed him how to do the backstroke.[10]

But while Le Piquey, on the Atlantic, and Vézelay, in Burgundy, occupied the summertime early on, the pull of the Côte d'Azur was not to be denied. After Badovici first introduced him to Villa E-1027, Roquebrune-Cap-Martin became the vacation destination he and Yvonne would head to, on close to an annual basis, throughout the 1930s. Gray had all but vacated the premises, having moved on, and was building yet another villa outside neighboring Menton on the Italian border. E-1027 was effectively under the ownership of Badovici, who allowed Le Corbusier and Yvonne to stay there as they wished. All was well, until one summer in 1938, when Le Corbusier decided the walls needed improvement.

Standing naked with paintbrush in hand, he splashed images of giant women, distorted in Picasso-like fashion, in a series of sexual positions. The main painting was inspired by a postcard and drawings he himself had made of Algerian women – the *femmes de casbah* – a few years earlier.[11] He brushed a total of eight unsolicited murals, inside and out.

Le Corbusier claimed he had authorization, but Gray, learning of it, was outraged, viewing it as defacement. A friend would later say it felt like a rape. Gray demanded that Badovici intervene and require that the architect pay for the removal of the artwork. Le Corbusier was unrepentant. He circulated photographs of his handiwork, which he said "burst out from dull, sad walls where nothing is happening." If it was vandalism, it was modernist graffiti, as he proudly labeled it. "An immense transformation, a spiritual value introduced throughout."[12]

It was up to Gray to interpret whether the women in provocative poses were a comment on her bisexuality or whether some kind of petty retribution was at work. Here was a woman who publicly said that the home was not a machine for living in and who dared to build something that many would later interpret as a better version of Villa Savoye. Yet after he painted the "Graffiti-Cap-Martin," Le Corbusier wrote to Gray, telling her how much he loved Villa E-1027, its organization and its charm. And the architect had well established that he viewed murals on walls as a carefully targeted architectural tool. He had recently completed a number of murals for the walls of Badovici's house in Vézeley, assisted by Fernand Léger.

For his part, Badovici initially seemed to indicate he liked the murals and praised them. But he also had an allegiance to Gray, who urged him to write a letter of admonishment. "What a narrow prison you have built for me over a number of years, and particularly this year through your vanity," scolded the Romanian, once among the architect's biggest fans.[13] The arrangement at Villa E-1027 soured, and once again a great friendship was torn asunder. Le Corbusier was not to be invited back. As he tried to convince the homeowners to sell him the property and settle the dispute for good, the war intervened. Italian soldiers, coming across the border on their way to occupying Monaco, set up an encampment at Villa E-1027, supposedly because of its military perspective as a lookout, though it was also, in the end, a great place to wait out hostilities and drink wine. Later, when the Germans took over the Côte d'Azur, the walls were riddled with bullet holes.

Trips to Roquebrune-Cap-Martin came whenever Le Corbusier traveled to the South of France – which occurred on several occasions in the years after the war – to vacation with Yvonne in Menton, to visit the modernist chapel that Matisse had designed in Vence, to meet with his colleague Josep Lluís Sert on an urban design scheme for Bogotá, and to oversee the construction of Unité d'Habitation in Marseille. When he was anywhere close to the area, he found the craggy, cactus-dotted slopes below the switchbacks to be irresistible. On one trip he even stopped in at Villa E-1027, which had been left in disrepair and was on its way to being sold, and did some restorative work on the controversial murals. He couldn't let go. In the summer of 1950, he rented a room in a shoemaker's cottage near the villa and began frequenting a restaurant called L'Étoile de Mer – the Star of the Sea. Little did he know the simple act of getting lunch would lead to extraordinary things.

He had been to the finest restaurants, from Buenos Aires to Paris to Rome, but from the moment he pushed open the saloon doors of L'Étoile de Mer, he knew it was a seafood shack he was destined to love. There were bottles of booze and wine on the shelves, alongside spices and mixing bowls, measuring spoons hanging down, and all kinds of framed letters and photographs on the walls. The dining area was outside, on a trellised terrace, populated by less than a half dozen tables. Heavy plates and pitchers of water and wineglasses occupied every inch of surface, keeping the simple white tablecloths and floral throws from fluttering off in the breeze. The luckiest diners had their back to the shack and looked out over the feast to the sea.

The owner, Thomas Rebutato, stood behind the bar. A retired plumber from Nice, he wore a beret and a white shirt wide open at the chest, and almost always had a Gitanes cigarette dangling from his lips. He had invested his savings to buy the land next to Villa E-1027, he told Le Corbusier, with the idea of building a summer holiday complex of modest one- or two-room cabins. The town could only increase in popularity, Rebutato figured, as a vacation destination. That's when he started cooking, putting together meals drawn entirely from the sea – grilled, simple and delicious. The architect asked if the restaurant owner could prepare a lunch for twenty people, as he planned to bring his team back for a working lunch.[14] If it was good, he promised to return faithfully.

The deal was the first in a lifelong business arrangement. If the friendly restaurateur with the thick Monégasque accent had any suspicions that he would give more than he would get in the relationship, he didn't seem to mind.

Le Corbusier did return, that year, the next year, and every year after that. He and Yvonne stayed at the shoemaker's cottage and lunched daily at L'Étoile de Mer, which he had offered to decorate – this time with clear permission. On the front of the bar he painted an eel, three starfish, a crustacean with dangling antennae, and a beefy grouper wearing a hat and smoking a pipe, a sly self-portrait. At the center was a combination of octopus and sun, with eight spindly arms, a Popsicle-shaped nose, and eyes and lips and teeth: his interpretation of L'Étoile de Mer. When he and Yvonne were there, Rebutato's son, Robert, went out just about every day and harvested sea urchins by the dozen – Yvonne's favorite. Le Corbusier sat down with the teenager and talked about the profession of architecture, which would ultimately be Robert's as well.[15]

Over wine and seafood with the owner, Le Corbusier made the pitch for a plan that would give him a place of his own. He would design five modernist bungalows on adjacent land owned by Rebutato, reserving one for him and Yvonne. Ultimately he worked the deal further, convincing the retired plumber to award him land right next door to the restaurant for an additional cabin, set apart from the others, as his ultimate vacation home. He sketched it in forty-five minutes on one of the white tablecloths on the terrace of L'Étoile de Mer and presented it as a birthday gift to Yvonne.

The *cabanon,* as it would come to be known, was outrageously simple for a man who had created so many complex urban design schemes and government headquarters. Yet it was not that different from the studio apartments he had stacked up in Unité d'Habitation. His palace of solitude was based entirely on the Modular, guiding the movements of man in constructed space. The space was 12 by 12 feet square and 7.5 feet high – the 2.26-meter height of the Modular Man with his arm extended. The inhabitants could move about within the space in a carefully calculated spiral of circulation. For the uninitiated, he wrote the formula on the wall, alongside yet another mural, this of a man and woman in abstract entanglement.

Part miniature log cabin, part shipping container, the *caba-non* accommodated one twin-sized bed platform for sleeping at the back wall; a breakfast table similar to the one he designed for the backyard at the Villa Le Lac in Vevey, supported by a single column; and a small stainless steel sink and a few shelves that constituted a galley-like kitchen. The toilet was in the corner in a space slightly smaller than the washroom of a commercial jet. There was storage built into the wall, under the bed, and even in the ceiling, which sported panels painted red, yellow, and green; pegs serving as coat hooks substituted for a closet. A square picture window at the front framed the view to the sea, the lush plants and trees, and Monaco in the distance, while another near the sink opened out to the side, where a bountiful fig tree stood. An additional narrow strip let more light in, and a sliding-door window at the back wall by the bed provided cross-ventilation. A strategically placed mirror on the kitchen cupboard reflected the view out the front.

The layout was based on the five holiday cabins he had designed on the other side of the restaurant, but Le Corbusier added many special touches for himself, beginning with the substitution of aluminum siding for rough-hewn logs for the exterior. The rustic planks, with the bark left on, were imported from Corsica, crafted along with the chestnut furniture by a carpenter friend and shipped to the site.[16] He personally guided the construction, completed by 1952, and when he moved in added only whisky crates – which doubled as seating and storage for his growing collection of driftwood, stones, shells, and bones – and, fittingly for any vacation home, an outdoor shower. Rebutato did all the plumbing, free of charge. The entire enterprise cost under $7,000.

If there was inspiration for the tiny masterpiece, it could be traced to the fishermen's cabins he admired in Le Piquey and the shack he shared with Marguerite Tjader Harris on the shores of Long Island Sound. The *cabanon* was also reminiscent of his huts for refugees and youth holiday camps, proposed for the Vichy government during the war.[17] But his appreciation for the primitive hut went deeper, to the core of his beliefs about architecture. In the simple dwelling, "not a piece of wood, in its form and in its force, not a string, is without a precise function," he wrote in 1928. "Man is economical. One day will this hut not become the Pantheon in Rome, dedicated to the gods?"[18]

The precise geometry and proportions, he believed, would lead to a healthy state of mind. He was uniquely proud of his technical accomplishment, the way he had utilized every inch of space, as an ultimate act of efficiency, using every trick that could possibly be pulled out of the architect's bag.[19]

None of it would have been possible without the Rebutatos. The *cabanon* was physically attached to L'Étoile de Mer, sharing a wall and symbolizing the relationship. The mural Le Corbusier had painted camouflaged a side door that led directly to the restaurant, as if they were adjoined hotel suites. He and Yvonne ate there every day. They were family, free to use the Rebutatos' boat, enjoying the company of their cat and dog, and, even though Le Corbusier was in his sixties throughout the time at the *cabanon*, virtually adopting young Robert as the son they never had. The boy not only dove for sea urchins for Yvonne, but he also helped Le Corbusier add to his collection of treasures, on one occasion producing a bone that they studied together, likening the marrow to the reinforced concrete the architect used in his famous projects around the world.

The days at Roquebrune-Cap-Martin settled into a comfort-able rhythm. The architect would swim twice a day, hiking down over the jagged rocks below to the sea. He padded around bare-chested, breathing in the salty, fragrant air. Yvonne was happiest there, holding court in headscarf and oversized jewelry on the terrace and lingering long after meals, her slender hands sport-ing dark fingernail polish, one hand holding a wineglass and the other an ever-present cigarette. Well known in town for her gift giving and playful antics, she was in many ways as revered as he was.

She complained, as she did at the penthouse at 24 rue Nun-gesser et Coli, that the accommodations were impossibly spare. It took the common sense of a spouse to reveal the preposter-ous sleeping arrangements—the narrow platform at the back wall for her, a mattress on the floor for him. On a visit from their friend Brassaï, the Hungarian photographer who, like Le Corbu-sier, had adopted a pseudonym, she exclaimed, "Brassaï, you're a witness, just look at the cell my husband keeps me in . . . just look! He makes me sleep . . . next to the washbasin. I wonder how I've managed to live for twenty years with this fanatic and put up with all his crazy notions."[20] But of course she kept com-ing back, by train and by car and, ultimately, by plane from Paris to Nice. It was her paradise, too.

It was only a matter of time before Le Corbusier allowed a little bit of work to intrude. With Robert's help, he built a simple studio a few steps away from the *cabanon,* a plywood shack with a slanted rolled-metal roof where he escaped to allow some pro-fessional thoughts to float in. The desk was a two-inch-thick block of wood painted white on two green sawhorses, set in front of tall six-paned windows that opened up like French doors; his stool was a whisky crate. He pinned sketches, plans, and draw-ings to the walls and placed some of his treasures—the *objets à réaction poetique,* as he called them—on a tidy bookshelf by the door. But there was no phone in the *cabanon* or the studio. If he needed to be reached, in only the most urgent of circumstances, he told everyone to call L'Étoile de Mer.

In the quest for his vacation home, Le Corbusier had capitalized on connections with others – Lipchitz's fisherman's cabin in Le Piquey, Badovici's house in Vézelay and Villa E-1027, and now Thomas Rebutato's plot of land around L'Étoile de Mer. There was something parasitic about the way he turned from house-guest to adopting places as his own, like marrying another man's woman: letting someone else make the great discovery and then moving in. Brilliantly, he arranged it so no one could make the same maneuver with him. The *cabanon* was so small, he could never have an overnight guest.

The very idea of a second home also was antithetical to the housing he was designing for the masses in cities. Not everyone could have a country house or a beach house; that was reserved for the elite. Still, at Unité d'Habitation, he attempted to create homes that had many of the benefits of the country: the light and fresh air, and easy access to recreation. And he had allowed himself the tiniest possible vacation home.

The five bungalows he built offered affordable efficiency, and for a time, he sought to provide a way for even more people of average means to enjoy Roquebrune-Cap-Martin. The project known as Roq and Rob – "Roq" for Roquebrune and "Rob" for Robert Rebutato – called for some two hundred apartments, or "cells," as he referred to them, each with a little balcony and a view to the sea, cascading down the slope near L'Étoile de Mer and Villa E-1027. It would have been a slice of Unité d'Habitation, slapped on the hillside. Though it was never built, the design concept was ultimately mimicked in resort hotels up and down the French Riviera.

It was the view – to the Mediterranean, to Monaco, the wild green growth and the craggy rocks – that Le Corbusier sought to provide to others. But he was well satisfied to enjoy it all for himself. It was a view that always seemed fresh, and it seemed to him that no one could possibly ever grow tired of it. The natural porch in front of the *cabanon* was an ideal promontory, a front-row seat for the theater of nature, the buckshot sunbeams poking down through the clouds by day, the moon shining a fat spotlight on the dark water by night.

So much of the rest of his life was torture amid the triumphs. At Roquebrune-Cap-Martin, he had landed, unequivocally, in a good place. He had good friends and delicious food, and Yvonne was happy. He had built a minimalist beach house that would be coveted for years to come by all those who dreamed of a simple, low-cost getaway of their own. It was modern architecture at its best. But mostly, it was home away from home.

"I'm so comfortable in my *cabanon*," he told a friend, "that I'll probably end my days here."[21]

7 ▪ THE CHURCH

It was the most unlikely commission for a man who wanted no part of organized religion, like William Blake writing *Jerusalem,* a pagan at Mass.

When two black-robed Catholic fathers first approached him in the spring of 1950 to build a church in the little town of Ronchamp, in the far east of France by the border with Switzerland, he told them no. Better to find an architect who actually believed in the institution, he said.

But another church official whom Le Corbusier had earlier befriended, Father Marie-Alain Couturier, was convinced the greatest living architect didn't really mean it. "What we need is a great artist," he implored in a letter following up on his colleagues' invitation, someone to create something new and daring and intensely beautiful.[1] He would have free rein to build whatever he wished. He need only pay a visit to the site, on a hilltop at the foot of the Vosges Mountains, and surely he would reconsider.

Bourlemont Hill, a summit fifteen hundred feet above a coal-mining village, had a long history as a sacred place. Pagans first climbed up to the perfectly flat plateau as a place to worship the sun, and were thought to have built a makeshift temple, a wisp of Stonehenge perched high. The steep slopes leading to the top were overgrown with wild rose and holly, acacia and oak trees; in the winter the grassy tabletop was shrouded in mist. The ascent was not so much a hike as a stairway to heaven.

For the Roman Empire, the location fulfilled more strategic than spiritual purposes. Soldiers set up tents on the hilltop, overlooking the ancient Roman road that ran alongside the valley below. The military outpost was the origin of the town's name, Ronchamp, meaning "Roman camp," and the road endures today as the main route from Paris to Basel.[2] With the arrival of Christianity, the site reverted to the sacred. There were legends of miracles there, of visions of the Virgin Mary. A sanctuary as early as the fourth century was succeeded by the first chapel, seven centuries later, which hosted a steadily increasing stream of pilgrims. Most came in September, in celebration of the birth of the mother of consolation and deliverance. They submitted themselves to her custody, seeking salvation for desperate causes, healing for sick children, and hope and release for faraway prisoners.[3] Statues were carved out of logs in her likeness, the wood winnowed down so they were light enough to carry around in processions.[4]

Another church was built at the valley floor, more easily reached by the families of the men moving to Ronchamp to work in the mines. The chapel on the hilltop was at one point put up for auction, when a consortium of forty families bought it and formed the Association de l'Oeuvre Notre Dame du Haut. The pilgrims kept coming – thirty thousand of them in one year – and church officials appointed a full-time priest, who added a cluster of five towers, the tallest, at the center, topped by a giant statue of the Virgin Mary made of zinc-coated oak. Though it looked like a castle, it was defenseless against nature and burned almost entirely to the ground when struck by a powerful lightning bolt in 1913. In the initial rebuilding plans at that time, local leaders envisioned a grand rebirth, a re-creation of the Basilica of the Sacré-Coeur in Paris, but a shortage of funds led to a less ambitious Gothic structure. The question of rebuilding was posed yet again in 1944, when the church was destroyed – this time by man – pummeled by a combination of German artillery and American bombardment during the liberation of France. The hilltop was taken, lost, and retaken, as the Allies moved toward Alsace. A French soldier saved a statue of Mary.

Out of the rubble, the local diocese and the regional government once again found opportunity. In the years after the war, leaders in the Catholic Church sought to inject some excitement in new church buildings, turning to the modern. More daring design had begun with Antoni Gaudí's Sagrada Família in Barcelona, Frank Lloyd Wright's Unity Temple in the Oak Park section of Chicago, and "free-form" churches in Germany and Italy that dared to tweak traditional elements, like the basilica. The Perret brothers – with whom Le Corbusier had apprenticed on his first stint in Paris – also broke the mold with the skyscraper-evoking industrial look of the Notre Dame de la Consolation in Le Raincy outside Paris. Father Couturier had been instrumental in the continuing effort of rejuvenating sacred art, and recruited Henri Matisse to design the simple white Chapel of the Rosary in Vence, near Nice, which Le Corbusier had visited while at Roquebrune-Cap-Martin. An even bigger statement, authentic and powerful and new, was needed at Ronchamp. And there was one man who could deliver that.

The friars, some of whom had traveled to Paris to inspect Le Corbusier's handiwork, including the Pavillon Suisse at the Cité Internationale Universitaire, were rewarded for their persistence. Within two months of being contacted, Le Corbusier was alone on that hill, picturing his ultimate act of visual poetry. Father Couturier was right. There was something about the place. He could feel it.

As a young man he had sketched dozens of cathedrals, temples, and mosques, but at no time did he reveal an explicit yearning to contribute to the august tradition of ecclesiastical design. Yet a church was the ultimate expression of architecture as he saw it: a place where, inside and out, a building could speak to its occupants and channel emotions. He sought the same kind of connection in his homes and apartment towers and government offices, but a house of worship was a singular opportunity for his stagecraft.

As with every other aspect of architecture, from ancient Greece to the Victorian age, Le Corbusier was a student of the design of the spiritual. The built environment of Christianity had a fascinating evolution. In the beginning, the church was in the home; worship was wherever people got together, even if it was just a family. When the religion was no longer outlawed, the business of building began in earnest, taking forms dependent on function, whether the monastic retreat high on a mountainside or the meetinghouse at the center of the village. Le Corbusier could appreciate the repeatable template that emerged, for the simple abbey of the local parish or the destinations of pilgrimage: an atrium and a basilica rising up over the altar, a rectangle anchored by a spire. Building through the Middle Ages fulfilled a greater mandate, to express the power and authority of the institution as the unshakable center of society. The result was some of the most monumental structures on the planet, built at enormous cost in money and manpower: vaulted ceilings, flying buttresses, ornate stained glass, statuettes and decorative friezes and gargoyles.

The great cathedrals were marvels worthy of admiration,

and he painted Notre Dame in moving detail. But when he visited Chartres near Paris, he was struck by the rigidity and forced nature of the project. There was a kind of disturbing overreaching; the building was trying too hard. "The cathedral of Chartres had the effect on me of the most terrible battle," he wrote to his friend William Ritter in 1917. "Never say that the Gothic is serenity. It's a poignant and gigantic struggle.... Chartres is a life of deliberate forces and demoniac optimism, of clenched fists and clenched jaws."[5]

If he were to build a church, he would do it differently. It would be simpler, a return to the ancient, at once more subtle and more powerful; something far removed from the gilded cathedrals of Europe. So it was that the very first sacred space he designed was to be in a cave.

The grotto at Sainte-Baume, in the South of France to the northeast of Marseille, was set in a limestone cliff two thousand feet high. It was the site of a legend about a witness to Christ's resurrection who held special interest for Le Corbusier: Mary Magdalene, the prostitute saint who washed the feet of Jesus with her hair. Traveling with her brother Lazarus from Palestine on a boat without a sail or a rudder, she landed at Saintes-Maries-de-la-Mer near Arles, where wild white horses galloped through the salt marshes, and converted all of Provence. Then she retreated to the cave, living naked and sustained by angels, praying in solitude for thirty years. She was the other Mary, a symbol of female power. Some deciphered Leonardo's *Last Supper* by reading her as Jesus's wife – no mere disciple, but a completion, the messiah's female counterpart.

Pilgrims, popes, and kings had been climbing up the massif at Sainte-Baume for centuries by the time Édouard Trouin, a surveyor and engineer who owned the land, was inspired to make the site a grander destination celebrating Mary, peace, and forgiveness. A basilica carved into the interior of the cliff, he believed, could rival Delphi, Jerusalem, and Rome. He sought out Le Corbusier in Paris in 1945, and the architect, eager for work following the war, was interested.

The plans for Sainte-Baume reveal Le Corbusier's first inklings of religion as theater. It was to be a journey through a series of spaces, a labyrinth leading to a sepulcher holding the body of Mary, who had been discovered in a crypt nearby. At the entrance would be the blinding light captured so well by Cézanne and, in the distance, the Mediterranean Sea. Inside the chambers, carved into the stone and shaped by rammed earth, the visitor would move through a cosmic play of shadow and light, a sine curve from day to night and back again: a meander, a winding path to self-discovery.[6] Trouin, who had papered all the walls and part of the ceiling of his Paris pied-à-terre with renderings of the project, envisioned not only a climactic shrine but also a museum, hotel, and theater; thinking like a Hollywood producer, he pictured the French sex symbol Brigitte Bardot playing Mary Magdalene. Skepticism among church officials turned quickly to outright opposition. The invisible architecture of peace and contemplation was never built.

Sainte-Baume was a disappointment, and though it was among many projects in the atelier's archives that were unexecuted, the experience made Le Corbusier wary of working with the Catholic Church. It was up to Father Couturier, who had supported and encouraged the development scheme at Sainte-Baume, to convince him that the Ronchamp project would overcome all obstacles. The very same priest who sat on Yvonne's whoopee cushion and laughed about it years before had become a good friend. Le Corbusier took him at his word that skeptics both in the town and in the church bureaucracy would be kept at bay.

In accepting the commission for Ronchamp, Le Corbusier also made a promise. His second attempt at designing sacred space would take everything to a new level — not only an entirely new look for a church, but a major turning point in his own style. His purist villas of clean lines and right angles had been beautiful but austere; his buildings up until 1950, when he agreed to build Ronchamp, conveyed the idea that they were there to serve a function. Eileen Gray had pointed out that the very practical rationale made the architecture feel a little cold. The Chapel of Notre Dame du Haut would billow and curve, and the faithful would not so much enter the building but experience it. The edifice was designed to connect on a different plane, to stir emotions and introspection, to break through to another side in an almost hallucinatory journey. While the Villa Savoye, with its occupants in golf attire clutching cocktails, evoked George Gershwin tunes, the soundtrack for the church on Bourlemont Hill was part Gregorian chant, part John Cage.

When the workers took away the last of the scaffolding in 1954, what stood was a curvy white dollop of whitewashed concrete sprayed from a cement gun, punctured by odd-sized windows at seemingly random locations, and topped by a bulbous roof, set at an angle like the dark hull of a boat, improbable, heavy, and thick, but looking for all the world like it was floating on air. Le Corbusier's creation appeared to have landed from outer space – yet somehow, as so many of the locals would come to say, as if it had been there all along.[7]

He had visited the site again and again, inspecting the rubble-strewn hilltop in a trench coat, and personally supervised the mixing of the local concrete, the delivery of African wood for the pews and the white stones from Burgundy for the altar. He climbed up on scaffolding and painted the glass in the recessed openings, and adorned the heavy main door, which swung open on a pivot, with a checkerboard of bright colors. Conjuring Ronchamp had been a singular thrill. It reminded him of when he first discovered the power of using color in architecture, splash-

In Paris as a young man, circa 1909, when he was an apprentice for the pioneering designers the Perret brothers. *© F.L.C. / ADAGP, Paris / Artists Rights Society (ARS), New York 2014*

Le Corbusier's sketch of the Acropolis, inspiration for his architecture, from his *voyage d'Orient*, 1910–11. *© F.L.C. / ADAGP, Paris / Artists Rights Society (ARS), New York 2014*

The Maison
Blanche, 1912.
One of the
first homes he
designed, for his
parents, on the
outskirts of his
hometown, La
Chaux-de-Fonds,
in northwest
Switzerland.
Anthony Flint

Amédée Ozenfant, second from left, was cofounder of *L'Esprit Nouveau*, the journal of the modern era. Le Corbusier is seated at the far right.

With Yvonne Gallis, the couture house model he would marry, at the beach in Piquey, in the early 1920s. © F.L.C. / ADAGP, Paris / Artists Rights Society (ARS), New York 2014

For his parents' retirement years on the shore of Lake Geneva in Vevey, Le Corbusier built the minimalist Villa Le Lac, also known as La Petite Maison. *Anthony Flint*

At 20 rue Jacob, the top-floor garret in the Latin Quarter where Charles-Édouard Jeanneret-Gris, as a full-time resident of Paris in the roaring twenties, changed his name to Le Corbusier.

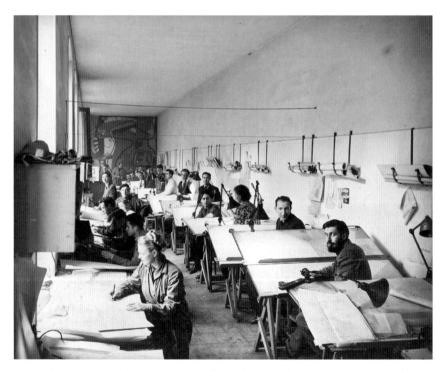

The studio at 35 rue de Sèvres, also in the sixth arrondissement—space rented from monks at a monastery next door to Le Bon Marché department store, beginning in 1924.

In 1925 Le Corbusier proposed razing the neighborhood known as Le Marais, replacing it with the towers, open space, and roadways of the Plan Voisin.
© F.L.C. / ADAGP, Paris / Artists Rights Society (ARS), New York 2014

Villa Savoye in Poissy, completed in 1929, affirmed Le Corbusier's role as a star architect and ushered in the International Style. *Anthony Flint*

On his 1929 trip to South America, Le Corbusier met the jazz singer Josephine Baker, here with others aboard the ocean liner *Lutetia*. © F.L.C. / ADAGP, Paris / Artists Rights Society (ARS), New York 2014

Charlotte Perriand, shown here with Le Corbusier and colleagues at the Bar Saint Sulpice in 1928, was a key collaborator, designing furniture and apartment kitchens. *Banque d'Images, ADAGP / Art Resource, NY*

En route to the 1933 meeting in Athens of Congrès International d'Architecture Moderne (CIAM), the political group Le Corbusier formed to promote modernism worldwide.
© F.L.C. / ADAGP, Paris / Artists Rights Society (ARS), New York 2014

Painting murals at E-1027, the modernist villa designed by Eileen Gray that Le Corbusier used as a vacation home in Roquebrune-Cap-Martin, between Nice and the Italian border in the South of France, throughout the 1930s. © F.L.C. / ADAGP, Paris / Artists Rights Society (ARS), New York 2014

Albert Einstein, who met Le Corbusier at Princeton University in 1946, praised the Modular, the architect's system for creating architecture that accommodates the movements of humankind. © F.L.C. / ADAGP, Paris / Artists Rights Society (ARS), New York 2014

Unité d'Habitation in Marseille, completed in 1952. An all-inclusive ocean liner on land that Le Corbusier envisioned as part of a vast Ville Radieuse, housing millions in cities all over the world. Anthony Flint

Touring Unité d'Habitation with Picasso in 1949, as the experimental apartment building in Marseille readied for opening. © F.L.C. / ADAGP, Paris / Artists Rights Society (ARS), New York 2014

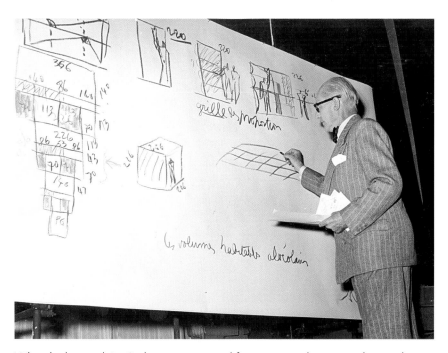

When he lectured, Le Corbusier never read from prepared notes, and instead drew on long strips of tracing paper on the spot. © F.L.C. / ADAGP, Paris / Artists Rights Society (ARS), New York 2014

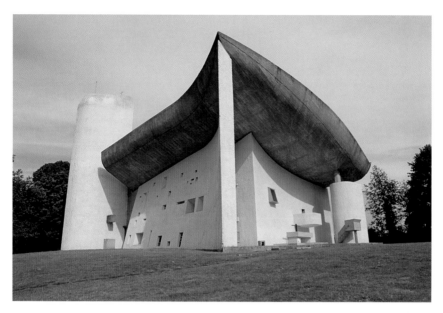

When Notre Dame du Haut de Ronchamp opened in 1954, the chapel was almost instantly an icon of twentieth-century modern architecture.   *Anthony Flint*

Light shining through the array of windows and thin line separating the walls and the crab shell–inspired roof at Ronchamp.   *Anthony Flint*

The terrace overlooking the Mediterranean at Étoile de Mer, the café where Le Corbusier and Yvonne dined on sea urchins and sipped wine, in Roquebrune-Cap-Martin.   © F.L.C. / ADAGP, Paris / Artists Rights Society (ARS), New York 2014

The inverted Couvent Sainte-Marie de La Tourette in Eveux, near Lyon in France, is a mecca for architects and an inspiration for scores of duplicates, including Boston City Hall.   Anthony Flint

One of the big picture windows at La Tourette, which was completed in 1960.
Anthony Flint

A monk's cell at La Tourette, including a private porch, wash basin, desk, and chair, in less than one hundred square feet.   *Anthony Flint*

The parliament building, completed in 1964, in the capitol complex at the planned city of Chandigarh, north of New Delhi. *Anthony Flint*

Le Corbusier at 24 rue Nung-esser et Coli, near Roland Garros sta-dium, in a portrait by the photogra-pher Yousuf Karsh taken in 1954.

© Yousuf Karsh

Karsh, who photographed many icons of the twentieth century, from Ernest Hemingway to Jacqueline Kennedy, found Le Corbusier reticent and reserved.
© *Yousuf Karsh*

With a rendering of Unité d'Habitation in the background, Le Corbusier made the cover of *Time* in May 1961. *Anthony Flint*

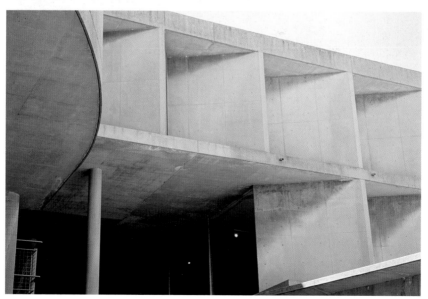

Le Corbusier's only building in North America, the Carpenter Center for the Visual Arts at Harvard University, in Cambridge, Massachusetts, opened in 1963. *Anthony Flint*

The *cabanon,* designed on the basis of the Modular, served as Le Corbusier's holiday getaway in his beloved Roquebrune-Cap-Martin. *Anthony Flint*

On the bench outside the *cabanon.* A lifelong swimmer, Le Corbusier waded into the water for the last time in August 1965. *Photograph by Lucien Hervé. The Getty Research Institute, Los Angeles (2002.R.41)* © J. Paul Getty Trust

ing reds and blues on walls to achieve "the power of blood, the freshness of the prairie, the brightness of sunlight or the depth of the sea and the sky. So many different forces at one's fingertips! It is pure dynamism, as I might say with equal justification were I writing of dynamite."[8]

The experience of discovering the building was carefully choreographed, beginning down below in the village, where it appeared, as the architect put it, as the seed sown of the acropolis, the white veils of the Mediterranean mimicking the undulating hills all around. The final steps to the chapel began near modest quarters for nuns, and the visitor marched up the last steep slope to the plateau, approaching from the southeast. The billowing roof – sweeping up from two sides to a peak that was anchored by a long, thin white column – was intended to draw the eye first.

He said he got the idea for the roof at Ronchamp from a crab shell. He was out on Long Island on his trip to New York in 1947, when he stepped on the shell and was impressed by its resilience. "On the drafting table is the crab shell I picked up," he wrote later. "It becomes the roof of the chapel: two connected concrete skins . . . hand me pencil and paper! It begins with a response to the site. Thick walls, a crab's shell, so as to enliven the too static plan with curves. So I pick up the crab's shell and place it on top of the walls."[9]

In terms of engineering, though, Le Corbusier designed the roof as much like the wing of an airplane he had detailed in his book *Precisions on the Present State of Architecture and City Planning,* published in 1930 at the brink of the jet age. Flat at the top and bowed out underneath, its interior was a hidden latticework of structural support, supplying incredible strength, while the outer membranes appeared feathery and fine. The plunges and angles and precarious tensions seemed to test the limits of any understood principles of engineering. And then there was his final touch: raising the roof up so there was about a four-inch gap between it and the top of the walls, further giving the impression it was floating, and letting extra light into the interior as well. The roof at Ronchamp was a marvel, the key element in a visual package that prompted observers to make a wide range of associations. The southeast corner of the church, the part of the building that visitors first saw, was the prow of a ship, a nun's hat, Noah's ark, a wind-filled sail, an ancient bark, a mushroom, a breaking wave, and even, for some, the foreskin of a penis. The open-ended interpretation was perfectly acceptable, for the most part, to Le Corbusier – and for generations of architects for years to come. People could see what they wanted to see, as long as they were responding emotionally.

Yet the exterior, by design, was only the beginning of the journey. More magic waited inside. The atrium, cavernous and tranquil, was awash in a matrix of colored horizontal shafts of sunlight, filtering through the jumble of recessed windows punched into the south wall, a mystical light show. At the juncture of the top of the walls and the ceiling – the gap that made the roof look like it was floating on the outside – a thin band of light glowed. And in the back, more bright beams shot through the semicircular band of windows at the top of the towers. The light beams appeared as if physical forms, with a mass all their own. The polished floor tilted down slightly, as if following the contours of the hill, funneling down to a spare altar. The dark wood rows of benches – Le Corbusier initially didn't want seating at all, believing that man should stand and pray – faced a blank wall punctured by a single square window surrounded by tiny dots of light. The curving entryway to an exterior pulpit, placed so that the clergymen could address the overflow crowds outside, was at the same height as the interior pulpit set off to the side, the preaching platform and stairs leading to it all of one concrete piece – like everything, securely anchored yet floating in space.

The stagecraft featured not only light but sound. The perfect acoustics allowed a whisper to be heard from the altar to the back of the room – and for human voices to soar and swirl and inhabit the space. Inside this church, Le Corbusier said, "they will be able to make incredible music, an unbelievable sound . . . music composed for the church, something new, not sad music; a loud noise, an unholy din."[10]

A journey into shapes and light and sound, the chapel was a symphony of warped planes and primitive contours intended to move the soul, to touch something deep within all those who entered its capacious volumes. It was a jolting inversion of the baroque, stripped clean of conventional elements. Le Corbusier fulfilled every specification by doing something different. He arranged for the bells to be hung from a separate structure off the back of the church. The rainwater collection system he was required to build – the plateau being unusually dry most of the year – took the form of bulging basins fed by sleek white spouts, his modernist gargoyles. Asked to create a monument to the French soldiers who died on the hilltop during World War II, he piled the stones from the destroyed church into a pyramid at the edge of the east lawn. There is no plaque or marker, just a simple statement – a precursor to war monuments for conflicts yet to come.

Only the nineteenth-century statue of the Virgin Mary – the one rescued by the French soldier – occupied a place of honor, in an alcove on the east wall.

When Pierre and Eugénie Savoye asked Le Corbusier to build them a country house, he delivered much more; he did the same with Ronchamp. The diocese officials could not say that they had not been warned, that there would be parallel messages, blurring the lines of Catholicism and other forms of mysticism, God and the Goddess. Le Corbusier's detachment from organized religion was no secret.

The principles that emerged from his Calvinist upbringing – orderliness, discipline, and the denial of excess – were useful guidance for life. Going to church on Sundays, however, held little appeal. His parents never pushed the ritual, attending church only on major holidays. His obligatory Protestant religious training was accomplished over several weeks in one summer, at the direction of his aunt Pauline.

As a young man, he had immersed himself in Ernest Renan's *The Life of Jesus,* purchased in Paris at the same time as Nietzsche's *Thus Spoke Zarathustra,* and begun to identify with the carpenter of Nazareth. Beside one passage – "Jesus is not a spiritualist; for him everything has a palpable realization. But he is a fulfilled idealist, for him matter is only the sign of the idea" – he scrawled a note in the margin: "And I herewith create everything anew! This is the feature all reformers have."[11] He would sometimes sign his name as "L.C." – coming close to the son of God's initials.

To the extent that he identified with any religious group, it was a band of rebels, marked as heretics and ruthlessly persecuted. The Cathars of Languedoc and Provence in the South of France believed in a simple way of life and a church without the gilded trappings of Rome. Also known as Albigensians, they were fervent believers in Mary Magdalene, whom Le Corbusier hoped to enshrine at Sainte-Baume. They were especially threatening not only as a splinter group but aligned in a potential north-south civil war in France. Pope Innocent III unleashed a withering crusade to rid the region of them, dispatching the Dominican Order to round them up and parade them naked through the streets, and to subject them to torture and target practice. In the

siege of one town, when a soldier worried that innocent Catho-
lics would be killed along with the heretics, a commanding abbot
replied that the troops should just kill everyone and God would
sort it out, coining the phrase used by merciless generals centuries later. The last of the Cathars fled into the Jura Mountains
of northwest Switzerland, a diaspora that Le Corbusier believed
informed the Jeanneret family tree. Maybe that was why he felt
drawn to the South of France and the Mediterranean: It was in
his blood. Identifying with rebels also suited him well.

And it was again Mary Magdalene, more than Jesus, who
captured his imagination. The twentieth-century Dominican
friars – the heirs of the crusaders who, ironically, awarded the
commission for Ronchamp – seemed to turn a blind eye to the
way that Le Corbusier's spiritualism veered off toward the occult. The "other Mary" was inherent in a panoply of mystical
forces he believed in, an alternate universe of music, color, mathematics – and sex.

He dove into the mystic by way of the ancient Greek myth
of Orpheus, who charmed the gods with his music, and demon-
strated to Plato and Pythagoras that the basis of the cosmos was
numbers and geometry – and that ultimately a kind of mathe-
matically based harmony is achieved by the fusion of man and
woman. The swollen volumes of the chapel at Ronchamp evoke
the life-giving womb, monument to the feminine – a tribute to
the Virgin Mary, Mary Magdalene, his wife, Yvonne, and, above
all, his own mother. In painted script, the words "Marie, shining
like the sun" appear on the pane of one prominent recessed window. Marie Jeanerret was like that to him: a beacon, a divining
light.

If the visiting pilgrims sought to be closer to God, they were
also, unwittingly, engaging in the journey of initiation that Le
Corbusier admired in the secret societies and Masonic lodges of
his day, prevalent in Paris and La Chaux-de-Fonds.[12] The archi-

tectural promenade at Ronchamp can be read as both a sensual journey and an immersion in the mystical proportions found in the Masonic square and compass – the next iteration of what Le Corbusier had called the poetry of the right angle.

"The obsession for symbols that lies deep inside me is like a yearning for a language limited to only a few words," he had written, after his odyssey through Turkey and Italy and Greece as a young man.[13]

What was undeniably true was the foundation of mathematics and geometry in his architecture, derived from the golden ratio, the basis for the Modular. Hidden in the chapel were the mystical powers of proportion, as if seen only with X-ray vision.

"The Modular everywhere," he said. "I defy the visitor to give the dimensions of the different parts of the building." The unseen blueprint appears in the lines on the floor and is buried in the canted walls.[14]

It was quite a trick, blending the Virgin Mary with the myth of Orpheus, the processionals of the Catholic Church with the Fibonacci sequence. The Le Corbusier code enveloped the atrium where the unwitting congregation sang hymns, an act of subversion. The pilgrims would come and go by the thousands. The Chapel of Notre Dame du Haut stood on the hillside like a monumental puzzle, never quite fully solved.

Suspicions of ulterior motives notwithstanding, Father Couturier, for one, only wanted more. Even as Ronchamp was being built, he commissioned Le Corbusier to build the monastery of Sainte-Marie de La Tourette, just outside Lyon in the hamlet of Éveux-sur-l'Arbresle. There the aging friar, dissatisfied with an initially hired architect's conservative plans, sought a place "to create a silent dwelling place for one hundred bodies and one hundred hearts" – a complex for teaching, for retreat, and for meditation.[15] Building such a refuge had swift appeal. "I have something of a monk's soul," Le Corbusier once told another clergyman.[16]

While the site for the chapel at Ronchamp was a flat hilltop, La Tourette would be tucked into a hillside, with forests at its back and sweeping views to open fields in front. Le Corbusier decided the building would not curve and undulate like Ronchamp, but instead it would take the form of a big rectangular box, oriented around a central courtyard, and anchored by a sanctuary at one end. The entrance was at grade, but the rest of the structure jutted out over the downward slope, held aloft by pilotis. The entire structure would be inverted, bigger at the top, shrinking and falling away at the bottom.

"I came here. I took out my little sketchbook as always," he wrote after first visiting the site in May 1953. "I drew the horizons, I determined the orientation of the sun, I sniffed out the topography. I decided where [the building] would be, since the place had not been determined yet. In making this choice, I committed either a criminal or heroic act. The first gesture to make was the choice, the nature of the site, and then the nature of the composition that we would make under these conditions.... Here, in this environment which is so mobile, so fluid, so shifting, descending, flowing, I said: I am not going to establish the position from the ground because it flees."[17]

Encased in reinforced concrete, his reliable *béton brut,* the exterior bristled with the rough texture of exposed stone, juxtaposed with huge panes of windows on the facade overlooking the countryside.

Specifications for the interior called for classrooms, a library, meeting rooms, and, above all, one hundred cells for the monks. Drawing from the Unité d'Habitation – as well as the monastery at Val d'Ema he so admired in Italy and the Cistercian abbey at Le Thoronet in the South of France – he set out the divine hotel rooms along the top two floors, hyperefficient quarters roughly six feet wide and twenty feet deep, accommodating a bed, a chest of drawers, a sink and mirror, and a desk. Each cell had its own balcony, where the monks could step out to contemplate the deep woods framing the site.

The attention to detail was painstaking, from the carefully laid out hallways and ramps to the garden on the roof. The cavernous chapel was illuminated by light barrels – conical skylights throwing down colored beams. The prohibition on clutter was absolute, with not so much as a crucifix to be added on to the interior decor. He had already taken care of that, with crosses inlaid in the walls and sculptural features throughout the building. Yet he wanted imperfections to show. When a worker installed a window upside down, he insisted it be left as is – to show, he said, that this house of God was made by imperfect man.

The interior of the monastery, he said, "displays a total poverty."[18] But he had once again achieved a convergence of simplicity and complexity, an architectural playground based on the Modular, his *cabanon* at Roquebrune-Cap-Martin a hundred times over, and a spiritual version of Unité d'Habitation as well.

Simplicity, poverty, and truth were likewise the stated requirements in the commission for the final church he would build, the Parish Church of Saint-Pierre, in Firminy, part of a postwar redevelopment scheme that included a stadium, a cultural center, a school, and housing – his final Unité d'Habitation apartment building. The church was to be the crown in that array, a giant squared-off cone made of concrete, completely blank all around, yet on closer inspection punctured with tiny openings to let light flow into the austere interior. Along with the light barrels at the top of the funnel, the effect was beams and ribbons and dots of light, thrown like water.

The designs for his last sacred space, in the end, remained largely on paper. Construction stalled when his main sponsor,

Eugène Claudius-Petit, stepped down as mayor of Firminy; the church would be completed forty-one years after Le Corbusier's death. La Tourette continued as a functioning monastery, though dogged by deteriorating concrete, leaks, and faulty wiring. It would become a prerequisite stop on the architectural pilgrimage tour, with students from all over the world photographing each other in the hallways and in the front entrance arch, arm raised up like the Modular Man.

But the pinnacle remained Ronchamp.

There had been sniping. The chapel at Ronchamp practically cried out to be mocked. A pioneering work of modern architecture, so new and radical and different, was almost reflexively pilloried. Some called it a bunker and a bomb shelter, others an "ecclesiastical garage." Local officials had second thoughts soon after the commission was granted; the mining industry was declining and people were out of work, and surely money would be better spent on making things right with them. Here was an out-of-the-way town making a big bet to put itself on the map – but that could wind up with a boondoggle.

Traditionalists in the Catholic Church were horrified. A German archdiocese noted "with dismay that Ronchamp was being met with an altogether positive response in the press," despite the church being "the height of innovation for its own sake, capriciousness, and disorder." Le Corbusier had "broken with the tradition of Catholic Church architecture with an unprecedented radicalism, and in many ways even violated the standard rules of architecture. . . . This church completely lacks the air of sanctity that must be demanded at all costs."[19]

Even those who supported the choice of Le Corbusier and wanted to like it found the end result disturbing somehow. The architect seemed driven to confuse and unsettle, said one Jesuit chaplain. "Everything is unresolved dissonance. There is no recognizable axis."[20]

Many fellow modernists were equally disappointed, though for very different reasons. For the average pilgrim, Ronchamp was all about the heart and not the head. Those immersed in the modernist project preferred the architect's mechanical and functional approach – house as machine – and buildings that intimidated, requiring more intellectual engagement. This place was too easily enjoyed. It was theater, to be sure – but a Broadway musical, not a serious play.

What an exquisite turn of events, for the man building his first church. He had managed to alienate both the conservatives in the religious establishment and those he considered allies in the avant-garde. He had to be doing something right.

The criticism faded away as a band played "La Marseillaise" and Le Corbusier made his brief remarks at the Ronchamp inauguration in 1955.

"In building this chapel, I wanted to create a place of silence, prayer, peace, and inner joy," he said. He thanked all the workers, suppliers, engineers, and administrators, and turned over a ceremonial key to the local archbishop, saying:

> A keen awareness of the sacred sustained our efforts. Some things are sacred, others are not, whether or not they are religious. Our workers ... were the ones who made this difficult oeuvre, meticulous, rough, strong in the means deployed, but sensitive, animated by a total creational mathematics of inexpressible space. Some scattered signs and a few written words speak praise to the Virgin. The cross – the real cross of torment – is installed in this arch; the Christian drama has thus taken possession of the place. Your excellence, I turn over to you this

chapel of loyal concrete, perhaps steeped in foolhardiness, certainly in courage, with the hope that it will find in you as in those who will climb the hill, an echo in what we have inscribed here.[21]

In the years to come, the Chapel of Notre Dame du Haut at Ronchamp would grace the covers of textbooks on modern architecture and become a destination for architectural pilgrims as much as, if not more so than, those coming to celebrate the blessed Virgin Mary. Long before Frank Gehry shocked the world with the curvy forms of his museum at Bilbao, Le Corbusier had broken through to a new realm of form. Some would come to call Ronchamp the first example of postmodern architecture – the movement that would emerge as a backlash to modernism, with a more playful approach and a rejection of the right angles and straight lines that Le Corbusier himself had established. In turn it led to a wave of biomorphic architecture, aided by computer-assisted design and software that Le Corbusier never had – buildings with even wilder undulations and bulging volumes reflecting the structure of natural organisms: architecture as zoology.

All his sacred spaces – at Ronchamp, La Tourette, and Firminy – accelerated the trend in psychedelic church design, from Oscar Niemeyer in Brasília to Richard Meier and the Jubilee Church in Italy. Like local civic leaders clamoring for a Gehry museum, many church officials longed for the attention and excitement that accompanied Ronchamp. It wouldn't take long for traditionalists to condemn the ecclesiastical arms race in design and plead for a return to the basics.

The inauguration of Ronchamp, however, was an unfettered celebration of the great achievement. Members of the crowd at the opening ceremony all but lifted Le Corbusier up on their shoulders. At a luncheon, he signed autographs on Ronchamp postcards, destined for the gift shop and visitor center in the years to come. His celebrity had moved into a new phase, a new dimension – as the creator of sacred space. "Your Corbu was being loved," he wrote to his mother, noting how everything unfolded so splendidly at the opening that June 1955. Though he was sixty-seven years old, he wrote to her once again with great pride and seeking approval. "All joy, beauty, and spiritual splendor. . . . Your Corbu was in the place of honor, at the top. Well regarded, liked. Respected. This was a difficult game to play. It's the most revolutionary work of architecture for a long time."[22]

Marie, shining like the sun, was nearly a hundred years old and remained the one person he wanted to impress most of all. She needed constant convincing. Like all the letters sent to Vevey, retelling adventures, noting appearances on radio and television, inviting Marie and his brother, Albert, to grand openings, there was little in the replies that acknowledged the path to greatness.

In his travels, Le Corbusier had taken to carrying around a copy of *Don Quixote*.

8 ▪ THE CITY

The Air India jet banked over the Himalayan plains, tilting the first-class cabin toward an expansive view of the northern region all the way up toward the foothills and Shimla, the former summertime capital of the British Raj. Rivers appeared as long muddy ribbons, with a thin stream of water in the center. The long stretches of flat, khaki-colored land were sprinkled with clusters of green bushes and trees and a few huts here and there. Le Corbusier looked down and remembered how he had, in a similar fashion from the Graf Zeppelin, surveyed Brazil, twenty years and a lifetime ago. That was a different kind of chaos, the rivers meandering wildly through the jungle. Now, over India, half a world away, he leaned close to the jet's oval window and pictured a grid to organize humanity, an order to be imposed on an increasingly crowded nation, and grand monuments befitting the new republic. The blank canvas was before him. There was earth to be moved.

On the descent to Delhi, the stewardess handed the hot towels around. It had been a long flight, from Geneva with a stop in Bombay, hours and hours in the air. He calculated that he had essentially spent an entire day in hurtling aluminum tubes. But flying was still a time that he cherished. He had climbed aboard some of the first passenger planes, Lockheeds and Fokkers and Boeings, their ribbed silver fuselages bright and shiny. Inside, the cabins were tidy and economical – so compelling he sketched them, detailing the consoles for air-conditioning and reading lights, and the pull-down overhead bins.[1] The interior organization confirmed the wisdom of the built-ins and other features maximizing the use of space in his apartments and the *cabanon,* just as the ocean liners he first used for international travel had been inspiring. And the plane provided splendid isolation, a time to read and think and reflect and draw, away from telephones and client meetings and the bustle of the atelier. Most of all, he could look out the window, from the ultimate observation deck, watching the wrinkles and folds of the landscape recede as he headed for the sky and the clouds.

The trip to the subcontinent was especially long but well worth it in every way. He was traveling to the place where he would achieve his lifelong dream at last: to build a city from scratch.

He knew that when he landed he would be well taken care of, as the VIP guest of the new prime minister. What a visionary Jawaharlal Nehru had turned out to be. A soldier in the Indian army, he made his way to the top of political power, just at the moment India was granted independence from the British Empire in 1947. After two hundred years of colonial rule, it was Nehru who would lead the fledgling democracy into the modern world. The population had grown to 350 million people, in the big cities of Delhi and Bombay and across the countryside – the vast majority staggeringly poor. In those plains running out from the foothills of the Himalayas, Nehru had the chance to make a statement, showing the world the bright future the nation would inhabit. And he had turned to Le Corbusier to get it done.

The region of northern India was known as Punjab, and nowhere were the tensions of the time more evident. With independence had come the partition, a bold redrawing of boundaries aimed at separating warring Muslims and Hindus and Sikhs. West Pakistan was created on one side, and East Pakistan – later renamed Bangladesh – on the other; Punjab was in the middle. The rearranging of millions of people was destined to be a violent and messy process, known to this day as not simply the partition but the tragedy of partition. Those who called the place home for years suddenly found themselves in the religious minority and had to flee. For India, the biggest test came in the case of Lahore – previously the provincial capital but, after 1947, part of Pakistan. Hundreds of thousands of families were wrenched from their homes and had to be resettled. And a new capital for the Punjab state was urgently needed.

The task promised a fresh start in all kinds of ways. Some advisers suggested building on the Victorian city of Shimla, but Nehru dismissed the idea. Shimla had powerful associations with the British regime – Rudyard Kipling wrote *The Jungle Book* there – and it was too close to the new, tenuous borders with Pakistan and China. Nehru sought a capital that would symbolize independent India's move to modernity, liberated from being a British colony – a new city "free from the existing encumbrances of old towns and old traditions," he said. "Let it be the first large expression of our creative genius flowering on our newly earned freedom."[2]

Nehru had his eyes on an alternate site, which he had surveyed from a plane as well: a flat area of fertile land nourished by two seasonal rivers, 150 miles north of Delhi. Amid the smattering of rural villages, little more than collections of shacks, was the temple of Chandi, the Hindu goddess of power. The prime minister decreed that the new modern city and the new capital for Punjab should be there, and it should be called Chandigarh. And he made his mandate clear: no neoclassical or Beaux-Arts grandeur, but rather the best of modern architecture and urban design, a city to break emphatically with the colonial past.

Stepping down the rollaway stairs to the tarmac, Le Corbusier, veteran traveler, shook off the jet lag and prepared to take on his latest commission. The warm air, the mist, the smells, the smoke – every signal was a step into another world. He traded his dark suit, bow tie, and porkpie hat for knee-length khaki shorts and shirt, and climbed into the passenger seat of a waiting Jeep. His driver took him north from Delhi, hitting the horn to clear the way of people and livestock, a custom that would be part and parcel of motorized travel in India for years to come.

Soon they were on the outskirts and into the bush. Barechested men in turbans herded goats and bulls along shallow waterways lined by dry reeds. They looked on sternly at the white-haired foreigner in round black spectacles. But when the Jeep's front tires got lodged in ruts on one section of road, a scrum of men appeared instantly to push the vehicle forward.

The destination was a clearing dotted with squat trees, mangos, Indian rosewood, and lemon eucalyptus, where canvas tents had been set up. Le Corbusier swung himself out and walked into the landscape, scanning the horizon. The sky was soft and the air was sweet with the flowers of the high desert. In the distance were the Himalayas, powerful and unblinking, overlooking the plain.

The encampment afforded colonial comforts, and Le Corbusier was delighted. His tent had a sturdy cot, and each morning a fresh bouquet of pansies was provided, as well as a new maidenhair fern for his buttonhole. His hosts ensured he was as relaxed as possible, given the enormity of the task before him.

Chandigarh was his to conjure, but it had not started that way. Nehru's first choice was a team led by an American.

Albert Mayer was an engineer for the US Army stationed in India during World War II when he met Nehru, then in the Indian armed forces. The two men talked about human settlement, and after the war Nehru invited him to return to plan new villages. When the prime minister first made his decision to build Chandigarh, Mayer was the natural choice to lead the project.

Trained at Columbia and MIT, Mayer had emerged as a city planner with a social conscience. The world's cities were growing rapidly, and as migrants poured in from the countryside, flocking to urban centers in search of a better life, they needed decent housing. With the urban theorist Lewis Mumford, Mayer founded the Housing Study Guild, a group of design professionals dedicated to solutions for the rapid urbanization of the twentieth century. Like Le Corbusier, he designed large-scale apartment buildings and was immersed in the challenges of public housing in New York City, where he was a founding partner in his planning firm. The answer was housing and more housing—but the big picture, the framework of infrastructure, was so often elusive. The congestion on the roadways of New York dismayed him. The trick was to make it all work, in a master-planned community, a New Town, where the components fit together and the unintended consequences were minimized. Command and control.

Mayer's partner in the commission was Matthew Nowicki, another Mumford protégé. Nowicki had, among other things, established the saddle dome design of sports arenas in the United States. A Russian-born Pole, he briefly manned antiaircraft

guns during the blitzkrieg and then went underground, teaching classes in town planning and architecture in a course he convinced the Nazis was about bricklaying. He had designed a sports
center and a casino by the time he teamed up with Mayer.

The two men were joined by two others, Maxwell Fry and
Jane Drew from London, modernists who were equally interested in building schools and housing. They settled on a basic
plan, after camping out in India for weeks, hoping to understand
the local culture and craft the architecture accordingly. They
envisioned a capital complex and, below, curvilinear roadways
snaking through residential districts. As a whole, the product
was a version of the Garden City that had become popular in the
United States, from Baldwin Hills Village in California to Green-
belt, Maryland. Inspired by the British urban planning theorists
Ebenezer Howard and Raymond Unwin, the goal was to create affordable satellite communities with an ideal population of
thirty-two thousand, combining the best of town and country.
The Garden City sought to be a collection of enough people in
one place to feel lively, yet spread out to give residents a feeling
of having plenty of personal space. Landscaping in the tradition
of Frederick Law Olmsted helped create the sense of pastoral
retreat. From the beginning, Chandigarh was destined to be an
American suburb in India.

Mayer was elated to see the noble experiment unfold. "I feel
in all solemnity that this will be a source of great stimulation to
city building and re-planning in India," he told Nehru. "But I also
feel that it will be the most complete synthesis and integration
in the world to date of all that has been learned and talked of in
planning over the last thirty years, but which no one has yet had
the great luck to be allowed actually to create. Yet I feel we have
been able to make it strongly Indian in feeling and function as
well as modern."[3]

Then the unthinkable happened. In the summer of 1950, Nowicki was killed in a TWA plane crash near Cairo, returning from the site. The decision was made to start over and reach out to new architects to lead the effort. Two representatives of the Indian government were dispatched to Europe to find a new leader. Eugène Claudius-Petit, the French reconstruction minister and later the mayor of Firminy, recommended Le Corbusier, and the question was posed to Max Fry and Jane Drew, who would continue to be a part of the project: What do you think of hiring the Frenchman? "Honour and glory for you, and an unpredictable portion of misery for me" was the reply.[4] The Indian emissaries headed for Paris and 35 rue de Sèvres.

The architect gruffly informed them that he could not possibly spend so much time in India, and if he took on the project he would work from Paris. His reputation for being difficult was well established. Yet his innovation and imagination were irresistible. Le Corbusier was reflexively playing hard to get; he had said no to Ronchamp at first, after all. But the value of building a city from scratch – even more so than designing a church – was self-evident. In ultimately getting to yes, he insisted on a number of conditions, starting with complete control, and proposed that his cousin Pierre Jeanneret act as the leader of the project team. The deal was sealed on a Sunday morning in Paris – something Le Corbusier immediately admired, that the newly independent Indians would work seven days a week.[5] Nehru was overjoyed. And by the beginning of the following year, 1951, Le Corbusier was on his way to India.

At the encampment, the atmosphere for him was both serene and supercharged. There he was, finally able to build a city, as he tried to do in Bogotá and Rio and Algiers. No one was willing to let him create an entire metropolis according to his modernist principles. Until Nehru.

It was a marvelous blank slate – there were no existing buildings to tear down, no urban fabric to rip up, no Le Marais to be bulldozed to make way for the Plan Voisin. Nor had a city been destroyed by fire or earthquake or war. There was simply nothing there. He had free rein. The plan was to make a government center and a town initially for 150,000 people, then 300,000, and, over time, the potential to accommodate a population of 500,000. It would serve people of all classes, including the very poor, who were to be provided a means to live there with dignity. As long as he met those specifications, he could organize everything however he chose. His theories about how human beings best functioned in urban settings, developed and fine-tuned over four decades, could finally be put into action, unleashed on the Himalayan plain.

The plans were in his head; he put them on paper as a man in a reverie. He had gone through the process many times before – at the clearing in Poissy, at the hilltop in Ronchamp – but his Chandigarh sketchbook was filled with page after page of all the elements of an entire city. There in the bearable and pleasant heat of February, the vision that was required was exponential. In choosing where everything should go, he was like a novelist facing a blank page. Before beginning, he needed to know how the story would end.

The Americans had the right idea in many ways. Putting the capitol complex at the top of the new city made sense. But the plan's curving streets and splotches of open space would not do. Mayer and Nowicki's plan, an attempt to replicate traditional Indian building styles, was too rambling, spread over twenty-one thousand acres or about thirty-three square miles – larger than Manhattan. The plan needed tidying; Le Corbusier tightened up the proposed city limits, and turned all the American team's curves into a strict grid – the most orderly and rational in all the subcontinent, right angles and straight boulevards everywhere.

The grid consisted of forty-seven blocks, each nine football fields wide and three-quarters of a mile long, stacked in a core of rows of nine across and five down – a chessboard of human settlement. It was the biggest golden ratio he would ever create. In a reflection of the highly structured arrangement, the blocks would become known as sectors, each with a number – such that a future resident might proclaim that he lived not by the park or by the big oak tree or in a neighborhood with a nineteenth-century name, but in Sector 16.

The functions of life were similarly divided into different areas on the grid – government buildings, institutions such as schools and hospitals, and commercial and residential areas. Parks would be spread throughout the grid, but the main recreational area would be adjacent to the capitol complex, around the big man-made Sukhna Lake that Le Corbusier took particular pleasure in planning, with a sailing pavilion and beach club, walkways, and landscaped grounds.

The capitol complex, however, was where he could really let his imagination run wild. The requirements were for three major buildings – a secretariat or administrative building for government workers, a place for the legislature to convene, and a building for the judicial branch – all to be set on a broad campus at the northeast tip of the grid. He pictured the citadel raised up and separate from the rest of the city, visible for miles. The ensemble would be monumental, and his signature architecture, all his own, inside and out. He was already envisioning the sculpture in concrete, fronting on reflecting pools and a sweeping plaza, the assembly chambers with a soaring ceiling, and the halls of power he would adorn with his original tapestries. He had come a long way since the designed-by-committee United Nations.

Everything would have its own place. He imagined a marketplace occupying the center of the grid, providing all the shops and services the residents would need, one after the other in continuous arcades. The institutional buildings – a university and medical center – were set to go in the southwest quadrant. The rest of the sectors were reserved for the homes, primarily compact, three-story apartments reminiscent of his worker housing at Pessac for Henri Fruges's sugar cube factory. Many would have their own little driveway in the back, as well as a yard. The residential districts would be very consciously set apart from the bustle of the marketplace and the official business of the new capitol.

There would be none of the clutter and squalor of Bombay. The geometry would take care of that, keeping everything neat and organized. He was determined to accommodate a large population efficiently and in harmony; once again, that orderliness gave rise to a kind of mystical power. At the same time he wanted to honor the simplicity of Hindu temples and peasant life, and create architecture throughout that was not European or American, but Indian. The final flourish he pictured was a centerpiece work of public art, a giant, open hand, palm tilted upward to the sky, suggesting tenderness, welcome, and open democracy.

Never before had the blank canvas been so tantalizing. In those days at the encampment, Le Corbusier sketched and walked through the sand and brush, turning the large Brazilian coin he had started to carry in the pocket of his trousers. He also carried a pocket-sized cutout of the Modular Man. Among the many photographs he posed for, one showed him holding the Modular Man up in the sunlight, with a broadsheet-sized paper showing the master plan for Chandigarh.

For a project that was going to require so much work, Chandigarh gave him peace. He had started the project a few years after turning sixty and felt both an energy and a serenity he had not enjoyed in years.

"I've never been so tranquil and solitary, absorbed by the poetry of natural things and by poetry itself," he wrote to Yvonne.

"We're on the site of our city under a splendid sky, in the midst of a timeless countryside. . . . Everything is calm, slow, harmonious, lovable – everyone addresses you in low, modulated tones."[6]

Every foray around the site convinced him that the Indian people, and the region, were tailor-made for the grand experiment. Being in India was magical. He toured the gardens of the maharajah of Patiala, immersed himself in Indian art, and frolicked with the monkeys that congregated in the town squares. He clowned around as he had done while visiting Chicago, placing his glasses on a rock that looked like a head with a craggy face. And he worked. "We are working as if possessed," he wrote to Yvonne. "I'm telling you, Von, I am making here, at last, the crowning work of my life, with these people, the Indians, who are extraordinarily civilized."[7]

Yvonne, of course, was in Paris. He was faithful only in his letter-writing to her; being on the road stirred the usual feelings of romance. In New York, there had been Marguerite Tjader Harris, and another American, Hedwig Lauber, a buxom blond journalist whom he saw at her flat in Zurich, stealing away for sausage and ham and wine.[8] His women had strict instructions: to resist the temptation to write deeply intimate things down and to mark envelopes "personal," lest the office secretary open their correspondence. Now, in India, it was the perfect time to get together with a pretty architecture student he had met in England at a meeting of CIAM. Minnette de Silva was conveniently nearby in Sri Lanka, then called Ceylon.[9] She revered the aging architect and impressed him by learning French so she could converse with him more. For him, she came to represent an idealized version of the East.[10] Nothing about aging was slowing him down, including his proclivity for the dalliance.

While he spent the small amounts of spare time that he had with de Silva, there were other exotic adventures – and additional commissions – that consumed his attention in India. He was invited to the center of the nation's textile industry, Ahmedabad, part-time home of Mahatma Gandhi, and where a number of artists and wealthy patrons were keen on modernism. He leaned on the considerable talents of Balkrishna Doshi, who had apprenticed at 35 rue de Sèvres and served as a key liaison and fellow builder at Chandigarh, to smooth the way for his trip to the city, between Delhi and Bombay in the Gujarat state. Heartily welcomed there, he was promptly awarded commissions for four buildings, beginning with a museum – a massive box uncharacteristically clad in red brick, raised up on pilotis – and two grand residences. The villa built for Manorama Sarabhai, a collector of contemporary art, featured vaulted ceilings of red clay tile and a concrete slide leading from one of the son's bedrooms to the swimming pool below. The weekend retreat designed ultimately for Shyamubhai Shodhan, the head of another prominent family in Ahmedabad, was a stack of geometric shapes rendered in concrete, seamlessly blending the interior with the tropical gardens outside. Le Corbusier was especially pleased with that creation, calling it a palace and a functional house. "With his money and some rough concrete and color, I have given him shade in the summer, sun in the winter, air circulating and cool in all seasons."[11]

The ultimate commission in Ahmedabad was issued by the Mill Owners' Association, a collection of wealthy cotton mill owners who sought a headquarters and convening place for workers, with whom they had established a progressive partnership. There Le Corbusier employed a series of slanted fins, forming his signature brise-soleil, in a four-story structure serviced by ramps and concrete staircases. The interior was airy and open, with no traditional doors or windows, and an elegant pavilion afforded spectacular views to the countryside all around. There, the man who was rapidly becoming India's favorite architect pictured "workers washing and drying their cotton materials on the sand in the company of herons, cows, buffaloes and donkeys, half immersed in the water to keep cool. Such a panorama was an invitation to attempt, by means of architecture, to frame views from each floor of the building – for the benefit of the staff in their daily work, for festive evenings, for night views from the stage of the assembly hall, and also from the roof."[12]

It was architecture to stir the soul, to enliven the daily functions of life in grand surroundings – just what he had in mind for Chandigarh.

Despite his protestation that he could not possibly leave Paris to oversee construction of the new city, Le Corbusier returned repeatedly to India, though he turned over the job of on-the-ground project manager to his trusted cousin. Pierre Jeanneret, who had moved past his disapproval of Le Corbusier's time in Vichy, was equally enchanted with India. The team, including Maxwell Fry and Jane Drew, based operations in a construction headquarters in the center of the city, in what would become Sector 19. The move there – from the initial set of tents and then accommodations in Shimla, which required an arduous commute – created an air of excitement as the new capital started to take shape.

The labor force brought in to execute Le Corbusier's plans – five thousand men, women, and children – recalled the building of the pyramids. The heavy building materials were toted in baskets, passed from worker to worker in firemen's brigades, and perched on heads. Trees of rebar sprouted up everywhere, alongside precarious scaffolding that from a distance looked like little more than skinny twigs. The crazy scene was both exhilarating and strange. In the evenings, he wrote to Yvonne. "Everyone sleeps under a thatch of reeds supported by two low walls, and at night the whole place fills up with children and men. This all happens on the site itself, in the dust, among bags of cement, bricks, etc., naked kids running around everywhere. The women never have a place of their own. These people are nomads."[13]

Befitting a city built from the ground up, completion came in stages, from 1953 to 1965. What arose was extraordinary and comprehensive. Every detail had been fawned over, from lighting to door handles to manhole covers, which sported a metal relief of the city grid. Pierre designed furniture for the homes and government offices made of sleek wood, rattan, and bamboo: tables and chairs and desks and bookshelves. He designed the pedal boats for use on the man-made lake as well. Le Corbusier created huge tapestries of colorful, abstract forms to go in the parliament and judicial buildings. At just about every rotary juncture of the street grid, a posted map provided orientation, identifying sectors by number. Even the trees were selected and planted with great care, their umbrella crowns choreographed to form arches of badly needed shade.

The opening ceremonies, as each building was completed, were true celebrations, punctuated by a formal service of tea. Nehru appeared in his trademark white cap and a sherwani, the precursor to his eponymous jacket. Le Corbusier wore a double-breasted suit and characteristic dark bow tie. The two men traipsed all around, marveling at the views and details. Nehru was delighted, tamping down skepticism among the reporters, who found the architecture strange and indecipherable. The architect could conduct himself with the utmost confidence; he had delivered. The capitol complex, above all, was an architectural wonder.

The secretariat building, hosting eight stories of administrative offices, conference rooms, and dining halls, stretched for nearly three hundred yards — the UN slab on its side. The facade — similar to Unité d'Habitation, coated with dozens of square brise-soleil — was topped by a roof that served as an observation deck and geranium garden. The legislative assembly building was the jewel in the crown, with a sweeping concrete parasol in front, evoking the curve of the horn of a bull. At the center of that rooftop, a parabolic chimney with a slanted top towered over the main legislative chambers, inspired by industrial cooling towers and the farmhouse chimneys he remembered from La Chaux-de-Fonds.[14] A reflecting pool in front provided a watery mirror for the monumental forms, which in turn seemed to mimic the grandeur of the mountains in the distance.

With the high court building, far across a massive plaza and lawn that Le Corbusier hoped would be filled with people for festivals and civic gatherings, the architect managed to impress himself. The facilities, containing eight courtrooms and offices, were framed by an overhanging cover, a long concrete umbrella, with three sculpted columns at the entrance painted green, yellow, and saffron: the colors of the Indian flag. The facade under the overhang bowed out as if the building were tilting in a hallucinatory haze. The high court, the first of the monumental capitol buildings to open, with an approving Nehru in attendance, was "quite simply extraordinary," Le Corbusier wrote to his mother. "It's an architectural symphony that surpasses all my hopes, gleaming and taking shape in the light in an unwearyingly unimaginable way. Seen close up or from afar it's a surprise, it knocks you out. It's been made of raw concrete, with a cement gun."[15]

The government buildings were the first to be occupied, and government workers populated the first blocks of housing. As the city was planned, so was its inhabitation. Le Corbusier provided a user's guide – essentially a set of rules – to guide life in the City Beautiful, as it became known. The purpose of the "Edict of Chandigarh" was to "enlighten the present and future citizens of Chandigarh about the basic concepts of planning of the city, so that they become its guardians and save it from the whims of individuals." The city "is planned to human scale. It puts us in touch with the infinite cosmos and nature. It provides us with places and buildings for all human activities by which the citizens can live a full and harmonious life. Here the radiance of nature and heart are within our reach." In addition to an exhaustive classification of the arterials and cross streets, and a list of acceptably "truthful" building materials (concrete, brick, stone), there was this ordinance: "Vehicular traffic is completely forbidden in the green strips, where tranquility shall reign and the curse of noise shall not penetrate." And: "No personal statues shall be erected in the city or parks of Chandigarh. The city is planned to breathe the new sublimated spirit of art. Commemoration of persons shall be confined to suitably placed bronze plaques."[16]

If the architect thought he could control the citizenry, the final phases of construction were a bad omen. Le Corbusier grew increasingly cranky in difficult dealings with the Indian project team, writing letter after letter expressing outrage at various blunders and wrongheaded proposals to modify his plan. In truth, there were no major violations of his artistic intent – the issues included appointments to committees, the placement of a berm or other landscaping, and delays in the provision of his fees. But the squabbles reflected the extent of Le Corbusier's emotional investment in the city he had created. He appealed to Nehru with urgent telegrams, claiming his vision was being terribly mutilated, until the prime minister essentially stopped talking to him.

There were some things – many things – that would not be controlled. The plaza would become barren and overgrown, and the judges would park their cars in the drained reflecting pool, which was impossible to keep full year-round because of water shortages. The citadel of grand monuments would be ringed with machine gun nests to protect its residents from hostile neighbors in Pakistan. Chandigarh, like other cities throughout India, would have beggars and slums, and the streets, which seemed so wide and ample in the early years that some observers wondered if they would ever fill up with cars, would be choked with traffic.

"Modern life demands, and is waiting for, a new kind of plan, both for the house and the city," he had written nearly forty years earlier, in *Vers une architecture*.[17] Yet it was as if no amount of planning could accommodate the realities of a burgeoning population or the whims of the individual the edict warned against. There was, as well, plenty of bad planning. The long blocks and great distances between homes and stores and workplaces virtually prohibited walking in the hot summer months. Similarly, every government office in the secretariat building would be jury-rigged with fans to make the workday tolerable.

But then as now, Chandigarh's distinction was that in a country of chaos, there was the foundation of order. In a nation emerging from the grip of colonial rule, democracy was honored with an acropolis of modern architecture. When the architect left India for the last time in 1956, he boarded the plane knowing he had given that gift.

9 ▪ THE UNIVERSITY

It was up to Harvard to bring Le Corbusier back to America.

Yet having the architect design a modernist building for the campus was the unlikeliest of propositions in the 1950s. Tradition engulfed the brick, stone, and clapboard campus, established in 1636, and change was carefully deliberated. The university's motto, *veritas,* Latin for "truth," signaled the gravity of the mission. There should be no sudden moves.

Well into the mid-twentieth century, an army of maids was deployed each morning to make up the all-male dormitory rooms; the Faculty Club was for gentlemen of Harvard only. There was a strict dress code for coming to dinner in the dining halls, where long, wooden tables were illuminated by chandeliers. A professor would not think of proceeding to the lectern in anything but a suit and necktie. Unmatched in business, economics, the humanities, and law, Harvard churned out MBAs and white-shoe law firm partners, presidents and CEOs and Nobel Prize winners.

The president, Nathan Pusey, was a classically trained historian and a kind though austere man, who seemed likely to embrace the status quo when he took office in 1953. Born and raised in Iowa, he was the first non–New Englander to lead Harvard, not that anyone could tell the difference from his Yankee predecessors, so sober his demeanor.

But change was coming, if in small increments. The trustees wanted him to focus on the liberal arts and undergraduate education, following the penchant of his predecessor, James Bryant Conant, for graduate programs. Pusey nearly tripled faculty and staff, raised salaries, ultimately oversaw the construction of thirty new buildings, and poured resources into the lesser-known education and divinity schools. He also opened doors to women, launching the first experiment in co-ed dormitory living. "Civilization is dead," one alumnus promptly announced.[1]

At the same time, he was convinced Harvard should be doing much more in the arts. There was a proud tradition, to be sure. Charles Eliot Norton was the first professor of art history named by any university in the country. Charles Herbert Moore, the landscape painter, famously taught Fine Arts 1 – painting, sculpture, watercolor, and drawing. The university's centerpiece art museum, the Fogg, opened in 1895, housed a prodigious collection of paintings, sculptures, photographs, and other media, from the Middle Ages to the current day. Picasso's *Guernica* was displayed for a time there.

But there was virtually no focused effort to have students make art. In the array of famously decentralized programs – Harvard's approach was to let schools rise up and sink or swim on their own, with "every tub on its own bottom"– there was never a fine arts school and never a thought of one. Art and design were conceded to places like the Rhode Island School of Design and Parsons. Pusey sought to explore the possibilities and formed a task force to make a comprehensive assessment of the arts at Harvard. In 1956 that panel produced *Report of the Committee on the Visual Arts at Harvard University*, a tidy volume with crimson binding, recommending a multimillion-dollar expansion; a new department of design with a curriculum blending art history, theory, and practice; and forward-looking programs for the future. "Perhaps at no moment in history since the invention of printing," the panel wrote, "has man's communication with his fellow man been so largely taken over by visual media as today."[2]

The new program needed a home, with plenty of well-lit studio space, a theater, and facilities for exhibitions. A new design center that served the entire university, it was decided, would be best located near the Fogg Museum and Robinson Hall, then housing the school of architecture, to create an "arts quarter" on campus. The task force penciled in a placeholder site between the Fogg and the Faculty Club, where an old wooden structure, the Farlow House, stood. Harvard's legions of wealthy alumni stepped up eagerly with support. Alfred St. Vrain Carpenter, a 1905 graduate and the owner of a successful pear-farming business called Topsides in Oregon, pledged $1.75 million. The new building would bear the family name.

Then there was the biggest question of all: What kind of building should it be, and who should design it? And for that, Le Corbusier was fortunate to have an old friend in high places.

When Josep Lluís Sert was a young man living in Barcelona, he picked up several of Le Corbusier's books in Paris while visiting his aunt. He became so enamored that he formed a fan club and invited the master to visit Spain in 1929. It was a glorious trip, as they toured the twirling and swirling works of Antoni Gaudí. Eventually, Sert worked at 35 rue de Sèvres and collaborated with Le Corbusier on several projects throughout his career. He was a member and, for a time, chairman of CIAM; he worked on the urban design scheme for Bogotá and he helped bring Picasso to Unité d'Habitation in Marseille. Settling in Cambridge, Massachusetts, and bringing his architectural practice there, he had become dean of Harvard's architecture school, just at the moment the university was deciding what the new arts center should look like. Sert informed Pusey and McGeorge Bundy, dean of the Faculty of Arts and Sciences, who was brought in to oversee the project, that he had an interesting candidate in mind.

In June 1958, he made his pitch. Le Corbusier was the most famous architect in Europe, perhaps in all the world. Yet he had no buildings in North America. How strange, he told them. It was like not having any Picassos in our museums.[3]

Pusey and Bundy were intrigued. The more they thought about it, the more the moment seemed right to do something daring. Down the street at MIT, Alvar Aalto's Baker House, an undulating dormitory overlooking the Charles River, had opened. Eero Saarinen, creator of the TWA Flight Center at JFK and the St. Louis Gateway Arch, built a striking chapel and auditorium, especially among the stately domes and neoclassical columns elsewhere on campus, further broadcasting MIT's commitment to modern architecture. Even more concerning, archrival Yale was attracting attention by mixing in modernism with the Gothic in New Haven. An art gallery by Le Corbusier's contemporary Louis Kahn became an instant classic as an icon of the International Style; Saarinen was signed on for two buildings; and Paul Rudolph, who was experimenting with complex forms and the use of concrete in a style ultimately known as brutalism, had just designed the school's art and architecture building.

Go ahead and see if Le Corbusier might be interested, Bundy told Sert, so Harvard could get in the game.

Sert felt a moment of dread, anticipating the drama, the fussy directives, and the ultimatums. His colleagues at Harvard didn't know what they were in for. But he followed through and got in touch with his old friend and mentor.

As Sert well knew, the master might well respond with an initial refusal. In 1953, he was a busy man and, finally, much sought after following the triumphs of Unité d'Habitation, Notre Dame du Haut in Ronchamp, Sainte-Marie de La Tourette in Éveux-sur-l'Arbresle, and Chandigarh. Most important, while he trusted his old apprentice, this was America calling – the country that had mocked him in 1935 and marginalized him ten years later in the UN project. Why should he return for more punishment? It was a small measure of comfort that the client was the world's greatest university, but still.

The official invitation, on Harvard University letterhead, was deferential and to the point. The university sought nothing less than an international meeting place to better integrate the arts and society, an ambitious synthesis to take place all in one special building. It should interest "the architect, the painter, and the sculptor in you to an equal degree."[4]

The budget was a maximum of $1.2 million for fifty-seven thousand square feet, with restrictions on height so as not to stir up opposition in the adjacent residential neighborhood or overwhelm the stately Faculty Club. The benefactors, the Carpenters, who were consulted continually and approved of the idea of Le Corbusier being the architect, wanted only "considerable area of trees, shrubs, and flowers" – pastoral cues that would soothe and inspire the young generations of artists. The studio space should be flexible, well lit, and well ventilated. The exhibition area should feel open.[5] But there was in fact very little in terms of specifications, making it just the kind of project Le Corbusier would be willing to take on. Open-ended and free rein was how he liked to do business.

Meeting with Sert over coffee in Paris to discuss the project, though, he had questions. Harvard was asking for many functions to be incorporated into a major work of modern architecture dropped down on little more than an acre, wedged between neoclassical buildings. It seemed to be a squandered opportunity to do something greater. "Such a small commission from such a large country," he said.[6]

Like a diplomat in cease-fire negotiations, Sert kept Le Corbusier talking. The Carpenter Center, he said, would have outsized importance at Harvard. After the gimcracks of Yale and MIT, it could be the American version of Ronchamp and every bit as exciting. As he had throughout his life, though, Le Corbusier focused on money. "What the hell do you think I care about becoming saviour or redeemer," he retorted; "it is necessary that those who employ me *pay*."[7]

There was, however, some indication that the Carpenter Center for the Visual Arts, as the building would be known, would indeed become a pivotal part of the future of the university. Little-known plans to expand the Harvard campus eastward, into the residential neighborhood just behind the building site, held the potential for a dose of urban renewal in Cambridge. The Carpenter Center would be the gateway, the spot marking the transition from the old to the new.

The commission was inherently compelling for other reasons. The center would be a place both of intellectual rigor and where young people actually made things. "A meeting place of head and hand," Le Corbusier would come to call it.[8] His favorite occupations – painting, drawing, and design – would flourish there, alongside sculpture and photography and film, and who knew what other pursuits and subversive thinking might lie ahead. It was to be a place where students and teachers mixed things up, where new ideas were born; perhaps even a school where a teacher like Charles L'Eplattenier would cultivate the next Le Corbusier.

Just before leaving for Roquebrune-Cap-Martin for the month of August in 1959, Le Corbusier added "Boston/VAC"– standing for visual arts center – to the list of projects at 35 rue de Sèvres

and assigned one of his best draftsmen, the Chilean Guillermo
Jullian de la Fuente. He also tapped Sigfried Giedion, one of the
original founders of CIAM and a teacher at Harvard and MIT, to
help manage the commission. Captain Giedion, as Le Corbusier
referred to him, would patiently work through the complicated
transatlantic relationship that the master whimsically called the
"American problem." One final bit of business was to demand an
increase in fees, to $50,000. He provided his bank account num-
ber for the money to be wired and waited for the Harvard officials to get back to him on their hands and knees, thankful that
the great master would conjure something in their midst, and
they better act fast before he changed his mind. "You have real
friends at Harvard . . . ," Sert assured him, "even if you royally
don't care a damn about them [or] this continent, etc.!"[9]

Passing through the arched portals into Harvard Yard, Le Corbusier and Sert let the din of Massachusetts Avenue fall away.
Before them were the crisscrossing walkways through the quadrangle, lined by scarlet oaks and American elms, and lorded over
by the statue of John Harvard, his outstretched foot polished
from being touched by thousands of students for good luck.
They passed the broad steps of Widener Library, the red brick
and bone-white spire of Memorial Church, and the stately Loeb
House, for many years the residence of Harvard presidents, until
they came to another redbrick wall and black-iron gates leading
out to Quincy Street. There the delegation of deans and trustees
waited, huddling in the November cold, men in dark suits and
narrow ties, every last one of them. Nathan Pusey reached out to
shake hands; there were polite introductions all around.[10] But Le
Corbusier was already drinking in the site.

To his left was the Fogg Museum, a hulking Beaux-Arts building occupying one end of the street, designed by a firm that included the great-grandson of the American master Charles

Bulfinch. To his right was the neo-Georgian Faculty Club, all red brick and white columns and eight-pane windows, built on the site of the former home of the literary giant Henry James. Across Quincy Street was Sever Hall, designed by H. H. Richardson, one of America's most revered architects of the nineteenth century, and Robinson Hall, built by McKim, Mead & White, City Beautiful specialists who had designed the Boston Public Library. Directly in front was the all-wood nineteenth-century Victorian Farlow House, an administrative building destined for demolition, with some of its occupants gamely gathered outside as well.

The visitor from Paris surveyed the site. He sized up Pusey. Then he shrugged his shoulders as if to say, *If this is where you want me to build, we'll build it.*[11] The architect opened a black notebook and began writing.

Given the tight space, the building would have to be tilted on a diagonal. That would give him a little more room for the two ballooning volumes he envisioned, gently curving like a nautilus shell. In between these two lungs, representing healthy circulation, he pictured a ramp gently ascending from Quincy Street, plunging through the upper floors, and descending back down to Prescott Street—and on to the new frontier, the expanded campus he had been promised. The pause at the top of the ramp would be like being in a tunnel in an aquarium, looking left and right into grottos and caves of artistic creation.

He had long favored the ramp as both a functional and a symbolic device, from the Villa Savoye to Moscow to Ahmedabad. In Cambridge, it would twist and turn like a sine curve, reflecting the twenty-four-hour cycle through dusk and dawn. The *route ascensionnelle* would also honor the walkways of the campus, which had fascinated him. Harvard Yard reminded him of a miniature version of his Ville Radieuse, the students moving through the open spaces and between the uniform buildings like vehicles on his highways. At a later meeting on campus, the university project team noticed that Le Corbusier was distracted, continually looking out the window. He told them he had witnessed something beautiful: the quadrangle empty one moment, brimming with life the next, as classes ended and the students had to get to their next one, moving seemingly in every direction, following their desired lines. The ramp at the Carpenter Center would take them to a new dimension, up off the flat ground. All those young minds would be lifted to ever-greater heights.

The building material would be a sand-colored concrete, in sharp contrast with the red brick and granite all around. There was never a question that Le Corbusier would use anything else – though he didn't think America was ready for the rough-hewn *béton brut* he had been employing. He promised the surfaces – some squared off and linear, other parts curving, reflecting the sun, collecting shadows – would be as smooth as a baby's bottom. He pictured bands of narrow vertical windows running from floor to ceiling, in staccato succession, like the frames of a film running through a projector, and a series of angled concrete fins, just as he had recently used in the Mill Owners' Association Building at Ahmedabad. The whole structure would be raised up on concrete stanchions, the reliable pilotis, which would rise up through the building and make the studio space feel like a peaceful clearing amid trees. From an elevated garden terrace, students and faculty could survey the traditional campus across Quincy Street, gazing out from the modernist promontory.

He was fully prepared not to like the experience. But being in Cambridge, its intelligentsia clustered in one zip code, a grouping reminiscent of Saint-Germain, was a pleasure. He held court at parties at Sert's home, sparkling in dark suit and a bow tie of blue and red flowers, and visitors hung on his every word. Giedion and another woman who had been part of CIAM attended as well. At one such event, everyone was drinking Pernod on the patio when a woman was briefly wedged in a pivoting door, and Le Corbusier called for a measuring tape to assess the conditions of the Modular – and soon the guests were measuring everything, from their feet to their rear ends.[12]

The students at Harvard loved him, too, just as the young people had thronged around him during his 1935 tour. The architecture school students threw a party for him in Robinson Hall and drew a picture of the Modular Man on a mural, along with a giant pair of round black eyeglasses, in his honor. He addressed the crowd from an interior balcony, in French and broken English – announcing, "One must have courage!" and "What spirit! *Une atmosphere morale!*"[13] Buoyant and giddy, soaking up the adulation, he flirted with the women and arm-punched the men. On his way out, noticing a student with pointy facial growth that reminded him of his painter friend, he tugged at the student's beard and said, "Farewell, Léger," before making an exit with a flourish.[14]

All his senses were as alive as ever. On the flights between Paris and Boston he gazed out the window and sketched the rugged Atlantic coastline; on the ground in Cambridge he was mesmerized by a white vapor trail stretching across the blue sky.

When it came time to view the final model, Pusey and the Harvard men gathered in Massachusetts Hall. The model, Sert thought, was quite rudimentary and would be eclipsed in workmanship by any number of students' work at the time. The dapper Spaniard translated Le Corbusier's comments and politely smiled as they began to understand that the crazy creation would soon be in their midst.

The ramp was a red flag for Pusey, purely as a practical matter. Would it not, he asked, become treacherous in the New England winters? Le Corbusier assured him he would cast in grooves to drain the moisture away. The Harvard president was also puzzled that there weren't more important activities planned for the ground-floor lobby; Le Corbusier had put the main exhibit space and the café up on the third floor, wanting the bustle to be aloft. The exchange was relatively tame. What Pusey didn't mention was how his colleagues had asked why the building couldn't be clad in red brick like most of the others on campus.

The plans received a warm reception among the faculty and the members of the arts task force, who had the sense that something truly historic was about to happen. "The 'old man' . . . has performed even better than we had all expected, and all of us here in Cambridge are in a state of euphoria," said one. "I don't know what we expected – some spidery drawings, some intricate diagrams – but we were quite unprepared for the breathtaking beauty of the . . . project," remarked John Coolidge, architectural historian in the fine arts department.[15]

In the five years of the project, from conception to completion, Le Corbusier made exactly two trips to Cambridge, lasting just a few days on each occasion. After going through the final details of budget and timetable, he left the actual construction to Sert and the Harvard project managers. It was just as well. Sert was the critical liaison between Cambridge and Paris, handling the brusque dispatches from across the Atlantic. "I absolutely reject cinder blocks for the building's interior: they are horrible!" the master scribbled on a set of plans modified by the Americans.[16] At another point, he objected to the suggested placement of mechanicals in too visible a spot for his tastes. This building, he wrote, is not a car. Sert channeled Le Corbusier, interpreting his instructions and making the architecture more practical.[17]

In construction, which began in 1962, extensive adjustments were necessary, from the windows to the air-conditioning ducts. William LeMessurier, who would become one of the nation's leading engineers of skyscraper design, helped the team of contractors navigate the complicated cantilevers and the structural support needed for the dirt, rocks, and plantings of the terrace garden. Metric measurements had to be converted to feet and inches; the slightest error would throw everything off. The use of concrete, just beginning to be a favored material for modern architecture around Boston, was particularly demanding for the workers. A team of builders of fishing boats from Nova Scotia was brought in to consult on how to sculpt the molds for the most challenging curves. When a cantilevered section required the support of heavy, clunky beams, they had to be artfully hidden, so that all that was seen were the pilotis flush against a smooth, flat surface. Most of the concrete could be poured into plywood forms laced with rebar, but many of the weight-bearing stanchions had to be packed manually.[18]

Le Corbusier's system of ventilation, working in concert with the innovative design of the windows, was also puzzling to the Boston-area workers, many of whom lived in simple triple-deckers. The architect wanted the studio space to be flooded with light, with strategically placed skylights and narrow floor-to-ceiling panes of glass. But he added little door-like windows for natural ventilation as well, which students could open in front of their workspaces. Air-conditioning, as Le Corbusier wrote to the project team, was "dear to Americans with their by now traditional sinus condition," a belittling statement from a man who suffered from the very same condition throughout his life. But HVAC – heating, ventilation, and air-conditioning – didn't need to be running all the time. The building was to be heated in the cold months, opened up in the spring and fall, and sealed as necessary only in the hottest times of summer, "if you sirs are not found completely naked on Cape Cod" at that time.[19]

Sert relayed Harvard's requests for fine-tuning and change orders to Paris, which Le Corbusier, spending more time painting at 24 rue Nungesser et Coli, largely ignored. As the price of the project, in classic fashion for a building by the master, soared over $2 million and kept climbing, the team on the ground was forced to sneak in cutbacks, eliminating a planned tunnel to the Fogg Museum and changing the type of exterior glass. Le Corbusier, skeptical that minor cost savings were really necessary for such a wealthy university, was as disapproving as he had been with the Indian team at Chandigarh. "Here, I become imperious and imperative," he wrote in another missive from 35 rue de Sèvres, "and demand that Boston admit that it is my drawings which determine the building."[20]

By 1963, the building was complete. All that was left was the landscaping – another point of contention, with Le Corbusier calling for wild raspberry bushes and Harvard insisting on a prim lawn and yew shrubs. And there was the final matter: whether Le Corbusier would come back for the ribbon-cutting. Harvard, where commencement was led by men in top hats and tails on the first Thursday of June, was planning an appropriate ceremony. There was an assumption that the architect would attend.

Le Corbusier thought about it but ultimately declined to come to the party in his honor, citing poor health, and other commitments, and recalling difficulties traveling to America. On a previous trip, at the consulate in Paris, he had refused to answer the question of whether he had ever been a communist.

The inauguration went on without the creator in the fall of 1963. The Carpenters were there, walking down the ramp, champagne glasses in hand. The benefactors were thrilled, seeing the building as "opening the door of future and present enjoyment to those who pass lightly through."[21]

The reviews were mixed. The final product, so striking and different from the neighboring buildings, appeared to some to thumb its nose to the rest of Quincy Street. "To proper Bostonians, this is bad manners," wrote Ada Louise Huxtable, architecture critic for the *New York Times*.[22] One professor sniffed that it looked like two grand pianos trying to make love.[23] The director of the Fogg fretted over the "white whale stranded on stilts in our midst."[24]

Yet for others, the Carpenter Center somehow fit in with its neighbors. It was just different, like a rockabilly song before a ballad on a music album. On the north side, the top of the structure exactly matched the cornice of the Fogg Museum. On the south side, the pilotis at the base of the building, sparse and subtle, segued to the sloping lawn and the traditional architecture of the Faculty Club. By day, the ramps were inviting from the street, and the windows set into the angled fins glowed mysteriously by night.

The building was eagerly occupied. Students flooded into the light-filled studios and got to work. They struck up conversations inside and out, relaxing in the café and on the terrace, just as Le Corbusier had planned. The bold statement of the architecture seemed to inspire creativity, including in the professors, whose classes were unlike most others at Harvard. The course on drawing was about seeing and perspectives; students were asked to sign their name, then sign it backward, then upside down.

There was photography and film and work in television, the study of the shape of sound. There were exhibits on radical new uses of color in design, "anonymous" art such as the baskets found at the market and bazaar, the sleek modern Thonet chair, and town planning in the Soviet Union. The center started publishing a journal called *Connection,* reminiscent of *L'Esprit Nouveau.* Everything was fair game; one student wrote a critical analysis of Le Corbusier's worker housing at Pessac. Most of all, the students worked with their hands, getting dirty with paint and plaster, with sawdust from cutting wood on the muscular machine stations set up in the studios. They learned to love the act of making.

The Carpenter Center was a beachhead in another way, as Harvard became more daring in its architecture. The first act of modern architecture had been Harkness Commons by Walter Gropius, who had apprenticed alongside Le Corbusier at Peter Behrens's studio and who became chairman of the architecture department at Harvard. But the Carpenter Center was a catalyst for further experimentation. Sert went on to design the massive and colorful Holyoke Center, now the Smith Campus Center, in the heart of Harvard Square, and the Peabody Terrace towers at Memorial Drive on the banks of the Charles River. Through the 1960s and 1970s, Quincy Street became its own architectural promenade. At the end of the street was William James Hall – the tallest building at Harvard, housing psychology, sociology, and anthropology – by Minoru Yamasaki, architect of the twin towers of the World Trade Center. Next door, the Australian architect John Andrews created Gund Hall, the iconic home for the Graduate School of Design, its top floors adorned with long ribbons of Villa Savoye–like horizontal windows and held up by tall pilotis. The school moved from the neoclassical Robinson Hall to the inverted concrete structure, where generations of architects in training would, appropriately, study and emulate Le Corbusier in the cascading trays of drafting tables.

Architects throughout Boston would also follow Le Corbusier's lead, notably at Boston City Hall, with its remarkable resemblance to the monastery at La Tourette. I. M. Pei, who had met the master at MIT some forty years earlier, took the UN building to the next level with his John Hancock Tower.

The legacy of the Carpenter Center, the only building Le Corbusier would ever build in North America, would inevitably become complex. There were some leaks and issues with humidity, and the concrete became discolored, requiring constant restoration. Some of the spaces outlived their usefulness as well. Working with their hands is still a mainstay for art students, but design ultimately moved into the realm of the digital, and computer screens didn't require illumination from skylights. Filmmaking, one of the most successful programs at the Carpenter Center, occurs in the dark, in its creation and viewing; the architecture doesn't matter at all.[25] The café, with its beautiful views of Harvard Yard, would close, unable to be sustained.

Through the tumult of the 1960s, plans of all kinds went awry. Pusey became embroiled in the campus protests and the student occupation of Massachusetts Hall. He resigned shortly afterward. The promise of innovation and creativity in the bolstered arts program he envisioned would morph into angry revolt.

The eastward expansion that Le Corbusier was promised never materialized; in the years to come, Harvard would focus its expansion in another direction, across the river, into the Allston area of Boston. There and all around the Harvard campus, the appetite, if not tolerance, of contemporary design lessened. The president at the beginning of the twenty-first century, Larry Summers, all but prohibited anything but traditional architecture, calling out the Carpenter Center as being especially ugly.

Yet over the years, the gift to America would endure. While in the pantheon of Le Corbusier's works it may be considered as the B side of a hit single, the Carpenter Center, as the only building by the architect on US soil, remains a treasure of architectural history, if not the visitor destination that is Frank Lloyd Wright's Fallingwater. The building spawned fierce protectors, although they were sometimes viewed as a particular brand of elitist, like those who would pay top dollar for a painting by Warhol.

Decades after it was completed, the defenders rushed forward when it was threatened. Harvard had decided yet again to bolster the arts, this time with a new museum, proposed for Memorial Drive near Sert's iconic Peabody Terrace. That plan was thwarted by neighbors, so the university sought to expand and renovate the Fogg Museum instead. The city of Cambridge required that the architect for this new scheme, Renzo Piano, maintain the museum's Georgian revivalist facade. The rest of the building, however, was to be completely gutted. And that required major operations in the rear of the Fogg – exactly where Le Corbusier's ramp came down, emptying out to Prescott Street.

The best engineering solution was to lop off the ramp about three-quarters of the way along its descent, encase it and ship it to be put in storage, and reattach it when the retrofit was complete. But the project advisory committee, populated by Le Corbusier aficionados, wouldn't allow the Carpenter Center to be violated. Instead the ramp was encased and the construction work on the Fogg went on around it, adding significant costs. Piano, designer of a visitor center tucked into the hillside at Ronchamp, might have anticipated that messing with the Carpenter Center wasn't tenable. A building completed in 1963 was afforded all the respect as one from forty or eighty years earlier. It was historic preservation flipped on its head.

The Renzo Piano project for the Harvard Art Museums would complete the extraordinarily diverse parade of architecture all along Quincy Street: William James Hall; Memorial Hall; Gund Hall; the renovated Fogg Museum; H. H. Richardson's Sever Hall; the Carpenter Center; and the Faculty Club. In a quarter of a mile, there would be contemporary and traditional and a combination of the two.

The man who started it all would know none of it – not the creativity the building inspired, nor the way it promoted other modern architecture on the Harvard campus and throughout Boston, nor the respect and recognition it would garner, right up

to the university's fiftieth anniversary celebration of the Carpenter Center. Yet it is safe to say he would not have been surprised.

"Creation is a patient search," he was fond of saying, so much
so that he made the phrase the title of a book.[26]

He had made his contribution. Skipping the ribbon-cutting
was the ultimate act of rising above, like not showing up for winning an Oscar. In declining the invitation, there was also the
whiff of revenge. For all his good feelings about Harvard, it was
one last snub of the country that had snubbed him.

But none of it mattered. The only long trip he was making in
those days was between Paris and Roquebrune-Cap-Martin. He
was spending more time alone in the *cabanon,* in his makeshift
studio, and at L'Étoile de Mer, sitting outside, looking out past
the rocks to the sea.

10 ▪ THE DEPARTURE

Yvonne was first to go, in 1957. What was remarkable was that she endured as long as she did. She was frail and gaunt at the end of her life, her eyes hollow, though still appointed with mascara. When she met socially with Le Corbusier and a group of friends, she would offer cigarettes around to each and every one of the group, seemingly every few minutes, even if the guests made it clear they didn't smoke.[1] It was as if she thought that of course they needed the tobacco in their lungs as much as she did, as surely as everyone lovingly gripped the cocktail glasses in their hands.

The onetime model had started using a cane after the beginning of her decline in the Vichy years. Virtually everything that ailed her, the arthritis and bone degradation and gastritis, was aggravated by what was clearly an addiction to pastis. Le Corbusier never confronted her alcoholism head-on. Instead he tried to coax her to eat better and take short walks of two hundred paces, but it was a pointless charade. She repeatedly injured herself, falling down drunk. She was malnourished and dangerously thin; in the end she lost all feeling in her legs. In the final years of her life, she preferred to keep the apartment dark, ashamed at her appearance – the antithesis of the light and air her husband craved for himself and mankind.

The marriage had many hallmarks of dysfunction. He could be rough with her. "You have no right to come here!" he once barked, when she entered a room at 24 rue Nungesser et Coli during his conversation with a professional colleague.[2] But she returned the favor and then some, letting loose with obscenities directed against him, often in the presence of others. He would go numb and resigned in the face of such fusillades, like a man who suddenly turns with great interest to washing the dishes in the middle of a full-scale domestic meltdown.

What he preferred was to remember how things started out so marvelously. Yvonne had a love for life in the early days in Paris, and on the trips to Le Piquey, taking the Voisin out for picnics under lone trees in the countryside. A fashion model from Monaco – it was hard to beat that. She put on her lipstick so it was in the shape of a heart! And he could actually talk to her, a big change from his years as a young man, so tied in knots as he was over women. Dating Yvonne was a big step up from his assignations with prostitutes – though there was a rumor he had actually met her in a bordello, a legend that the Gypsy from Monaco made no effort to deny.[3]

But once he had her, the bird in hand, he looked elsewhere. His philandering was far and away the biggest unspoken theme of the relationship. His cheating ranged from one-night stands to enduring relationships, especially with Marguerite Tjader Harris. The double life was part and parcel of the European tradition of keeping mistresses, but nonetheless required great energy and effort – scheduling the dates and times of assignations, and keeping all correspondence secret. Yet he also convinced himself that Harris might possibly coexist with Yvonne, literally right next door. He and his American lover discussed her financing the initial scheme to build holiday cabins on Thomas Rebutato's land in Roquebrune-Cap-Martin and inhabit one herself. The deal was abruptly called off, without explanation. It takes a village, but wife and mistress on the same shore was clearly too outrageous, even for him.

There is no evidence Yvonne ever knew outright about any or all of his extramarital relationships, though it is hard to believe she had no inkling. His long absences couldn't have helped but eat away at her, as much as she busied herself with tidying the apartment. Self-medicating might have been a matter of survival, facing so many nights alone. The real question, he might have thought, was why she would stick with him for three long decades. She made no secret that he drove her crazy – their home awash in bright light and bare white walls, the prohibition on adorning anything with so much as a tea cozy, the spartan arrangements at the *cabanon*. They had virtually no common interests, and early on, she made it clear she didn't want to talk about work when they were at home. There were never any children of their own to focus on; she seemed to be interested in having a family, but he would have nothing of it, preferring "adopted" sons like Harris's boy, Hilary, or Robert Rebutato – sons for whom, ultimately, he did not have to be responsible. What was there to stay for? Ultimately, the fact of the companionship itself, comfortable and comforting, was life sustaining. Right through to the end, when her broken body relented, in a Paris clinic at four in the morning, at sixty-five years old. She died holding his hand.[4]

The closeness Le Corbusier felt became evident, in ghoulish fashion, during the funeral arrangements. First Le Corbusier had the body brought home from the clinic in Paris where she died, and put her on display at 24 rue Nungesser et Coli. "Look how lovely she is," he told surprised visitors who came to call, including Charlotte Perriand.[5] Others were equally horrified when he slipped behind the curtain at the crematorium ceremony in Paris and retrieved from her ashes a bone – an intact cervical vertebra that had survived the inferno. It was tucked in a rolled-up newspaper and ultimately shown all around, kept in his pocket, and placed on his work desk.[6] With Yvonne, though with little else, he was unapologetically sentimental. A part of her would be with him always.

The final resting place was high above the *cabanon* at Roquebrune-Cap-Martin's cemetery, overlooking Coco Chanel's villa, reached by the trademark perilous switchbacks of the area. A stonemason friend milled the concrete tomb, which was placed about halfway up the steeply sloping graveyard, where the Rebutatos and a few others from the area who knew and loved Yvonne stood in silence. Yvonne was at peace. Le Corbusier was seventy years old. As the solemn small group attending the funeral surely noticed, there was a space on the front of Yvonne's memorial tomb. The aging architect had reserved it for himself.[7]

Back down at the *cabanon,* he was composed and matter-of-fact, writing Marie and Albert, noting various business matters, and urging his brother to come see the "Electronic Poem" at the Philips Pavilion, an avant-garde exhibition in a sweeping, tentlike structure he had designed for the upcoming Expo '58 in Brussels.

Having his wife die before his mother was unusual for any man, though it seemed like Marie would go on living forever. She had become stocky in her dotage, her skin leathery and splotchy, her hair pure, brazen white. With her ever-present eyeglasses and half-pouting, half-surprised expression, the resemblance to her younger son was striking, while Albert looked more like her late husband, Georges, who had died more than thirty years before. In September 1959, the brothers threw Marie a hundredth birthday party in Vevey. The event, at the Villa Le Lac, was covered by a major Swiss newspaper. In fact, she was ninety-nine, but Le Corbusier, anxious to celebrate the centennial sooner, had fudged the birth date by a year. They sang and laughed, and Marie took a turn at her beloved piano.[8] He had traveled all night from India to be there.

The following winter, in 1960, she died. Marie had spent a full century of life first in La Chaux-de-Fonds and then on the shores of Lake Geneva, while the ritzy Swiss Riviera built up all around her. As she did the dishes she looked out over Lake Geneva, through the horizontal band of windows her son had designed for her. She had been the stoic matriarch, the source of the family's income in lean times, thanks to her highly sought-after piano lessons. A century of stoicism – and tormenting her son with perceived indifference, in ways neither of them fully reconciled. It was Albert, of course, who stayed at home all the years Le Corbusier was building his career around the world, who was at her side when she finally succumbed. Le Corbusier traveled to Switzerland immediately, and watched the black car take the coffin away from Villa Le Lac in a steady and silent snow.

The relationship between mother and son was peculiar to the end. He boasted to her not only about professional accomplishments but also his sexual conquests. The details of his time with Josephine Baker are known because he wrote it all in letters to his mother. He drew himself nude for her. In a letter to his brother after the funeral, he recounted a dream he had of her, waiting on a train platform, all in pink.[9] He sketched a picture: Marie, shining like the sun, a sexy goddess he had honored at Ronchamp.

When his father died, years earlier, Le Corbusier had been badly shaken. Turning to drawing as always in times of joy and pain, he sketched Georges on his deathbed. The grief enveloped him like a fog, a cold he couldn't shake. It was an uncomfortable feeling for a man dedicated to controlling things, to be at the mercy of an emotional force that refused to be managed. When his mother died, he could not help but see she had lived a long and full life. He had grown more reconciled to death. Including facing his own.

And so he was alone. In Paris, he continued to paint in the mornings in his studio at 24 rue Nungesser et Coli, wearing the same untucked black-and-white-checked shirt, turning out canvas after canvas, the right arm propped up with the left. He was happiest doing what he thought might bring him the same fame as Picasso and Léger, though it never did. Most afternoons he made the dutiful journey to the atelier at 35 rue de Sèvres. His architecture was what was still so much in demand, perhaps even more so than ever.

Each new section of Chandigarh that opened up brought accolades. The Japanese were equally thrilled with his National Museum of Western Art in Tokyo, set in a campus that recalled a downsized version of the UN compound. The museum building was a big box with few windows but with an interior exquisitely designed for the display of art.[10] The Tokyo commission was a satisfying coda, based in part on the concepts he had for the "infinite museum" that he had proposed decades earlier for the banlieues of Paris.[11]

In France, the town of Firminy was also in a thrall. There he had designed not only the dramatic church that was the encore for Ronchamp and La Tourette, but the last of the Unité d'Habitation apartment buildings and an elementary school with an angled, diving facade that evoked the prow of a ship. Throughout the latter half of his career, he kept coming up with new forms. Ronchamp broke the mold, followed by the curves and billows of Chandigarh and the Philips Pavilion, and then the vaulting tiled arches of the Maisons Jaoul, a pair of private residences in Neuilly-sur-Seine.

The master's ability to come up with new ideas was especially admired in Italy, eager to claw back in the long reconstruction following World War II. After his long-ago entreaties to Mussolini, he picked up where he had left off. The Olivetti company, making the pivot from typewriters to the new frontier of calculators and computers, needed a new headquarters. Le Corbusier created an elongated version of the rectangular slab of Unité d'Habitation, accompanied by a parabola tower, amoeba-like sculptural features, and ramps around the base, all of it raised up on pilotis. The site of the futuristic complex, meant to inspire research and innovation, was in the town of Rho, outside Milan.[12]

Venice recruited him to build a giant hospital complex for the severely ill in the San Giobbe neighborhood, presenting a unique challenge to build by and over water. His solution was a thatched patchwork of steel and concrete, horizontal and sprawling, a set of dominos at right angles around square courtyards, an inner logic. While his trusted assistant Guillermo Jullian de la Fuente took the lead on the project, Le Corbusier was feted during a site visit by the Italian government and business leaders, in suits and sunglasses, crowding around him, eager to get a picture taken with the celebrity architect.[13]

The invitations for commissions came in from everywhere. Rivals on the world stage could bitterly disagree about a range of issues, but they had one thing in common: a fondness for Le Corbusier. Fidel Castro wanted him to design a building in Cuba. He proposed a stadium and sports complex for Baghdad. At the same time, President John F. Kennedy hoped to inaugurate a massive redevelopment in New York City.

That project, thirty-five acres of undeveloped land on the West Side of Manhattan between Fifty-Seventh and Seventy-

Second Streets, was the kind of grand planning he was hoping for when he first visited America. It was a vast stretch along the Hudson River that required no demolition, on a strip at the edge of Manhattan's urbanization, almost exactly opposite the United Nations on the other side of the island. The prized real estate was controlled by the Amalgamated Lithographers of America Union, which sought a giant mixed-use complex with residences, stores, offices, a library, parks, and playing fields. Hilary Harris, Marguerite's son, who rode in the rumble seat when the architect and his mother zoomed around the parkways of Fairfield County and New York City, offered to appeal to Le Corbusier to design it. Hilary had interned at 35 rue de Sèvres and become a filmmaker, and hoped to capture the incredible act of city building as a documentary. President Kennedy, whose enthusiasm for modernism was tempered only by the more traditional architectural urgings of his wife, wanted to christen the project personally. He would have gladly stood by Le Corbusier's side. But the aging architect said no. He was getting too old to deal with another complicated commission in America.[14]

It didn't really matter how many new commissions he got anyway. He had long since started on a victory lap. Charles de Gaulle awarded him the Legion of Honor in a ceremony where he was described, flatly, as the "world's greatest architect." He sat for Yousuf Karsh, joining the pantheon of twentieth-century icons the Armenian photographer captured, from Churchill and Hemingway to Helen Keller and Elizabeth Taylor. (The only other architect Karsh had photographed was Frank Lloyd Wright.) The sitting for the portrait was in 24 rue Nungesser et Coli. Le Corbusier chatted briefly about various features in the flat, like the spiral staircase, proudly noting it cost him only $200. But then he clammed up. He posed for the portrait in his double-breasted three-piece tweed suit, with bow tie and white pocket square, propping his glasses up on his forehead. Karsh had photographed presidents and prime ministers and movie stars and popes, being sure to break the ice and get comfortable with them before he started shooting. But it was as if Le Corbusier had been challenged from so many different directions over the years that he didn't want to say anything further that could be misconstrued.[15]

The only place that seemed not to welcome him fully, late in life, was Paris. He enthusiastically entered the competition to build on the site of the Gare d'Orsay on the banks of the Seine, a grand terminal for suburban trains that had fallen into disuse and disrepair. Towering glass facades were splintered and broken, and the trash-strewn main concourse was being used for parking cars; the signature frieze of the god Mercury's face seemed forlorn, looking down on the Legion of Honor Museum next door. Responding to a call for proposals to redevelop the site, Le Corbusier submitted a rendering for a 330-foot slab that recalled the UN building and his massive, unbuilt tower for Algiers. Together with low-slung structures at the base, the complex would hold a conference center, hotel, exhibition space, and multiple meeting rooms.[16]

The competition was equally audacious – one rival proposed a swirling vertical torch, shaped like a giant cone – and the chosen design, by René Coulon and Guillaume Gillet, was a horizontal version of Le Corbusier's tower, stretching for several blocks. The redevelopment would overlook the Louvre and the Jardin des Tuileries, wincing on the other side of the river. Ultimately, the city reconsidered the entire idea, instead refurbishing the Gare d'Orsay as a stunning museum, where visitors wait in hour-long lines to view the works of Cézanne and Monet. The Musée d'Orsay stands as one of the most beloved and popular destinations in Paris – salvaged and reinvented, saved from the wrecking ball. At the time, however, Le Corbusier viewed the rejection of his proposal as more evidence that, ever since the Plan Voisin, his name evoked fear in the city he called home.

It was time to slow down anyway, and there was no better place to do that than in Roquebrune-Cap-Martin. His movements there had become a fixture of the little town. The young girls giggled at seeing him clamber about, making his way along the beachfront, plodding, in his circular black glasses, looking not so much like the mystical black raven as a sharp-featured, wise, old owl.[17]

"Don't take the trouble with an ugly old man like me," he told a photographer who was biding his time before another appointment. "It would be better for you to take pictures of Princess Grace, just behind that rock, or Brigitte Bardot at Saint Tropez."[18]

Around the *cabanon*, if he thought of himself as Don Quixote, he was equal parts Robinson Crusoe. With Yvonne gone, the place was being inhabited in the way it was best intended: by one man, Thoreau-like, living alone. Some days the Rebutatos would deliver meals to him on a table, out in front of his little house. He would sit there, on a bench, bare-chested, wearing a white cap, looking out over the sea.

There was time to think back on his career. His plans had so often been greeted with an almost violent reaction. He had been called a madman, a tool of Lenin and a lackey for real estate developers – branded both a communist and a capitalist, sometimes in the same year. The world of architecture was astonishingly cutthroat. For every Villa Savoye and Ronchamp, there was the League of Nations, Palace of the Soviets, Rio, Bogotá, and Algiers. Of the three hundred projects he designed, seventy-eight of them were built – not an unusual record for a major architect, but far fewer physical manifestations than enjoyed by his American rival, Frank Lloyd Wright.

Le Corbusier felt everything deeply – the triumphs and the disappointment. Nobody knew what it was like, living life with the volume on high, the dials turned all the way up. He was constantly thinking, analyzing all the world with his X-ray vision, like a meteorologist who could never just see clouds and sun, but barometric pressure and air mass.

The rushing fire hose turned on those around him. One colleague might get a dressing down after spending all night on drawings, while another, a new father, received a gift basket, anonymously delivered on Christmas Eve. He seemed incapable of expressing sympathy either way, missing the usual cues for how others might be feeling. After the bitterest exchange, he would carry on as if nothing had happened; one did battle and then went back to the corner of the ring. It was no accident he referred to himself on several occasions as a boxer. He also knew that in basketball – another sport he enjoyed – some players reach their peak performance only when they play angry.

A colleague in the atelier, André Wogenscky, recalled receiving Le Corbusier as a guest at his home and introducing him to his German shepherd, Puck. The architect first caressed the dog but then gripped the nape of his neck, tighter and tighter. His host, alarmed, asked why he was doing it and warned that the dog would bite him. "I love to feel how far I can go" came the reply.[19]

If he had regrets about how he had conducted himself through his life, he never revealed them. The closest he came to a confession was in a car on his last visit to New York City in 1961. He had agreed to give a lecture and accept an honorary degree at Columbia University, after months of negotiations over fees and travel requirements. A big group of students enthusiastically greeted him at the airport, and he was whisked to the Plaza by limousine to drop off his bags, and then to 116th Street and Broadway, where thousands of students and proud parents assembled in front of the rotunda in a driving rain. Le Corbusier asked for a mortarboard and made it plain he wouldn't accept the degree without it. Taking the honorific sheepskin, he then unfurled it and used it as an umbrella, to protect his head from the rain, allowing the ink to blur in splotches. On a later car ride from Morningside Heights, he seemed to try to explain why he was such a curmudgeon. "You may wonder why I am so difficult," he said, gazing out the rain-dappled window to the crowded streets of Manhattan as the city whirred by. "I find it essential in architecture to be this way."[20]

What was also undeniably true was how much the me-against-the-world posture worked against him. Since he started off virtually every interaction with the assumption that he was about to be undermined, or his genius and authority were somehow questioned, the end result, over time, was for others to minimize contact. Even his biggest fans had to steel themselves to deal with him, approaching with only the most necessary inquiries, couched in language so as not to offend. Some, like Nehru, would reach a point where they avoided him entirely. He burned through many relationships in this way. The remote and mercurial personality, part and parcel of his inspired genius, led one biographer to suggest a mild autism.[21]

By the summer of 1965, his interactions with others seemed to be in final spasms. Jerzy Sołtan, another key hire at the atelier who would go on to be an influential teacher at Harvard and MIT, recalled visiting the master in July,

> on the eve of his departure from Paris for his customary August vacation. By that time, his wife had already passed away. I visited him at the atelier. The "sacred" rhythm of his day had by then changed considerably. Indeed, now it was reversed. Corbu spent the mornings at the rue de Sèvres and was too tired in the afternoons to move around

much. But one felt that he did not want to admit any major changes in his life. He knew, and everyone around him knew, that his heart was in bad shape.

From the atelier, we took a taxi to his home, at rue Nungesser-et-Coli. We had lunch there. Corbu offered me a drink. The sun was resplendent on the terraces. All sorts of plants were in bloom. Far away, Mont Valerian was vibrating in the summer heat; nearby, bees and flies buzzed around. . . . What will you have? Something light. Perhaps a Dubonnet. And you? Corbu poured himself a double pastis, hardly taking any water. It is a deadly beverage, and I protested mildly. Corbu dismissed my grumbling. He was smiling but serious. As long as he was alive he would not allow himself to be pampered. As long as you live, live with gusto! After luncheon, however, he weakened visibly. Yes, he thought he would lie down. A Mediterranean siesta — nothing more. Kindly, but firmly, he saw me off.[22]

The following day, the architect went to Saint-Germain for lunch at the apartment of his longtime doctor, Jacques Hindermeyer, traditionally scheduled before the ritual holiday emptying of Paris. The two men talked about many things, including what each would do if they swapped professions. Le Corbusier suggested he would let people die with dignity. After Hindermeyer returned from a phone call, he found his guest had taken off his shirt. "I don't feel well," Le Corbusier said, "it's as if there were rats in the plumbing." Grabbing his stethoscope, the doctor found the architect's heart to be in complete arrhythmia.[23]

Hindermeyer couldn't convince him to call off his trip to Roquebrune-Cap-Martin or even to give up swimming. But Le Corbusier did promise he would limit the exertion to one swim a day, at noon. The architect took the plane from Paris to Nice the next day, and traveled by car to his holiday retreat.

In letters of late, he was dwelling on how everybody must die sometime, and that death was a beautiful thing when one has lived an active life. He said he felt tired, though not tired like an old man, more of a man of fifty. His brother, Albert, remained concerned. In late August, Le Corbusier wrote to him, assuring him that the Rebutatos were being attentive to his need for a healthy diet and ample rest and relaxation. "They treat me as if I were a stick of barley-sugar."[24]

One thing struck Robert Rebutato as odd, however, in late summer of 1965. The man who had been like a second father to him gave him a manuscript to deliver to Paris. Rebutato had become a part of the atelier by that time, following his dream to build great architecture like his mentor. He would be happy to do it, he said, but pointed out that Le Corbusier would be back in Paris himself long before Rebutato could complete the errand. But the old master insisted – in retrospect, leading Rebutato to believe he had other plans.[25]

In earlier days, he would walk to the ocean straight from the adjacent terrace of L'Étoile de Mer, making his way along a rocky path to the jagged outcroppings at the water's edge. He would jump in with an aggressive dive and get back out on the rocks with equal effort, as the waves slapped against him. One day, after a friend watched with concern how hard a time he was having getting out, the proud architect told him that God was simply toying with "playboys like me"– seeing how much fight was left.[26]

On August 25, 1965, he emerged from his front door and looked out over the Mediterranean. The plants and trees bounced in the breeze. That summer, he had started taking another route, along the path parallel to the railroad tracks, down to the sweeping crescent of pebbles and dark sand of the main beach at Roquebrune-Cap-Martin. His feet sank into the stew of pebbles, broken shells, and sea glass. Wading in was always a challenge, through the shifting mounds of rocks and pebbles, and into the gently pounding surf. When the water was up to his hips, he lunged forward to begin swimming. His crawl, self-taught at Le Piquey forty years earlier, was mechanical and rhythmic, arms bent at the elbow, fingertips spearing into the water, one side and then the other.

The waves carried him up and down, just like the Atlantic had three and a half decades earlier on the *Lutetia*. The water was buoyant with salt, its thickness keeping him afloat. Yet swimming in the open ocean there was not for the timid. Unlike a jog on a country road, there was no place to stop and rest out in the uncompromising water.

He was little more than a hundred yards offshore when the first jolt came, and he could no longer move his arms and legs. As his head bobbed underwater, he might have seen the sea urchins, which years ago Robert Rebutato had brought back to L'Étoile de Mer for Yvonne, nestling into hiding places, their dark spikes poking out. In the last moments, they would have blotted and merged like spilled China ink on tracing paper, until everything was black.

Two young men from north of Paris, vacationing at Roquebrune-Cap-Martin, discovered the limp body floating facedown at 10 a.m. that sunny August morning in 1965. Simon Ozieblo and Jean Deschamps, out swimming themselves about twenty-five yards from shore, said they thought they saw someone struggling in the waves a short time earlier. They brought the man to the pebble beach, and Ozieblo, feeling a faint pulse, attempted mouth-to-mouth resuscitation. But it was clear to him death was already doing its work. A little trickle of blood streamed from the corner of Le Corbusier's mouth. A rescue team from the local fire department arrived and gave him oxygen and a shot of solucamphre to try to revive him. Nothing.[27]

LE CORBUSIER EST MORT, the headlines read throughout France. The Rebutatos' German shepherd was inaccurately identified in some newspaper photo captions as the architect's own. It made for a good portrait, though: the faithful dog, waiting for the master who would never return.

At the inquest, the cause of death was determined to be cardiac arrest – just as Jacques Hindermeyer had warned. The defiance of his doctor's orders, as well as several other hints dropped prior to that summer of 1965, suggested to many that the walk to the sea was an orchestrated suicide – willfully expected, if not that day, the next, or the day after that. He sought tight control over every aspect of his professional and personal life; it would not be a stretch to believe he would choreograph how he would die. Though always in far better physical condition than Yvonne, he grimaced when, in her later days, she had to be cared for in a special car in the train from Paris to Roquebrune-Cap-Martin, and taken from the train station to the *cabanon* in a wheelbarrow, there being no wheelchair handy. He made several comments indicating he did not want to languish incapacitated in his dotage. In his conversation with Hindermeyer that final summer in Paris, he said that if he were a doctor, he would assist people in dying with dignity. And as the scholar Kenneth Frampton notes, there is an Albigensian tradition – the Cathars from whom Le Corbusier was convinced he was descended – of sacred suicide, of preparing for the afterlife with a final sacrament at one's deathbed, then speeding the process of death by fasting and refusing water. "How nice it would be to die swimming towards the sun," he told his atelier colleague Jerzy Sołtan.[28] Like Hemingway, he had seen enough. One thing was certain. He planned to end his days at Roquebrune-Cap-Martin.

He left no specific requests for a grand funeral, and indeed remarked at one point that such a ritual would be a masquerade.[29] But France had big plans for its adopted son. His body was taken on a funeral route befitting a fallen president, from Roquebrune-Cap-Martin to the town hall of Menton, the nearest major municipality, where he lay in state, and then to the sacred space he designed, the monastery at La Tourette outside Lyon, for another night. The monks gathered around in silent appreciation for the man who had created their unique place of meditation and prayer. Later, in Paris, a black car took the casket to 35 rue de Sèvres, and dozens crowded around to get a glimpse. In an elaborate procession into the courtyard of the Louvre on the dark night of September 2, 1965, twenty soldiers wearing crisp side caps and carrying flaming torches marched in perfect cadence alongside the casket, draped with the French tricolor trimmed in gold tassels. With three thousand in attendance inside and outside the museum's Cour Carrée, André Malraux, Charles de Gaulle's minister of culture, eulogized the world's greatest architect as an innovator, someone who challenged the status quo and revolutionized the field. At the same time, quoting Le Corbusier himself, he had "worked for what mankind needs most today: silence and peace." The Paris newspapers hailed the man who "achieved control of the sun" and, although he once proposed razing the center of the city, "liberated us from a tyrannical past."[30]

When the last of the pomp and ceremony died down, his remains were brought back to Roquebrune-Cap-Martin, the architect's final resting place, at his request, at the tombstone he designed and intended to share with Yvonne. The cemetery sat on a steep hillside like a set of ballroom stairs, with a collection of graves on each level; the tombstone faced inland, inviting a gaze to the names in memoriam, framed by the backdrop of the blue Mediterranean Sea. One constant was Robert Rebutato, standing beside the grave marker, just as he had done at Yvonne's funeral, acting as a master of ceremonies, honoring the extraordinary man who befriended him some fifteen years earlier.

It was not long before the honors emerged, suitable for a major public figure. His visage graces the ten-franc Swiss banknote. A square in the capital of Bern was named for him, as was a street in Geneva and in Roquebrune-Cap-Martin. In Saint-Germain, the triangle formed by the boulevard Raspail, the rue de Sèvres, and the rue de Babylone was given the name of Place Le Corbusier. Yet most of those hurrying by the Hôtel Lutetia or Le Bon Marché don't actively think about how the world's greatest architect once worked in that corner of the sixth arrondissement. The best of his work is more seamlessly part of the culture. Somehow, the modern was already within and without, just as he had planned.

EPILOGUE

■ ■ ■

The Legacy

On a late afternoon in November 2013, as students at Harvard University's Graduate School of Design geared up for another long night working on models and renderings in preparation for withering studio reviews, Kanye West, the multiplatinum recording artist, appeared at the bottom of the five levels of workspaces known as the "trays." The crowd gathered around and on the stairways, jostling beside the drafting tables to hear what the rapper had to say. "I just wanted to tell you guys: I really do believe that the world can be saved through design," he said. He went on to say, "And I know that there's traditionalists that hold back the good thoughts and there's people in offices that stop the creative people. . . . I really appreciate you guys' willingness to learn and hone your craft, and not be lazy about creation. I'm very inspired to be in this space."[1]

A few months earlier, the iconic performer was more specific in how he was inspired by the process of design and by one architect in particular. Le Corbusier, he said in an interview with the *New York Times,* challenged the status quo and broke with the past, starting fresh and clean and spare. His own music, West said, similarly embraced that daring simplicity. "I'm a minimalist," he said, "in a rapper's body."[2]

That a fan of Le Corbusier could be found inside Gund Hall, home of Harvard's prestigious architecture school, was unsurprising. Generations of architects have been inspired by Le Corbusier, and many, with mixed results, have copied his designs. Walk into the offices of any architect practicing today, and chances are the *Oeuvre complète* will be on the bookshelf. That a popular entertainer like Kanye West endorsed the architect, however, signaled something more expansive.

In his day, Le Corbusier was the original star architect, catapulting the profession into the realm of celebrity, as public intellectual and leader of a cause. He was a pioneer in self-promotion, publicity, and communicating his ideas; his five points of architecture – from freeing the ground to the open plan – was a typical act of reducing complex themes to bumper sticker simplicity. His approach to the built environment was comprehensive – not just a style of building, but an extensive system of beliefs and standards encompassing transportation, economics, politics, domestic functions, human happiness, public health, and affordable housing. His prescription for human habitation began with the Modular, informing the design of the individual home, and moved seamlessly along a kind of nesting of scales, all the way to the aggregation of homes and workplaces and commerce that makes up entire cities. All the while, he was a writer, a painter, a sculptor, a drawer, and a public speaker. He did it all.

But the passing of time has not been kind. For every fan, there is a vocal detractor. He is widely reviled as a destroyer of cities, his scheme to wipe out central Paris mocked as preposterous. For many, his attributes embody the worst of contemporary design: an obsession with form, driven by utterly misguided notions of how people actually interact with architecture, live in their homes, or look to find the front door. Worst of all, he is in danger of being forgotten entirely, lost to obscurity. In the United States, Frank Lloyd Wright is much more identifiable as a pioneer of modern architecture and as the archetype of the architect, writ large. The author of a book about Le Corbusier must continually test for any glimmer of recognition of the subject; beyond a tight-knit group of scholars, he is simply not widely known. Despite his extensive influence across the landscape of America, in corporate office parks and downtowns, few on these shores have any idea who he was. It is a safe bet that fans of Kanye West had to look him up – and that they were curious why their idol would single him out.

The matter of Le Corbusier's legacy – the view of his influence, good and bad, and what kind of man he was – had no greater choreographer than Le Corbusier himself. His attention to public relations ensured that his comprehensive approach to design would be characterized just the way he wanted it to be long after his death. Like a man running for president already thinking of what will go in his library, he starting plotting early on about how his collected works, papers, letters, and renderings might be gathered all in one place.

In 1949, he wrote to a friend:

One can conk out at any time of life.... With my wife's agreement, I have arranged to leave what I own to the poor. Now, what I own can at best be used as something to light the fire with. Here at 24 rue Nungesser et Coli (and even at 35 Sèvres in a cellar), I have substantial archives of all kinds: drawings, writings, notes, travel diaries, albums, etc. I don't want some hooligan happily pillaging it all, and destroying series whose value depends on their being complete . . . the aim of this letter is to set you thinking and to request you – when the time comes – to take immediate possession, or rather, immediate control of my archives, so as to protect them from being wrongfully scattered.[3]

Without direct heirs, he spent the last fifteen years of his life conceiving and implementing, down to its smallest details, the project of a foundation that would bear his name. "I here declare, for every eventuality, that I leave everything that I possess to an administrative entity, the 'Fondation Le Corbusier,' or any other meaningful form, which shall become a spiritual entity, that is, a continuation of the endeavor pursued throughout a lifetime," he wrote in January 1960.[4]

The Fondation Le Corbusier was formally established in 1968, housed at the Maison La Roche, built in 1923–25 for the Swiss-born art collector Raoul La Roche, and adjacent to Maison Jeanneret. When La Roche moved there it was on the outskirts of Paris, but today the compound, at the end of a narrow lane in the sixteenth arrondissement, is around the corner from a bistro selling lunchtime steaks for seventy-two euro. Maison La Roche was converted to a museum, where visitors can tour the entire building and also view some of Le Corbusier's artwork. In the archives are some eight thousand drawings, 450 paintings, and hundreds of papers, letters, and plans. Le Corbusier the artist left all of that and more, including forty-four sculptures and twenty-seven cartoons for tapestries,[5] as well as the ephemera owned by individuals – the college student who kept a long strip of lecture notes, or the woman given a watercolor portrait, which the architect routinely dashed off when the subjects struck him as particularly attractive.

The foundation itself is housed in Maison Jeanneret, and includes every book ever written about Le Corbusier and everything written by Le Corbusier. The latter category is substantial; he wrote no fewer than thirty-four books over his lifetime, plus those published posthumously, including the autobiographical *Le Corbusier lui-même* – the edited manuscript he asked Robert Rebutato to deliver to Eugène Claudius-Petit in Paris just before his final walk to the sea. He was also a prolific writer of private letters, to his mother, famously, as well as to people like William Ritter and other friends, where he poured out his soul, reflecting on what was happening at various stages of life. It is a vast record both professionally and personally.

His public persona was carefully controlled, a constant exercise of exuding confidence and never compromising, befitting a polemicist. In private, particularly as a young man, he was tortured by self-doubt bordering on depression. He soared high and loved life and architecture when times were good, but deeply felt the lows, wallowing in disappointment, and harboring decades-long grudges. Irascible to the end, he is not remembered fondly in many quarters, and his time in Vichy raises deeply disturbing questions. His efforts to downplay – or outright erase from the record – his interactions there seem especially shameful in light of details exposed by the biographer Nicholas Fox Weber, which leave little question of his zeal to join the regime. His comments about Hitler and Jews, and his associations with fascists and extreme right-wingers favoring eugenics, made his loss of credibility inevitable. Switzerland's largest bank, UBS AG, pulled an advertising campaign centered on the architect in 2010, and Zurich reconsidered naming a square for him next to the central train station.[6]

Steadily, however, Le Corbusier's buildings – among the seventy-eight in twelve countries, out of some three hundred he proposed[7] – are being restored and turned into visitor destinations. Many have become historic landmarks and pilgrimage sites for anyone interested in architecture. Ronchamp, the site of Renzo Piano's visitor center set in the hillside beneath the chapel, is the most popular, with eighty thousand visitors per year, followed by Villa Savoye, which was saved from the wrecking ball after World War II when the town of Poissy wanted to use the site to build a school, with forty-five thousand annual visitors. Maison La Roche attracts twenty thousand visitors per year, according to the Fondation Le Corbusier. France recently invested millions in the restoration of the monastery at La Tourette. Unité d'Habitation in Marseille, bouncing back from a fire in 2012, is still home to more than a thousand people, and visitors can experience life there by renting an apartment through Airbnb or staying at the Hôtel Le Corbusier, with its swank 1950s-style bar and restaurant serving nine-course French meals. For people wishing to stay in the smallest rooms, the manager says she always first inquires, "Are you in love?" An art gallery recently opened in the gymnasium Le Corbusier designed on the rooftop.

The guided tour of Unité d'Habitation in Nantes-Rezé fills up every Saturday, and visitors march through a model apartment. The complex at Firminy, including the church that was only completed posthumously in 2006, is yet another stop following in the architect's footsteps, as well as Roquebrune-Cap-Martin, where the town provides guided tours of the *cabanon* and adjacent studio. For years it was left completely open, but it was only recently closed off with a chain-link fence and locked gate after evidence of vandals was discovered. L'Étoile de Mer is still right next door; vacationers can rent the five modernist holiday cabins, also given landmark status, and Eileen Gray's Villa E-1027, with Le Corbusier's offending murals restored for public viewing as well. A film starring the singer turned actress Alanis Morissette, telling the story of the triangle of Gray, Jean Badovici, and Le Corbusier, was produced in the renovated home and grounds.

In Switzerland, the country of his birth, Maison Blanche, the house lovingly built for his parents, has been adopted by a nonprofit organization and is tenderly cared for, inside and out. His other early villas in La Chaux-de-Fonds are all happily inhabited to this day as private residences. The building where he was born is marked only with a plaque, the apartment occupied; a retail joke shop occupies the ground floor. Le Corbusier, architecture, and town planning are all big themes in the remote Swiss city, where arguably the sole other attraction is a watch museum. A train ride away in Vevey, the Villa Le Lac, or La Petite Maison, just down the street from the Nestlé headquarters and at the foot of the hills hosting fantastically expensive resort hotels, is also open to the public on weekends. The modernist trailer, occupied by the architect's mother and then his brother, is being honored with a careful, ongoing restoration that includes a painstaking analysis of wall colors and the appearance, over time, of the backyard garden that is the site of Le Corbusier's infamous picture-frame opening overlooking Lake Geneva.

In Zurich, the Heidi Weber Museum–Center Le Corbusier was completed in 1967, the result of a commission requested by the interior designer, art collector, and patron who became a singular devotee of Le Corbusier's life work. They met in Roquebrune-Cap-Martin in 1958, and she asked him to design the exhibition pavilion and art gallery to house his sculptures, tapestries, furniture, and books. He obliged with a colorful temple in steel and glass, with a sleek inverted roof design. Weber, who claimed to have sold all her belongings and home to see the project through, faithfully hosted photography exhibits and lectures on urban design.

Chandigarh is not on the typical tourist's itinerary for India, and the capitol complex, ringed by machine gun nests, requires permission slips signed by no fewer than three different offices. The City Beautiful marches on pretty much as Le Corbusier intended – though with a population twice as big as Nehru had initially planned and, like everywhere in India, still growing. Some informal settlement, or slums, has inevitably infiltrated the rigid long blocks, and the traffic is as bad as elsewhere in the subcontinent. The Fondation Le Corbusier led an application for

UNESCO status for Chandigarh along with additional Le Corbusier sites in other countries. In the meantime, door handles and
furniture and even manhole covers from Chandigarh routinely
show up for sale at auction houses and on eBay. For example, in
2011 the Wright auction house put an upholstered teak sofa up
for sale for $25,000, along with a rosewood file rack from an ad-
ministrative building for $15,000.[8] The Chandigarh sell-off has
been widely criticized by the Indian government and Le Corbusier devotees, of which there are many in India. The affront is
palpable: that the work of the great master, in bits and pieces,
would go to the highest bidder.

It is perhaps the ultimate irony that the country where he is least
known, and where he felt he was rebuffed in the 1930s and 1940s,
is the place where the influence of Le Corbusier is so readily
seen. The scheme of the Plan Voisin of 1925 became the template
for post–World War II urban renewal in American cities – towers in the park and highways through downtowns. The Unité
d'Habitation apartment building was replicated, albeit badly, in
sprawling campuses of public housing towers in cities across the
country, from the Bronx to the South Side of Chicago.

Every highway through a city, every concrete downtown
parking garage, and every government center complex that rose
up in the era of urban renewal owes a debt to Le Corbusier. New
York's master builder, Robert Moses, took Le Corbusier's vision
and built public housing towers and superblock apartment buildings like Washington Square Southeast, south of Washington
Square Park, and used his rationales to build the Cross Bronx Expressway and to propose other crosstown expressways bisecting
Manhattan. Moses's models for the Mid-Manhattan Expressway
were straight out of Le Corbusier's drawings – the elevated roadway sweeping past buildings' upper stories, sometimes going
straight through the buildings, with deliveries and pedestrians

relegated to a separate plane. In cities large and small, whole swaths of old neighborhoods were wiped out, as Le Corbusier had proposed for central Paris, to make way for highways and wide arterials, and cruciform housing towers set in open space. The highway-and-arterial system of America's suburbs, similarly, is pure Le Corbusier. The US traffic engineers who built the nation's system of collector roads and highways essentially adopted the grid of Chandigarh wholesale. This, in turn, became the framework for suburban sprawl.

The modernism that Le Corbusier pioneered has been mimicked extensively. Corporate firms and city governments in pursuit of the modern look have snapped up copycat designs by graduates of architecture schools who swooned over him. Developers embraced his style as well because it was relatively cheap to build; the lack of ornament and the use of concrete ended up saving money, whether for a condominium tower or a giant corporate headquarters near a highway off-ramp. And cities across the land took their cues from Le Corbusier. At one intersection in downtown Washington, DC, the buildings at all four corners display Corbusean elements: concrete columns or pilotis, smooth and unadorned concrete facades, and angled or dimpled windows just like those at Unité d'Habitation or the assembly building at Chandigarh. The horizontal bands of tinted fenestration, borrowed from the Villa Savoye, are ubiquitous in thousands of boxy buildings in suburban corporate office parks.

There were other major forces of modernism, of course. Mies van der Rohe's plain glass skyscrapers define downtowns. Frank Lloyd Wright inspired the ubiquitous ranch home on the suburban cul-de-sac. The rivalry between Le Corbusier and Wright flared up from time to time, with Wright highly critical of Le Corbusier, though Le Corbusier never returned fire. They shared much in common – including a love for romance – though they took different approaches, and the common denominator was surely their posture of break-the-mold innovation. The man from Paris had a bit more continental flair; if Frank Lloyd Wright was Bill Gates, Le Corbusier was a bit more like Steve Jobs – and his Villa Savoye was the architectural equivalent of the iPhone. One little-known fact is that Le Corbusier was considered for the commission that Wright won for the Solomon R. Guggenheim Museum in Manhattan. His proposal was for ramps moving up through exhibition space, but at right angles.

The extensive impact of Le Corbusier's designs in America might be unknown to the average citizen, but his fiercest critics know exactly how influential he was and blame him for the worst excesses and foibles of modernism. The urban theorist Jane Jacobs, who moved from Scranton, Pennsylvania, to Greenwich Village in the 1930s, led a powerful backlash against all his urban planning ideas. In an essay published in *Fortune* magazine in 1958, she delivered a harsh, reality-based critique of Le Corbusier's Radiant City as exactly the wrong approach for regenerating America's downtowns. (It would become the basis for her seminal 1961 book *The Death and Life of Great American Cities.*) "[These cities] will be spacious, parklike, and uncrowded," she wrote. "They will feature long green vistas. They will be stable and symmetrical and orderly. They will be clean, impressive, and monumental. They will have all the attributes of a well-kept, dignified cemetery. . . . These projects will not revitalize downtown; they will deaden it."[9]

Assessing the housing towers and windswept plazas in East Harlem, central Philadelphia, and elsewhere, Jacobs revealed an inconvenient truth: that the developments sketched on the drafting tables of planners were devoid of life in reality. Residents longed for the corner stores that had been wiped away. They felt insecure in the big open spaces. The ingredients of good urbanism, she said, were exactly the opposite of Le Corbusier's prescription: the uses, or functions of urban life, should be mixed together, not separated, whether stores, residences, or workplaces. The ideal density was not in sixty-story towers but in the blocks of attached five-story brownstones of Greenwich Village, with front stoops allowing "eyes on the street" and the bustling activity of the "sidewalk ballet." Wide streets and highways killed urban life; streets must accommodate pedestrians and bicyclists, and urban neighborhoods should be oriented around transit, such as buses, subways, or light rail. Le Corbusier's grand plazas and monumental blank walls eradicated human activity; short blocks featuring a diversity of uses – like those in Greenwich Village or, for that matter, Le Marais – were the necessary components of a healthy city. Finally, there should be no top-down planning with master builders unilaterally bulldozing and building according to what they think is best. Citizens must be integrated into the planning process to help shape their communities.

Jane Jacobs's principles are part and parcel of the dominant approach to urban planning today, and *Death and Life* has become a bible. Human-scaled, mixed-use, transit-oriented neighborhoods are the template of what is known broadly as "smart growth," which has an environmental basis as well, as it reduces reliance on the private automobile that Le Corbusier and his contemporaries envisioned. The sustainable city, oriented around the reduction of carbon emissions amid the looming specter of climate change, is the goal of urban planning now.

The physical and psychological destruction of urban renewal – whether the Upper West Side in Manhattan, at the site of the present-day Lincoln Center, or the West End at the Government Center complex in Boston, both bulldozed in the late 1950s – marked a dark time for city building. And those redevelopment schemes were precisely the kind of razing that Le Corbusier advocated for the center of Paris nearly a century ago. The prominent urban planning project of today is to repair that dam-

age: to fill in the sweeping plazas, dismantle the elevated highways traversing cities – the Central Artery in Boston, the Park
East Expressway in Milwaukee, the Embarcadero in San Francisco, the Alaskan Way Viaduct in Seattle – and replace public
housing towers with smaller-scale, more fine-grained urbanism.
The towers in the park – derisively known as "the projects" – have
come down one by one, including Cabrini-Green in Chicago and,
perhaps most famously, Pruitt-Igoe in St. Louis. Built in 1954 by
Minoru Yamasaki, the architect of the World Trade Center, the
Pruitt-Igoe complex of thirty-three large apartment buildings
set in open space rose up on bulldozed land as a public housing
solution in a declining industrial city. But the development became a haven of crime and drugs, essentially unlivable, and its
demolition began in 1972. The implosion of the structures, documented on film, became a symbol of urban planning gone wrong,
an example of how real people inhabited spaces in a very different manner from what designers intended. Seen from above,
Pruitt-Igoe is a carbon copy of the Ville Radieuse. The apartment buildings, although they were stripped down and lacked
the amenities that Le Corbusier intended, were horizontal slabs
inspired by Unité d'Habitation. There was no clearer indictment
of the great architect's urban planning schemes than what occurred in St. Louis, and planners across the land have essentially
pronounced: never again.

For all the symbolism of Le Corbusier's Modular Man – the figure representing human-centered design – the complaint about
the architect's creations was that they were in fact often quite
ill-suited for humans: passageways and doorframes too narrow,
bedrooms too cramped, and sinks too shallow, splashing water
on those who turned on the tap. His system of brises-soleil often
failed utterly, baking inhabitants who were forced to jury-rig
apartments and offices with fans and tarps. Roof-and-wall junc-

tures were seldom watertight. And what leaves many unsatisfied is not a technical glitch, but the very nature of modernist design. The bourgeois sofa was, in the end, more comfortable than the club chair that came out of rue de Sèvres, just as worn-in sneakers feel better than high heels. The horizontal strip window, framing the view outside like a painting, turned out to be often annoyingly restricting. Arguably, humans prefer to look out a traditional vertical window, which frames the upright human body. Le Corbusier critiqued the dimensions of buildings, interiors, and furnishing of the nineteenth century, and now his substitutions have been found wanting. In the journey back to the future, many of the elements of his revolution can be read as a diversion and a waste of time. From the blank walls of brutalism – taken from the French *béton brut* but doubling as an aesthetic description – to horizontal windows, the modernist project is seen by many in the design professions as an unfortunate dead-end, a failed experiment that left so many cities scarred, something to be fixed and forgotten.

The ferocity of the antimodernism backlash extends to the present day and contemporary design. With neo-traditional town planning and architecture ascendant, a cottage industry of critics has emerged. Le Corbusier made a splash with groundbreaking designs, with the Villa Savoye and Ronchamp; in just about every case, he was criticized at the time for outlandishness. But while the Chapel of Notre Dame du Haut was labeled an "ecclesiastical garage" and the Carpenter Center likened to two grand pianos having sex, the pillorying of contemporary architecture has only grown more intense. Buildings are likened to pickles (Norman Foster's Swiss Re Building in London) and highway overpasses (Rem Koolhaas's Seattle Public Library) and, in the case of Zaha Hadid's proposed Qatar soccer stadium, vaginas. Doomsayer James Howard Kunstler maintains a popular blog called *Eyesore of the Month,* lambasting the products that the descendants of Le Corbusier turn out for ugliness and dys-function. In this unhappy dynamic, the emperor has no clothes.

Because Le Corbusier pushed the extremes of structural engineering and the use of new materials and construction methods – all without a computer, which today's architects swear by – it is not surprising that there would be flaws; Frank Lloyd Wright weathered the same complaints from his clients at Fallingwater as Le Corbusier did with the Savoyes. But today, design flaws by architects seem to be seized on with particular relish. There is a certain delight in identifying how new forms might look interesting but are hopelessly impractical. The walls and windows leak; buildings with flat roofs collapse from the weight of heavy snow; gathering places are either drafty or bake in the sun. Building managers tape up handwritten signs to guide visitors who can't find the front door. A skyscraper in London, at 20 Fenchurch Street, was nicknamed the "Death Ray" tower because sun reflecting off its glass facade melted cars parked on the street below. At I. M. Pei's John Hancock Tower, the tall-est building in Boston, the architect who met Le Corbusier as a young man was mercilessly mocked after window panes popped out and crashed to the sidewalk below; to this day, the base of the tower is an inhospitable wind tunnel. A common sight is a skateboarder wielding a custom-made, handheld sail, who finds the streetscape ideal territory for propulsion. At Frank Gehry's Stata Center at MIT, the slanting and nose-diving configuration of the offices of Noam Chomsky made the über-intellectual dizzy just sitting at his desk. He had been relocated from Building 20, a World War II–era tilt-up structure that suited him just fine.

At the root of much of the skepticism is the way that today's "starchitects," such as Gehry, Koolhaas, and Daniel Libeskind, seem intent on outdoing each other with radical, head-turning designs. So-called biomorphic architecture, where the build-ings appear as undulating blobs – in the Netherlands, the shiny, oozing Son-O-House by Lars Spuybroek is an example – make Ronchamp look quaint and tame by comparison. The obsession with form in architecture schools and among many contemporary designers is seen as the ultimate indulgence, and it raises a concern that goes to the heart of what an architect should be in the twenty-first century: the solo magician imposing his will, as portrayed by Gary Cooper in the film version of Ayn Rand's *The Fountainhead*, or a more collaborative, less self-obsessed agent of change. The world doesn't need wavy shapes and headline-grabbing museums to make cities appear to be "world class," the critique goes; the world needs sustainable cities and affordable housing.

Alastair Parvin, a young designer based in London who is part of a team behind WikiHouse, an open-source construction set that allows free downloads of blueprints for parts produced in 3-D printing – "a really big IKEA kit" – suggests an end to the era of elite, well-paid lone architects working for rich clients creating individual buildings. "We're moving into this future where the factory is everywhere, and . . . the design team is everyone," he says.[10] The marriage of technology and the tradition of community barn raising, applied to the desperate needs of today's cramped and overwhelmed cities, could create a kind of crowdsourced architecture. In that world there is little place for a figure like Le Corbusier, choreographing and controlling every small detail. But in that sober and serious world, there is no room for a work of art like Ronchamp, either.

And yet modernism endures, on the shelves at Target and in the showrooms of IKEA, in the shelter porn of *Dwell* magazine, and on design blogs and Pinterest. The National Trust for Historic Preservation recently began a campaign to celebrate modern architecture – even going so far as to propose landmark status for many midcentury modern buildings. Eighty years later, the Villa

Savoye remains a beautiful machine for living in. Rooftop terraces and open-plan living rooms and carports are so ubiquitous that they are accepted without much thought of the pioneering designer who originated them. There is much that works and much to be learned from Le Corbusier – and it's in danger of being tossed aside, a baby thrown out with the modernist bathwater.

Nor is the question settled of how much Le Corbusier really is to blame for what followed him, in architecture and urban planning. Badly mimicked versions of Unité d'Habitation, without any of the careful calibrations for the number of occupants and the accompanying amenities, whether a bakery or a school, may have been destined to fail from the outset. Americans in particular failed to follow the instructions in the owner's manual. And Le Corbusier's comprehensive approach distinguishes him from the craven one-off production of new, interesting forms.

"Le Corbusier did everything, and did everything well. He was a true master," says the Miami-based Cuban architect Andrés Duany. He "planted the seed" for much in contemporary architecture with Ronchamp, the assembly building at Chandigarh, the random surface agitation of Unité d'Habitation, and the ramps angling up from ground to rooftop in his proposed Palais de Congrès in Strasbourg, France. But, Duany says, there was always something deeper in Le Corbusier's overarching approach to the built environment. "Everything was mutually supportive, part of an immersive environment – theory, economics, politics, aesthetics, philosophy. The starchitects today are more like one-trick ponies. What is the philosophy of Richard Meier or Frank Gehry? They don't have an urbanism. They just have shapes."[11]

Duany is an unlikely fan. He is a founder of the Congress for the New Urbanism (CNU), dedicated to neo-traditional town planning, mixed-use development, and Jane Jacobs principles – exactly the opposite of Le Corbusier's urban planning prescriptions. But there is much to admire, beginning with

CIAM – the Congrès International d'Architecture Moderne that Le Corbusier founded, which was the organizational template used as the basis for the CNU. Like CIAM, CNU has a charter, convenes regularly, and seeks to influence government to support its anti-suburban sprawl agenda – just as CIAM sought to convince mayors and other political leaders to embrace modernism. That effort was incredibly successful in embedding the modernist blueprint worldwide, Duany says. "It was the last paradigm that changed the world. From the traffic engineering to the ways to think about the city, a check against a standard model, for things like density and FAR [floor to area ratio]. It was a common language for people all over the world to talk to each other."

There is a certain symmetry in the New Urbanists' modeling a mission on the very force they are fighting against. But CIAM was successful, and for nonideological pragmatists, that's all that matters. "I was brought up on Le Corbusier," says Duany. "I adore his stuff. I can't help it."

Lance Hosey is another designer who one would not associate with the cold functionality of the Plan Voisin. But Hosey, chief sustainability officer at the architecture firm RTKL and author of *The Shape of Green: Aesthetics, Ecology, and Design,* also recognizes how Le Corbusier was on to something with the Modular. Though there were surely flaws in the measurement standards that failed to allow for bigger bodies to move through doorways and spaces, the foundation of the Modular, the golden mean, endures as an almost metaphysical guideline for good design. Hosey is immersed in a new science of design that identifies why the magical proportions – about 5:8 – are aesthetically appealing to humans: a page in a book, an iPhone, the facades of Notre Dame and the Parthenon, the face of the *Mona Lisa*.[12] The geometry and mathematics that informed Le Corbusier's mystic belief system are foundational, including fractals and chaos theory – the organic form of a tree branch, a lightning bolt, a river delta, or a Jackson Pollock painting. It turns out there may well be a universal truth in good design, and that good design makes us happy, helps us heal faster, and reduces stress. In delving into Pythagoras and the Fibonacci sequence, Le Corbusier sought to produce a pattern language for optimal environments all around us. The utopia on the sixtieth floor of the towers of the Plan Voisin, with the garden terraces and expansive views, was the gift of happiness he tried to bestow. His critics never made it to that place; they could not get beyond the audacious destruction that required it.

For the twenty-first-century city, however, among the greatest lessons to be learned from Le Corbusier are his design innovations in housing, and his recognition of the grand scale necessary to accommodate millions of people moving into cities each year.

The reasons those contributions are important is because the urban century has arrived, in dramatic fashion. More than half the planet's population currently lives in cities. That ratio will rise toward two-thirds between 2050 and the end of the century – an urban population of at least six billion, out of a total global population of nine billion. The fate of many of those six billion people – the current population of the entire planet – will hinge on how well cities are designed: the integration of housing and basic infrastructure, whether parks and open space, street grids and transport systems, basic sanitation and sewage systems, drinking water, and technology and information systems.

The megacities of the future will not be London or New York City or Tokyo; they will be in China, India, and Africa. They will not be populated by ten million people or even twenty million people; they will consist of forty million people and more.

And most cities are woefully unprepared for the massive population growth that is under way. Shlomo Angel, a professor at New York University and visiting fellow at the Lincoln Institute of Land Policy, has documented the way that cities worldwide have pushed outward. In his books *Planet of Cities* and *Atlas of Urban Expansion,* Angel urges better planning to make that expansion more sensible. The alternative is that migrants will live in substandard conditions of slums, and once that happens, cities will never be able to catch up and retrofit. Angel, who is advising the UN agency UN-HABITAT on urban expansion in the developing world, recommends that political leaders look fifty years into the future, plan a grid of major transit boulevards approximately a half mile apart, and act now to acquire and plot out periodic open space. They should be realistic about the vast amount of urban land that will be required. Le Corbusier, he says, may have been criticized for the specifics of the Plan Voisin, but in terms of the large-scale planning that cities of the future will need, he had the right idea. He was thinking big. The burgeoning growth of cities requires a regional vision.

First and foremost, all of those millions of primarily poor people – streaming into metropolitan areas overwhelmingly in the developing world, in Asia and sub-Saharan Africa – are going to need decent, affordable housing that can be built quickly. That, too, was Le Corbusier's project, fine-tuned in the Ville Radieuse and culminating in Unité d'Habitation. In his case, people needed immediate shelter after the destruction of World War II. In the case of the twenty-first-century megacity, migrants from the countryside will need housing as they seek a better life for themselves and their families.

The superefficient and compact apartments in Marseille were based on two basic principles: that each individual home could be arranged to provide all the living space that people needed, and that the collection of living units – the bottles in the wine rack – could be mass-produced and prefabricated to cut costs. The goal is the same as boutique hotels like the Hudson in New York, with its super-small rooms – to pack in the maximum amount of human habitation in a finite amount of space. That is what the world's cities will need to calibrate. The planning term "density" seems dreadfully dry, but in fact it is a central notion in the urban future – choreographing density that is just right, not too little and not too much. The goal is to make cities function efficiently and lay the groundwork for human happiness. The density of Unité d'Habitation in Marseille is about 125 people per acre – about the same, overall, as Paris and New York. Every city is different, and it may not be wise to try to establish a minimum standard, but as a practical matter, the future of the metropolitan region may hinge on maintaining about the same average density as Marseille. The design of the apartments and the building, within a framework of amenities, is critical. Well-designed density is dense without feeling dense at all.

Critically, Le Corbusier sought a repeatable urban form, orderly and efficient, on a grid that was infinitely expandable and made up of well-designed components that made living a pleasure. He understood that not every person on the planet would be able to have his or her own house on a plot of land, and took steps to accommodate that reality.

Some reject the very idea that any planner or architect should play God and try to impose order on the planet's growing cities. Like Jane Jacobs, some theorists claim that top-down planning and large apartment buildings are destined to fail, and that instead, human settlement should be allowed to organize itself organically – manifested in the phenomenon known as informal settlement. The United Nations estimates that 1 billion people live in slums, shantytowns, and favelas. In sub-Saharan Africa, an estimated two-thirds of all new arrivals in cities go straight to the slums, setting up shacks of corrugated tin and cardboard on occupied land with no formal ownership or title. It is all too easy to romanticize the slums, especially for those who don't live in them day after day. They are places of functioning economies and ingenuity – but also zones of crippling poverty, suffering, and disease, lacking basic services such as sanitation, drinking water, and electricity. The planet can do better.

As an alternative, the density and efficiency of Unité d'Habitation is already being embraced. New York City's "micro-housing" initiative included a design competition for living spaces for single people as small as three hundred square feet – in the same range as a studio in the Marseille building. The city recognized a growing housing crisis, where residents were doubling and tripling up in existing housing stock, creating worrisome conditions; other American cities, such as San Francisco and Boston, have followed suit in promoting more diversity and compactness in the design of urban living. And, of course, Asian societies such as Japan have been perfecting superefficient housing and hotel rooms for some time.

Sometimes Le Corbusier is credited in the contemporary configuration of superefficient housing. Bjarke Ingels, the Danish architect and founder of the Bjarke Ingels Group, directly attributes inspiration to Le Corbusier in such creations as the 8 House, a kind of combination of Unité d'Habitation and the unexecuted Roq and Rob holiday apartments envisioned for the hillside of Roquebrune-Cap-Martin. Each apartment in the 8 House has views, indoor and outdoor space, and a sense of light and air, yet they are all set in the context of significant density. Sometimes Le Corbusier is unseen but omnipresent, as in a collection of apartment buildings recently proposed for Kuala Lumpur. The towers are narrow at the bottoms and flare out at upper stories, freeing up the ground for parks and lush gardens. The architect, Thomas Heatherwick, discusses the scheme as if it were an original idea.

No matter. What's important is that fresh ideas and new approaches to city building continue to percolate. The massive project of urban expansion, the breathtaking growth of cities worldwide, will require a commensurate furious pace of innovative thinking. Le Corbusier's process of vision and his approach to problem solving are instructive. He viewed design as a work of art, yet was still pragmatic. He would go down paths and then turn around or back out and try something else. He loved to be at construction sites; he was always making adjustments in real time, on the fly. He was fundamentally disruptive, refused to accept the status quo, and innovated with a sense of urgency.

"Creation is a patient search," Le Corbusier said. In the business of human settlement, the search for effective solutions continues. Disparaged and derided, the architect with the round black eyeglasses actually has much to offer. His ideas and his template for disruption have value that has been obscured by the withering dismissal of those who see him as the destroyer of cities. The planet needs to make room for him, to welcome him back into the conversation. He comes in peace.

ACKNOWLEDGMENTS

The person who deserves the most credit and gratitude in the creation of this book is someone who knows all about the enterprise: my wife, Tina Ann Cassidy, author of two nonfiction works (one on the history of childbirth, the other a look at one year, 1975, in the life of Jacqueline Kennedy Onassis). A lifelong journalist—we met at the *Boston Globe*—she read the manuscript and made helpful comments. And while she would flag this as a cliché, she held down the fort. As a matter of scheduling, we switch off in writing books because the household would implode if we tried to do it at the same time. Professional and domestic responsibilities, including raising three sons, seemed to expand exponentially during my turn this time. I am grateful for her love and support and for the way she kept it together while I spent time sequestered in our top-floor writing nook, affectionately known as the Eagle's Nest, and was shamelessly absent for two fellowships in Europe. All the while, the Flint boys careened and wrestled like lion cubs. Even the weather was more severe.

In the final stages of the process she signed up to run the Boston Marathon, leaving me further in awe.

My oldest son, Hunter, reached the milestone of senior year and prepared to head off to college, while middle son, George, learned to pronounce Le Corbusier and assessed the difficulty of assembling the Villa Savoye LEGO kit. The youngest, Harrison, said he wanted to return to Paris and became an accomplished artist, his fantastic creatures not unlike the abstractions painted at 24 rue Nungesser et Coli. They continually asked if I was finished with my book because at that point we could get a dog. How that sequence was established remains unclear.

My mother, Mary Alice Flint, another editor in the family, provided encouragement and support, as did Julia Flint, and George and Emily Flint. My in-laws, Jack and Gloria Cassidy, happily and fearlessly welcomed Harrison and George for extended getaways and playtime with cousins at Sunrise Road.

My agent, Richard Abate, is most responsible for the concept of this book. Le Corbusier made a cameo in *Wrestling with Moses,* and Richard always believed he deserved a similar narrative treatment – to let more readers in on the secret, who he was and what made him tick. Making architecture and urban design more accessible has been our singular mission, through the honorable tradition of telling a good story. Ed Park, my editor at Amazon Publishing, helped achieve that goal in so many ways, tightening my writing and bolstering the many theatrical moments in the narrative. He was cheerful, firm, and encouraging throughout.

I can think of no better place to be in my post-newsroom career than the Lincoln Institute of Land Policy. From urbanization in China to resilience and climate change, the Lincoln Institute is immersed in the critical issues of the day. My thanks go to everyone there for all their forbearance. Gregory K. Ingram and Armando Carbonell have taught me much about economics, urban form, the analysis of empirical data, and the dangers of reaching conclusions too quickly. Visiting fellow Shlomo "Solly" Angel, author of the Lincoln Institute publications *Planet of Cities* and *Atlas of Urban Expansion,* continues the noble cause of helping megacities in the developing world prepare for their much more populous future. I also thank Joan Youngman, Martim Smolka, Dennis Robinson, Levering White, Jim Holway, Peter Pollock, Tom Thurston, and especially Katie Lincoln, Dione Etter, and the board of directors of the Lincoln Institute.

There were two other institutions that enabled me to write this book: the American Library in Paris and the Rockefeller Foundation's Bellagio Center.

Charles Trueheart and Anne Swardson, Grant Rosenberg, and everyone at the American Library in Paris allowed me to experience the city Le Corbusier called home as the first writer in residence and visiting fellow there. Being in Paris facilitated one introduction after the other, whether Patrice Tocme, who recalled her friendship with Le Corbusier and Yvonne, or Alan Marty, a surgeon turned writer who has become an expert in occupied Paris in World War II. The propinquity I experienced there recalled what I imagine was the norm in the 1920s. Marty suggested meeting at Café Josephine, where Le Corbusier had his lunch with the Germans in 1944. During dessert, who should walk by but Robert Caro; we chatted about how Le Corbusier had influenced the power broker Robert Moses. It was also at the American Library in Paris that I met Jerry Fielder, curator of the Yousuf Karsh Estate, whom I thank for allowing the use of the portrait of Le Corbusier. I owe a special debt to Clydette and Charles de Groot and the de Groot Foundation for supporting the fellowship and introducing me to so many interesting people (two seats over at the dinner table? That's Tolstoy's grandson). Library supporter Leslie de Galbert kindly provided shelter in a Corbusean tower in the fifteenth arrondissement built on the former Citroën assembly grounds, overlooking the Seine. Most days I'd take the 42 Bus across the Champ-de-Mars past the Eiffel Tower, and never got so jaded so as not to look up.

It all would not be possible without Virginie Alvine-Perrett, who welcomed me to Paris on an earlier research trip and introduced me to Charles Trueheart. She also led me to Monique Valery, niece of Pierre Savoye, who treated me to lunch at her flat by the Luxembourg Gardens. Neighbor and all-around disruptor John Werner, who brought me into the world of TED and TEDx, exercised one of his finest moments in networking by making the initial connection.

It was an equally audacious idea to steal away for a defined period of time to focus on writing, in the summer of 2013. It could have been in a cabin in the woods, but instead it was the Villa Serbelloni at the Rockefeller Foundation's Bellagio Center. Its mission is to bring together practitioners and scholars who foster international understanding – my focus being how Le Corbusier's efficient housing designs might help burgeoning cities in the developing world – and the diverse collection of fellows is as inspirational as the Lake Como landscape. My thanks go to Rob Garris, Pilar Palacia, Elena Ongania, and the great group that came together for that magical time – days writing shirtless in my room and getting feedback over limoncello at night – including Paul Reickoff, Lauren Hale, Hal Hill, Golnar Adili, Louis Wenger, Gill Shepherd, and Anthony Spires.

I had many guides as I retraced the steps of the world's greatest architect. The Fondation Le Corbusier is every bit the presidential library Le Corbusier had envisioned, and has been energetic in supporting the restoration and protection of his buildings as cultural heritage sites. I would like to thank executive director Michel Richard as well as Arnaud Dercelles and Isabel Godineaux. Myrianne von Buren and Edmond Charriere took me through the Maison Blanche, the neighborhood where the young Charles-Édouard Jeanneret-Gris first practiced his craft, and introduced me to the watchmaking capital of La Chaux-de-Fonds. The curator at Villa Le Lac, Patrick Moser, also welcomed me at Corseaux, and related with justifiable pride the great care taken in restoring and preserving this gem of modernism on the banks of Lake Geneva. My thanks also extend to the staff at Le Mirador Kempinski hotel, a memorable stop on the funicular, and the staff at the Switzerland tourism office.

In France, my thanks go to the staff at Villa Savoye, 24 rue Nungesser et Coli, La Tourette, and Ronchamp, and to Emmanuel Georges at La Maison d'Hôtes du Parc at Ronchamp, the Hôtel Le Corbusier at Unité d'Habitation in Marseille, the residents of Unité d'Habitation in Nantes-Rezé, Patricia and Marine Marinovich at the Hôtel Le Roquebrune, the Roquebrune-Cap-Martin tourist board, and especially Robert Rebutato. It was a trip through the looking glass to have our picture taken in front of the bar of L'Étoile de Mer, even as I so desperately wished I had paid more attention in Anthony Coppola's high school French class. Caroline Fletcher Graham provided invaluable guidance on all things South of France and beyond.

Pratap Talwar, principal at Thompson Design Group (where I am also thankful for the wisdom of Jane Thompson), guided my passage to India, along with Kiran Kapila, who made critical arrangements for me to take in Chandigarh. I am grateful to the University of Thane to have me included in its conference on urbanism as well.

Harvard University's Graduate School of Design has become a special place for me, not least of all as the scene of my Loeb Fellowship, but also for the Le Corbusier library in Special Collections of the Frances Loeb Library. I am grateful for the wisdom and assistance of Inés Zalduendo, Mary Daniels, Jim Stockard, Sally Young, and Alex Krieger. William J. Curtis provided special insight about the Carpenter Center, which celebrated its fiftieth anniversary while I was writing the chapter on Le Corbusier's only building in North America.

Barry Bergdoll, architecture curator at MoMA, and Jean-Louis Cohen, the preeminent Le Corbusier scholar, conjured a compelling and theatrical exhibition and accompanying volume, *Le Corbusier: Atlas of Modern Landscapes,* that both appealed to newcomers who had never heard of Le Corbusier – something I have tried to do with this narrative – while also providing a new lens, that of landscape, for specialists. The New York American Institute of Architects' Center for Architecture convened a two-day workshop that provided special insights into Le Corbusier's complicated relationship with that city.

There are a great many scholars with much more knowledge and insight than me, and of course many books about Le Corbusier that tend to break off specialized pieces of his life and career. There are books about Le Corbusier and the car he designed, his churches, his love of the beach, and his relationship with the occult, just to name a few. My gambit was to create a more accessible full biography. Several authors aided me in this task with their admirable work, including Jean-Louis Cohen and Timothy Benton (*Le Corbusier, Le Grande*), Mardges Bacon (*Le Corbusier in America*), H. Allen Brooks (*Le Corbusier's Formative Years*), William J. R. Curtis and Eduard Sekler (*Le Corbusier at Work*), and Nicholas Fox Weber (*Le Corbusier: A Life*).

I am grateful as well for the guidance, conversation, and fact-checking of Robert Campbell, the *Boston Globe*'s Pulitzer Prize–winning architecture critic, whom I met when I was just starting out at that great newspaper and have been trying to keep up with ever since. My recognition and appreciation extends to fellow authors Mitchell Zuckoff, Brian McGrory, and Alex Prudhomme; and Jeff Struzenski, Chris Lutes, Tim Love, George Thrush,

Robert Yaro, Dan Keating, John Redd, Nora Taylor, Ron Fleming, Richard Cheek, William Strong, Chip von Weise, Chris Wall, John King, John Fraser, and Bradley Frazee.

Le Corbusier's reference to his work as a "patient search" has had great resonance. An author, like an architect, strives to design an experience. And writing this book has been a singular and sometimes tumultuous journey. In August 2013 my sister, Melissa Ann Cappella, died following a two-year battle with breast cancer. She was stalwart and possessed a mischievous sense of humor, and she was a rebel. I didn't always agree about the institutions she challenged, but I admired how she, like Le Corbusier, would not blithely accept the status quo. This book is dedicated to her memory, and to disruptive spirits everywhere.

Anthony Flint

Palm Beach, Florida

February 2014

NOTES

Introduction. The Ascent

1. Josephine Baker and Jo Bouillon, *Josephine,* trans. Mariana Fitzpatrick (New York: Harper & Row, 1977), p. 81.
2. Jean-Louis Cohen and Timothy Benton, *Le Corbusier, Le Grand* (London and New York: Phaidon, 2008), p. 254.
3. Tim Benton, *The Villas of Le Corbusier, 1920–1930* (London and New Haven, CT: Yale University Press, 1987).
4. William Wiser, *The Crazy Years: Paris in the Twenties* (New York: Atheneum, 1983).
5. John D. Rosenberg, ed., *The Genius of John Ruskin,* 2nd ed. (Charlottesville: University of Virginia Press, 2000), p. 91.
6. H. Allen Brooks, *Le Corbusier's Formative Years: Charles-Edouard Jeanneret at La Chaux-de-Fonds* (Chicago: University of Chicago Press, 1997).
7. Ibid.
8. Le Corbusier, *Precisions on the Present State of Architecture and City Planning* (Cambridge, MA: MIT Press, 1991), p. 91.
9. Sambal Oelek, *L'enfance d'un architecte* (Paris: Éditions du Linteau, 2008).
10. Brooks, *Le Corbusier's Formative Years.*
11. Nicholas Fox Weber, *Le Corbusier: A Life* (New York: Alfred A. Knopf, 2008).
12. Ibid.

13. Ivan Žaknić, ed. and trans., *Journey to the East: Le Corbusier,* rev. ed. (Cambridge, MA: MIT Press, 2007), p. 216.
14. Cohen and Benton, *Le Corbusier, Le Grand,* p. 184.
15. Ibid., p. 99.
16. Weber, *Le Corbusier: A Life,* p. 15.
17. Ibid., pp. 292, 294–95.
18. Ibid., p. 294.

1. The Roar

1. Flora Samuel, *Le Corbusier: Architect and Feminist* (Chichester, West Sussex, England, and Hoboken, NJ: Wiley-Academy, 2004).
2. Noel Riley Fitch, *Walks in Hemingway's Paris: A Guide to Paris for the Literary Traveler* (New York: St. Martin's Press, 1989).
3. Le Corbusier, letter to William Ritter, 1917, Fondation Le Corbusier, Paris, France.
4. Weber, *Le Corbusier: A Life.*
5. Ibid., p. 143.
6. Cohen and Benton, *Le Corbusier, Le Grand,* p. 112.
7. Le Corbusier, letter to his parents, March 1918, Fondation Le Corbusier.
8. Cohen and Benton, *Le Corbusier, Le Grand,* p. 112.
9. Weber, *Le Corbusier: A Life.*
10. Cohen and Benton, *Le Corbusier, Le Grand.*
11. Ibid.
12. Ibid.
13. Le Corbusier, "Plan Voisin, Paris, 1925: The Street," Fondation Le Corbusier, available at http://www.fondationlecorbusier.fr/corbuweb /morpheus.aspx?sysId=13&IrisObjectId=6159&sysLanguage=en-en &itemPos=150&itemSort=en-en_sort_string1%20&itemCount=215& sysParentName=&sysParentId=65.
14. Ibid.
15. Le Corbusier, *The City of Tomorrow and Its Planning,* trans. Frederick Etchells (Cambridge, MA: MIT Press, 1971 [1929]).
16. Le Corbusier, *Urbanisme* (Paris: Flammarion, 2011 [1925]).
17. Marybeth Shaw, "Promoting an Urban Vision: Le Corbusier and the Plan Voisin" (master's thesis, Massachusetts Institute of Technology, 1991).
18. Le Corbusier, *The City of Tomorrow and Its Planning,* p. 258.
19. Ibid.
20. Willet Weeks, *The Man Who Made Paris Paris: The Illustrated Biography of Georges-Eugene Haussmann* (London: London House, 1999).

21. Stephane Kirkland, *Paris Reborn: Napoléon III, Baron Haussmann, and the Quest to Build a Modern City* (New York: St. Martin's Press, 2013), p. 117.
22. Ibid, p. 191.
23. Weber, *Le Corbusier: A Life.*
24. Le Corbusier, *The Final Testament of Père Corbu,* ed. Ivan Žaknić (New Haven, CT: Yale University Press, 1997), p. 21.
25. Charlotte Perriand, *A Life of Creation: An Autobiography* (New York: Monacelli Press, 2003), p. 23.
26. Antonio Amado, *Voiture Minimum: Le Corbusier and the Automobile* (Cambridge, MA: MIT Press, 2011).
27. Perriand, *A Life of Creation.*
28. Ibid.

2. The Masterpiece

1. Author interview with Monique Valery, Pierre Savoye's niece, in Paris, October 11, 2013.
2. Jean-Louis Cohen, *Le Corbusier: An Atlas of Modern Landscapes* (New York: Museum of Modern Art, 2013).
3. Josep Quetglas, *Les Heures Claires: proyecto y arquitectura en la villa Savoye, de Le Corbusier y Pierre Jeanneret* (Sant Cugat del Vallès, Barcelona, Spain: Associació d'Idees, Centre d'Investigacions Estètiques, 2008).
4. Dominique Amouroux, *The Villa Savoye* (Paris: Éditions du Patrimoine, 2011).
5. José Baltanás, *Walking through Le Corbusier: A Tour of His Masterworks* (London: Thames & Hudson, 2005), p. 13.
6. Cohen and Benton, *Le Corbusier, Le Grand,* p. 29.
7. Jean-Louis Cohen, *Le Corbusier, 1887–1965: The Lyricism of Architecture in the Machine Age* (Cologne: Taschen, 2006).
8. Cohen, *Le Corbusier: An Atlas of Modern Landscapes,* p. 60.
9. Ibid., p. 62.
10. Cohen and Benton, *Le Corbusier, Le Grand.*
11. Brooks, *Le Corbusier's Formative Years,* p. 238.
12. Cohen and Benton, *Le Corbusier, Le Grand.*
13. Cathleen McGuigan, "A View with a Room," *Architectural Record,* September 2013, http://archrecord.construction.com/community/editorial/2013/1309.asp.
14. Cohen, *Le Corbusier: An Atlas of Modern Landscapes,* p. 262.
15. Linda Wagner-Martin, *Favored Strangers: Gertrude Stein and Her Family* (New Brunswick, NJ: Rutgers University Press, 1995), p. 179.

16. Jacques Sbriglio, *Le Corbusier: la Villa Savoye* (Paris: Fondation Le Corbusier; Basel and Boston: Birkhäuser, 1999), p. 45.
17. Ibid.
18. Le Corbusier, *Precisions on the Present State of Architecture and City Planning.*
19. Sbriglio, *Le Corbusier: la Villa Savoye.*
20. Ibid., p. 97.
21. Le Corbusier, *Toward an Architecture,* trans. John Goodman (Los Angeles: Getty Research Institute, 2007), p. 235.
22. Weber, *Le Corbusier: A Life,* p. 580.
23. Cohen, *Le Corbusier, 1887–1965,* p. 53.
24. Cohen and Benton, *Le Corbusier, Le Grand,* p. 282.
25. Weber, *Le Corbusier: A Life,* p. 580.
26. Le Corbusier, letter to his mother, April 29, 1934, Fondation Le Corbusier, as cited in Cohen and Benton, *Le Corbusier, Le Grand,* p. 286.
27. Author interview with Monique Valery in Paris, October 11, 2013.
28. Eugénie Savoye, letter to Le Corbusier, September 7, 1936, Fondation Le Corbusier.
29. Eugénie Savoye, letter to Le Corbusier, October, 11, 1937, Fondation Le Corbusier.
30. Amouroux, *The Villa Savoye.*
31. Le Corbusier, letter to Pierre Savoye, [1937], Fondation Le Corbusier.
32. Author interview with Monique Valery in Paris, October 11, 2013.

3. The Debut

1. Mardges Bacon, *Le Corbusier in America: Travels in the Land of the Timid* (Cambridge, MA: MIT Press, 2001).
2. Geoffrey T. Hellman, "From Within to Without," *The New Yorker,* April 26, 1947.
3. Ibid.
4. Le Corbusier, *When the Cathedrals Were White: A Journey to the Country of Timid People* (New York: Reynal & Hitchcock, 1947), p. 35.
5. Le Corbusier, "A Noted Architect Dissects Our Cities," *New York Times,* January 3, 1932.
6. Hellman, "From Within to Without."
7. "French Architect Shows Work Here," *New York Times,* October 25, 1935.
8. Bacon, *Le Corbusier in America,* p. 55.
9. Hellman, "From Within to Without."
10. Bacon, *Le Corbusier in America.*

11. Ibid., p. 61.
12. Cohen and Benton, *Le Corbusier, Le Grand.*
13. Le Corbusier, *When the Cathedrals Were White,* p. 142.
14. Bacon, *Le Corbusier in America,* p. 99.
15. Ibid., p. 115.
16. Cohen and Benton, *Le Corbusier, Le Grand.*
17. Le Corbusier, *When the Cathedrals Were White,* p. 168.
18. Cohen and Benton, *Le Corbusier, Le Grand,* p. 302.
19. George A. Dudley, *A Workshop for Peace: Designing the United Nations Headquarters* (New York: Architectural History Foundation; Cambridge, MA: MIT Press, 1994).
20. Charlene Mires, *Capital of the World: The Race to Host the United Nations* (New York: New York University Press, 2013).
21. Dudley, *A Workshop for Peace.*
22. Kenneth Frampton, "Le Corbusier's Designs for the League of Nations, the Centrosoyus, and the Palace of the Soviets, 1926–1931," in *Palais de la Société des Nations, Villa les Terrasses, and Other Buildings and Projects, 1926–1927* (New York: Garland Publications; Paris: Fondation Le Corbusier, 1982).
23. Dudley, *A Workshop for Peace,* p. 48.
24. Cohen, *Le Corbusier: An Atlas of Modern Landscapes.*
25. Raul Barreneche, "Oscar Niemeyer, 1907–2012," *Architectural Record,* December 11, 2012.
26. *A Workshop for Peace* (Peter Rosen Productions with UN Department of Public Information, 2011), United Nations Webcast film, 54:01, posted September 7, 2011, http://www.unmultimedia.org/tv/webcast/2011/09/a-workshop-for-peace.html.

4. The Opportunist

1. Roger Price, *A Concise History of France* (Cambridge: Cambridge University Press, 2014), p. 298.
2. Hervé Laroche, "Divided France," *History of the Second World War,* Part 42, 1973.
3. Weber, *Le Corbusier: A Life,* p. 427.
4. Michael Robert Marrus and Robert O. Paxton, *Vichy France and the Jews* (New York: Basic Books, 1981), p. 53.
5. Weber, *Le Corbusier: A Life.*
6. Cohen and Benton, *Le Corbusier, Le Grand.*
7. Ibid.
8. Ibid., p. 236.

9. Carola Hein, *The Capital of Europe: Architecture and Urban Planning for the European Union* (Westport, CT: Praeger, 2004).

10. Le Corbusier and Pierre Jeanneret, *Oeuvre Complet de 1910–1929* (Zurich: Les Editions d'Architecture [Artemis]), 1964.

11. Eric Paul Mumford, *The CIAM Discourse on Urbanism, 1928–1960* (Cambridge, MA: MIT Press, 2000).

12. Cohen and Benton, *Le Corbusier, Le Grand.*

13. Ibid., p. 85.

14. Author interview with Alan Marty, author of *A Walking Guide of Occupied Paris: The Germans and their Collaborators* (forthcoming), in Paris, October 11, 2014.

15. Robert Fishman, *Urban Utopias in the Twentieth Century: Ebenzer Howard, Frank Lloyd Wright, Le Corbusier* (Cambridge, MA: MIT Press, 1982).

16. Laurence Bertrand Dorléac, *Art of the Defeat: France, 1940–1944* (Los Angeles: Getty Research Institute, 2008).

17. Cécile Desprairies, *Paris dans la collaboration* (Paris: Seuil, 2009).

18. Ibid.

19. Laroche, "Divided France."

20. Peter Clericuzio, "Le Corbusier and the Reconstruction of Saint-Dié: The Debate over Modernism in France, 1944–46," *Chicago Art Journal* 20 (2010): 46–71. Available at http://www.academia.edu /1879022/Le_Corbusier_and_the_Reconstruction_of_Saint-Die_ The_Debate_over_Modernism_in_France_1944-46.

21. Weber, *Le Corbusier: A Life.*

22. Ibid.

5. The Comeback

1. Cohen and Benton, *Le Corbusier, Le Grand,* p. 418.

2. Cohen, *Le Corbusier, 1887–1965,* p. 58.

3. Weber, *Le Corbusier: A Life,* pp. 569–70.

4. "Unité d'Habitation, Marseille, France, 1945," Fondation Le Corbusier, http://www.fondationlecorbusier.fr/corbuweb/morpheus.aspx ?sysId=13&IrisObjectId=5234&sysLanguage=en-en&itemPos=58& itemCount=78&sysParentId=64&sysParentName=home.

5. Cohen and Benton, *Le Corbusier, Le Grand,* p. 420.

6. "Corbu," *Time,* May 5, 1961.

7. "Happy Hive," *Time,* February 2, 1948.

8. "Unité d'Habitation, Marseille, France, 1945."

9. Lance Hosey, "Why We Love Beautiful Things," *New York Times,* February 15, 2013.

10. Cohen and Benton, *Le Corbusier, Le Grand*, p. 379.
11. Le Corbusier, *Le Modulor: essai sur une mesure harmonique a l'echelle humaine applicable universellement a l'architecture et a la méchanique* (Basel: Birkhäuser, 2000 [1950]), p. 17.
12. Ibid., p. 58.
13. Ibid.; "Unité d'Habitation, Marseille, France, 1945."
14. Jacques Sbriglio, *Le Corbusier: The Unité d'Habitation in Marseille* (Basel: Birkhäuser; London: Springer, 2004).
15. "Happy Hive."
16. "Corbu."
17. Ibid.

6. The Getaway

1. Jean-François Lejeune and Michelangelo Sabatino, eds., *Modern Architecture and the Mediterranean: Vernacular Dialogues and Contested Identities* (London and New York: Routledge, 2010), p. 94.
2. "Monaco," *The World Factbook,* Central Intelligence Agency, https://www.cia.gov/library/publications/the-world-factbook/geos/mn.html.
3. "Disparition Le Pirate de la nuit s'en est allé, et l'insouciance del la Côte avec," *Nice-Matin,* March 17, 2010, http://www.nicematin.com/article/societe/disparition-le-pirate-de-la-nuit-sen-est-alle-et-linsouciance-de-la-cote-avec.2241.html.
4. "Film Traveller Côte d'Azur: Film Memories at Hotel Le Roquebrune," YouTube video, 3:37, posted by "Jonathan Melville," April 9, 2013, http://www.youtube.com/watch?v=RAVwVauLmh8&list=PLzEhxUIQ8G_hkgw7ea9izEyKaAtob3ar6&index=4.
5. Judith Thurman, "Scenes from a Marriage," *The New Yorker,* May 23, 2005.
6. Alice Rawsthorn, "Eileen Gray, Freed from Seclusion," *New York Times,* February 24, 2013. Additional reference is the exhibit catalog: *Eileen Gray* (Paris: Centre Pompidou, 2013).
7. Alastair Gordon, "Le Corbusier's Role in the Controversy over Eileen's Gray's E.1027," *Wall Street Journal,* August 19, 2013.
8. Niklas Maak, *Le Corbusier: The Architect on the Beach* (Munich: Hirmer, 2011).
9. Weber, *Le Corbusier: A Life,* p. 240.
10. Ibid.
11. Alan Read, ed., *Architecturally Speaking: Practices of Art, Architecture, and the Everyday* (New York: Routledge, 2000).
12. Samuel, *Le Corbusier: Architect and Feminist,* p. 37.

13. Read, ed., *Architecturally Speaking*, p. 147.
14. Weber, *Le Corbusier: A Life*.
15. Author interview with Robert Rebutato in Roquebrune-Cap-Martin, August 30, 2012.
16. Cohen, *Le Corbusier: An Atlas of Modern Landscapes*.
17. Cohen, *Le Corbusier, 1887–1965*, p. 63.
18. Cohen, *Le Corbusier: An Atlas of Modern Landscapes*, p. 222.
19. Ibid.
20. Weber, *Le Corbusier: A Life*, p. 580.
21. Cohen, *Le Corbusier: An Atlas of Modern Landscapes*, p. 222.

7. The Church

1. Flora Samuel and Inge Linder-Gaillard, *Sacred Concrete: The Churches of Le Corbusier* (Basel: Birkhäuser, 2013), p. 82.
2. Danièle Pauly, *Le Corbusier: The Chapel at Ronchamp* (Basel: Birkhäuser, 1997).
3. Association de l'Oeuvre Notre-Dame du Haut, *Ronchamp: The Pilgrimage Church of Notre-Dame du Haut by Le Corbusier*, trans. Katherine Taylor (Regensburg, Germany: Schnell & Steiner, 2008).
4. Ibid.
5. Le Corbusier, letter to William Ritter, 1917, Fondation Le Corbusier.
6. Samuel and Linder-Gaillard, *Sacred Concrete*.
7. Author interview with Emmanuel Georges, proprietor, La Maison d'Hôtes du Parc, Ronchamp, August 28, 2012.
8. Pauly, *Le Corbusier: The Chapel at Ronchamp*, pp. 121–22.
9. Maak, *Le Corbusier: The Architect on the Beach*, p. 16.
10. Samuel, *Le Corbusier: Architect and Feminist*, p. 120.
11. Weber, *Le Corbusier: A Life*, p. 67.
12. J. K. Birksted, *Le Corbusier and the Occult* (Cambridge, MA: MIT Press, 2009).
13. Žaknić, ed. and trans., *Journey to the East*, p. 179.
14. Deborah Gans, *The Le Corbusier Guide* (Princeton, NJ: Princeton Architectural Press, 1987).
15. Samuel and Linder-Gaillard, *Sacred Concrete*, p. 124.
16. Ibid., p. 123.
17. Cohen, *Le Corbusier: An Atlas of Modern Landscapes*, p. 218.
18. Adrian Forty, *Concrete and Culture: A Material History* (London: Reaktion, 2013), p. 188.
19. Maak, *Le Corbusier: The Architect on the Beach*, p. 9.
20. Ibid.

21. *Chapelle Notre-Dame du Haut Ronchamp,* Association Oeuvre Notre-Dame du Haut, 2012, http://s343802320.onlinehome.fr/_valide/chapelle/wp-content/uploads/2012/01/DP_anglais.pdf.
22. Cohen and Benton, *Le Corbusier, Le Grand,* p. 574.

8. The City

1. Cohen, *Le Corbusier: An Atlas of Modern Landscapes.*
2. Lawrence J. Vale, *Architecture, Power, and National Identity* (New Haven, CT: Yale University Press, 1992), p. 106.
3. Ibid., p. 107.
4. Weber, *Le Corbusier: A Life,* p. 536.
5. Ibid.
6. Ibid., p. 542.
7. Ibid., p. 545.
8. Ibid.
9. Dennis Sharp, "Obituary: Minnette de Silva," *Independent,* December 14, 1998.
10. Cohen and Benton, *Le Corbusier, Le Grand,* p. 518.
11. Cohen, *Le Corbusier: An Atlas of Modern Landscapes,* p. 382.
12. Ibid., p. 384.
13. Weber, *Le Corbusier: A Life,* p. 597.
14. Brooks, *Le Corbusier's Formative Years.*
15. Cohen and Benton, *Le Corbusier, Le Grand,* p. 489.
16. *Edict of Chandigarh, Statute of the Land,* Museum of the City of Chandigarh, Chandigarh, India.
17. Le Corbusier, *Toward an Architecture.*

9. The University

1. Andrew L. Yarrow, "Nathan Pusey, Harvard President through Growth and Turmoil Alike, Dies at 94," *New York Times,* November 15, 2001.
2. Gökcan Demirkazik, "A Bauhaus Return to the Carpenter Center," *Harvard Crimson,* March 5, 2013.
3. Eduard F. Sekler and William J. R. Curtis, *Le Corbusier at Work: The Genesis of the Carpenter Center for the Visual Arts* (Cambridge, MA: Harvard University Press, 1978).
4. Ibid., p. 46.
5. Ibid., p. 43.
6. Ibid., p. 47.
7. Ibid.

8. Ibid., p. viii.

9. Ibid., p. 49.

10. Ibid.

11. Ibid.

12. Ibid.

13. "Corbu at Harvard," *Time,* November 30, 1959.

14. Sekler and Curtis, *Le Corbusier at Work,* p. 52.

15. Ibid., p. 96.

16. Le Corbusier Correspondence CCVA, Sert Collection, Frances Loeb Library, Harvard University, Folder E-34.

17. Author interview with Robert Campbell, Pulitzer Prize–winning architecture critic, March 30, 2013.

18. Author interview with William J. Curtis, architectural historian, April 17, 2013.

19. Sekler and Curtis, *Le Corbusier at Work,* p. 169.

20. Ibid., p. 174.

21. Ibid., p. 218.

22. Ada Louise Huxtable, "Bold Harvard Structure; Le Corbusier's Carpenter Visual Arts Center Collides with Colonial Charm," *New York Times,* May 28, 1963.

23. Author interview with William J. Curtis in Cambridge, April 17, 2013.

24. Sekler and Curtis, *Le Corbusier at Work,* p. 53.

25. Author interview with Robert Campbell in Cambridge, March 30, 2013.

26. Le Corbusier, *Creation Is a Patient Search* (New York: Praeger, 1960).

10. The Departure

1. Author interview with Patrice Tocme, a friend of Le Corbusier, in Paris, October 1, 2013.

2. André Wogenscky, *Le Corbusier's Hands* (Cambridge, MA: MIT Press, 2006), p. 27.

3. Weber, *Le Corbusier: A Life.*

4. Ibid.

5. Ibid., p. 18.

6. Ibid.

7. Ibid., p. 713.

8. Ibid.

9. Ibid.

10. Le Corbusier, "Musée National des Beaux Arts de l'Occident a Tokyo" (1956), proposal booklet for the Musée National d'Art Occidental, Tokyo, Japan, Fondation Le Corbusier.

11. Le Corbusier, "Musée du XXe Siècle" (1931), proposal booklet for the Musée du XXe Siècle, Nanterre, France, Fondation Le Corbusier.
12. Le Corbusier, "Rho Olivetti" (1964), proposal booklet for the Olivetti Centre de Calculs Électroniques, Rho, Italy, Fondation Le Corbusier.
13. Hashim Sarkis, *Le Corbusier's Venice Hospital* (Munich: Prestel, 2001).
14. Le Corbusier, letter to Marguerite Tjader Harris, February 1963, Fondation Le Corbusier.
15. Author interview with Jerry Fielder, curator and director of the Estate of Yousuf Karsh, Paris, October 1, 2013.
16. Le Corbusier, "D'Orsay – Paris" (1961), proposal booklet for the Hôtel et Palais des Congrès, Paris, France, Fondation Le Corbusier.
17. Author interview with Patricia Marinovich, co-owner of the Hôtel Le Roquebrune, Roquebrune-Cap-Martin, August 27, 2012.
18. Weber, *Le Corbusier: A Life*, p. 763.
19. Wogenscky, *Le Corbusier's Hands*, p. 8.
20. Mary McLeod, "Le Corbusier and Columbia, 1961" (presentation, "Le Corbusier/New York" Symposium of the American Institute of Architects New York Chapter, Museum of Modern Art, and Center for Architecture, New York, June 8, 2013).
21. Weber, *Le Corbusier: A Life*.
22. Jerzy Sołtan, "Working for Le Corbusier," in *Le Corbusier: The Garland Essays*, ed. H. Allen Brooks (New York: Garland, 1987), p. 16.
23. Weber, *Le Corbusier: A Life*, p. 9.
24. Ibid., p. 764.
25. Author interview with Robert Rebutato, in Roquebrune-Cap-Martin, August 30, 2012.
26. Weber, *Le Corbusier: A Life*, p. 703.
27. Le Corbusier, *The Final Testament of Père Corbu*.
28. Ibid., p. 25.
29. Weber, *Le Corbusier: A Life*, p. 11.
30. Ibid., p. 13.

Epilogue. The Legacy

1. Scott Lapatine, "Watch/Read Kanye West's Lecture at the Harvard Graduate School of Design," Stereogum, November 17, 2013, http://www.stereogum.com/1569581/watchread-kanye-wests-lecture-at-the-harvard-graduate-school-of-design/video/.
2. Jon Caramanica, "Behind Kanye's Mask," *New York Times*, June 11, 2013.
3. "History," Fondation Le Corbusier, http://www.fondationlecorbusier

.fr/corbuweb/morpheus.aspx?sysId=19&sysLanguage=en-en&
itemPos=1&sysParentId=19.

4. Ibid.

5. Cohen and Benton, *Le Corbusier, Le Grand.*

6. Bradley S. Klapper, "Nazi Praise Sparks Swiss Rethink of Le Corbusier," Associated Press, October 6, 2010.

7. Cohen and Benton, *Le Corbusier, Le Grand.*

8. Julie Lasky, "Chandigarh on the Block," *Design Observer,* March 28, 2011, http://changeobserver.designobserver.com/feature/chandigarh-on-the-block/25948/.

9. Jane Jacobs, "Downtown Is for People," *Fortune,* May 1958; republished September 18, 2013, http://features.blogs.fortune.cnn.com/2011/09/18/downtown-is-for-people-fortune-classic-1958/.

10. Alastair Parvin, "Architecture for the People by the People," TED Talk, 13:11, filmed February 2013, http://www.ted.com/talks/alastair_parvin_architecture_for_the_people_by_the_people.html.

11. Author interview with Andres Duany, in Miami, January 6, 2014.

12. Hosey, "Why We Love Beautiful Things."

INDEX